The Book of
NORTH TAWTON

Celebrating an Ancient Market Town

ALISON BAKER, DAVID HOARE
AND JEAN SHIELDS

HALSGROVE

First published in Great Britain in 2002

Frontispiece photograph: *The Square, 1875. Note the Town Post which was moved to make way for the Jubilee Clock Tower in 1887.*

British Library Cataloguing-in-Publication Data
A CIP record for this title is available from the British Library

ISBN 1 84114 156 9

HALSGROVE

Halsgrove House
Lower Moor Way
Tiverton, Devon EX16 6SS
Tel: 01884 243242
Fax: 01884 243325
email: sales@halsgrove.com
website: www.halsgrove.com

Printed and bound by
Bookcraft Ltd, Midsomer Norton

PREFACE

We would like to thank everyone who has helped in the preparation of this book, whether with recollections, photographs or other memorabilia, and all those ever ready to answer countless questions. We have been overwhelmed with the amount of material given to us and although we are unable to include it all, we hope to incorporate much of it in future local history exhibitions.

Our special thanks go to the Town Council, who have helped us to obtain a grant from the Lottery Fund to cover our expenses and for allowing us to browse through their archives which has proved most useful. We are also very grateful to Neil Hallam for giving us a character reference (!) in order to obtain the Lottery grant and for providing us with much information on the school.

The late Dorothy Stoneman and her husband Bill, both keen local historians, deserve a special mention in kindling our interest in the subject and collecting much valuable information, which they have passed on to us.

We owe a debt of gratitude to those people who have previously written about North Tawton, firstly William Skinner who produced a booklet on the town in the 1930s. He was followed by the late Revd Henry Fulford Williams, who had strong family connections with North Tawton and spent some of his childhood here. He contributed articles and papers to both the *Transactions of the Devonshire Association*, and *Devon & Cornwall Notes and Queries*, and later published one of his papers in the former as a booklet entitled *North Tawton, a Devon Market Town*. He also gave his original notes, dated 1954, to St Peter's Church and we are grateful to the churchwardens for allowing us to make full use of them and those of Walter Mortimer.

The late Walter Mortimer, churchwarden for many years who, as well as publishing a book on the history of our town, also left his notes and other material to the church. This included a scrapbook, a typescript copy of diaries kept by the Pillman family, dating from 1777 to 1834, extracts from which are included in the following pages, together with some reminiscences of Revd Robert Hole.

Bob Parker has drawn our maps, for which we are most grateful. Others who have allowed us to use their research include Russell Wright regarding the Gospel Hall, Rose Dadds for information on the United Reformed Church, and the family of the late Reg Farley who have allowed us to use material from his book on the cricket club.

Others who have helped include Joan Geering, who has very kindly read through the text and edited it for us, Edna Eglinton who has done likewise with the section on St Peter's Church, and Ann Adams who has helped with the first chapter and provided information on her ancestors, the Budd family. David Bale has provided much information on the 1939–45 war and the Royal British Legion, while Peter Bentley (former Senior Engineer, NDWB) has done the same regarding the North Devon Water Board. Gregory Distribution have kindly allowed us the use of their photocopier and Ann Hoare has helped in countless ways, not least with her enthusiasm.

Several people have lent us scrapbooks containing newspaper cuttings and photographs, some of which are undated and unattributed; while others have lent us copies or enlargements of photographs, where there is no means of knowing the name of the original photographer. In other cases, although the name of a photographer is known to us we have been unable to trace him, and we apologise for all such omissions.

North Tawton is an ancient town with much history and we do not pretend that we have discovered more than a small fraction of it. But we hope to have preserved some items of information and photographs that might otherwise have been lost, which may encourage others to dig deeper and discover more.

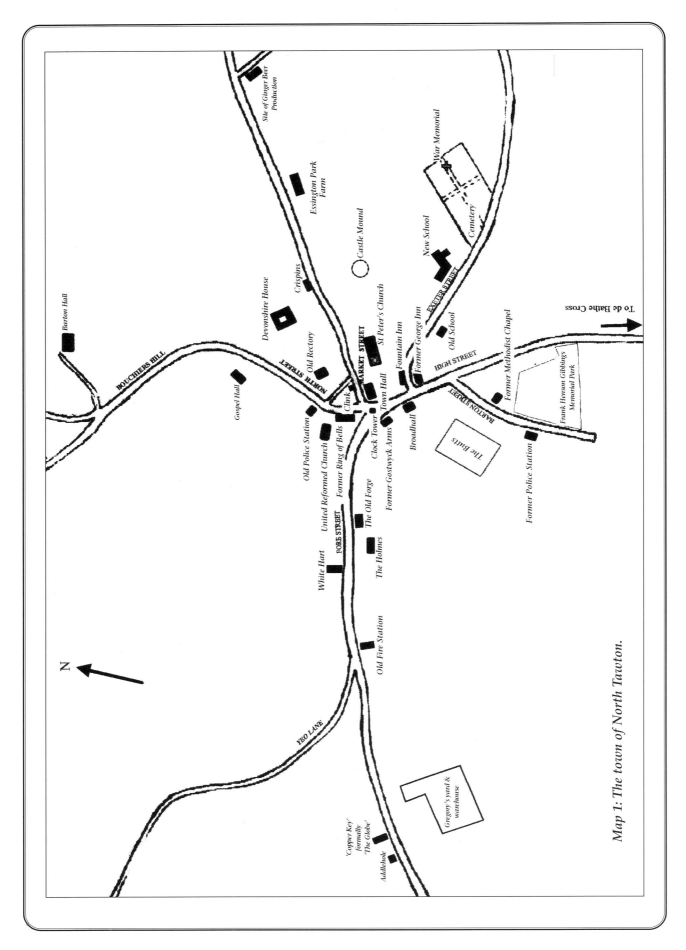

Map 1: The town of North Tawton.

CONTENTS

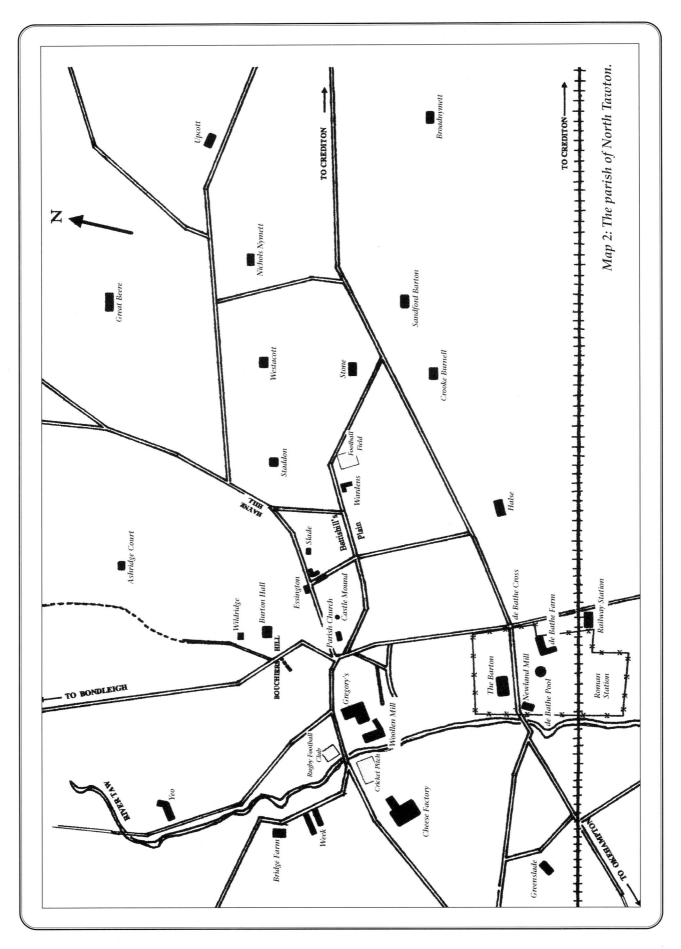

Map 2: The parish of North Tawton.

N

TO CREDITON

TO CREDITON

Upcott

Nichols Nymett

Great Beere

Westacott

Staddon

HAYNE HILL

Slade

Essington

Ashridge Court

Wildridge

Burton Hall

BOUCHIERS HILL

Parish Church

Castle Mound

Battishill's Plain

Wardens

Football Field

Stone

Sandford Barton

Crooke Burnell

Broadnymett

Halse

TO BONDLEIGH

RIVER TAW

Yeo

Rugby Football Club

Gregory's

Cricket Pitch

Woollen Mill

Bridge Farm

Week

Cheese Factory

The Barton

Newland Mill

de Bathe Pool

de Bathe Farm

de Bathe Cross

Railway Station

Roman Station

Greenslade

TO OKEHAMPTON

Chapter 1

SETTING THE SCENE

North Tawton is a small former market town in the centre of Devon, 20 miles from Exeter and within easy reach of Dartmoor National Park. At its highest point it is 203 metres above sea level. The River Taw flows through it and gave it its name, Taw being Celtic for 'silent one'.

The area of the parish is 5,963 acres. The population has waxed and waned over the years, gradually increasing from the Domesday estimate of a few hundred to 759 in 1750, rising to between 1,500 and the maximum of just over 2,000 in 1871, when the woollen industry was flourishing and the railway had arrived. It then fell back again to around 1,200 for much of the twentieth century until climbing back to 1,500 at the 1991 census, when the number of households was 601. At that time the unemployment level of five per cent compared well with neighbouring parishes. At the time of writing the result of the

Aerial photograph of part of Roman site at North Tawton, showing 'crop marks'.
The Barton is in the right foreground. (Photograph F.M. Griffith, Devon County Council, 3 July 1984. Copyright reserved)

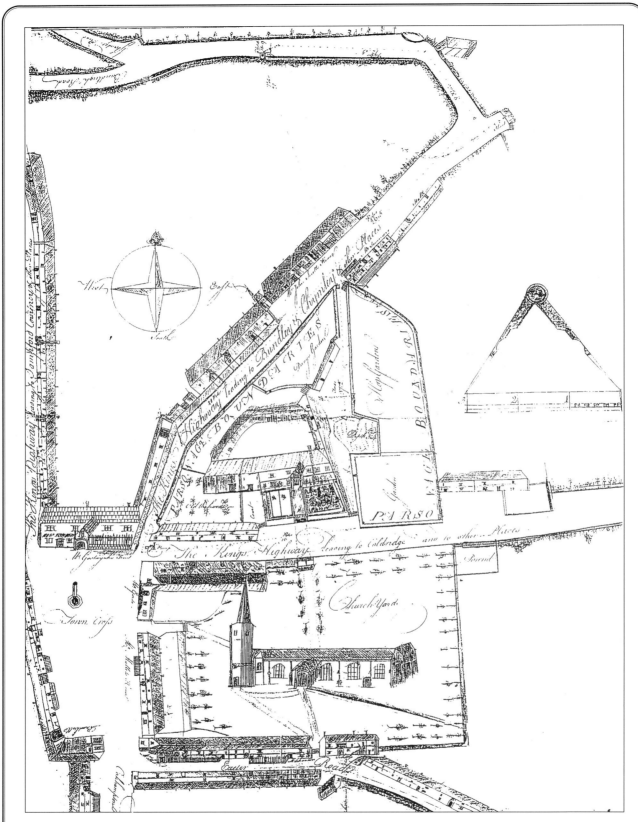

Map 3: The churchyard, parsonage, and The Square, c.1780. (Courtesy of John Arundell)

2001 census has not yet been released.

There is no doubt that Stone-Age man was here; two polished stone axes were found near the cheese factory, indicating that a Stone-Age settlement of some sort was present in the area. There have also been identified some Bronze-Age (roughly 2000–500BC) burial mounds near The Barton and some ring ditches, which may be of this date or later from the Roman period. Flints have been found in the vicinity. At Stone Farm, near the A377, some Bronze-Age remains have been identified.

The Romans reached Exeter in about AD50 and stayed for roughly 350 years. During this time they advanced westwards and the crossing of the Taw at Newland was probably of sufficient importance to be defended. It has been known for many years that there was a Roman road and a Roman fort in the parish, the latter just south of the railway line with the road stretching eastwards from it for several miles towards Bow, following the straight line of a hedge. However, in the last 20 years much more has been discovered by aerial photography, which shows up 'crop marks' *(see page 7)*. These indicate where the ground has been disturbed, causing the vegetation growth to vary, for example a crop grown on thinner soil over an impervious surface such as a wall will appear stunted and lighter in colour compared with the lusher growth found on deeper, moister soil over a buried ditch. Subsoil, once broken, never fully recovers its consistency; aerial photography shows up these differences, especially in times of drought.

The Roman site at North Tawton is now considered to have been much larger and more important than originally thought. It is an extensive settlement with a complex structure, as yet not fully understood, which has never been properly excavated. It extends on both sides of the A377 road from near de Bathe Cross to Newland Mills. There is evidence of more than one phase of building, including large and small military enclosures, which are thought to have been two marching or temporary camps, not used simultaneously, and one large or two smaller forts. This suggests that the Romans returned here on one or more occasions and that it was an important Roman base; it is one of the largest such sites in the South West.

The biggest enclosure is thought to be a vexillation fortress. These were campaigning bases holding between 2,500 and 4,000 troops, both legionary and auxiliary. Two possible sites of a bath house have been located, together with a tile found at the site south of the railway. There are also three double ditched features present, the purpose of which is open to speculation. In addition, a Roman coin was found in 1908 in the river near Newland Mills which probably dates from the first or second century AD.

It is thought possible that the place name 'Nemetostatio' mentioned in Roman writings referred to North Tawton, but other places, in particular Bow and Bury Barton at Lapford, have been suggested. 'Statio' refers to a posting station or a tax gathering point. The whole complex is on the private land of farms of The Barton and de Bathe and is a Scheduled Monument, which is protected by many regulations, among which is the prohibition of the use of metal detectors on the site.

Of the Saxons we know little, but it is possible that they built the church, and the fact that North Tawton gave its name to a 'hundred' suggests it was probably important in Saxon times. A hundred was a Saxon division intermediate in size between a manor and a county, roughly equivalent to the district of today. Originally it was equal in area to 100 hides, a hide being a variable acreage depending on the fertility of the soil.

Domesday Survey

There are six identifiable holdings in what is now North Tawton parish which were mentioned in the Domesday Book, a survey compiled in 1086, 20 years after the Battle of Hastings. William the Conqueror sent out men to record all his lands and everything in them. This was double checked and rough drafts made (the one for the South West called the Exon Domesday still exists), and then the fair copy was made by a scribe in Winchester. The manors are arranged by hundred, and the hundred of North Tawton covered many parishes as we know them today, which sometimes causes confusion in identification.

The manors (names Anglicised) listed which are now in the parish *(see Map 2)* are as follows: Tawton, (Great) Beere, Broadnymett, Crooke, Greenslade, and Nicholls Nymett. The King himself held the manor of Tawton, but the rest were granted by him to various Norman followers, the barons, in return for service, especially military service. They in turn sublet to others lower down the social scale

For each manor there was listed the name of any tenant and sub-tenant, the acreage, the number of men and the type and number of animals. For instance, the manor of Tawton which probably included the town lands, also Week, Staddon and The Barton, had land for 30 ploughs (a plough consisted of a team of oxen), 40 acres of woodland, 30 of coppice, 40 of meadow and 5 of pasture. There were 31 villagers, 28 smallholders, 3 serfs (landless men), 10 cattle (it is thought that the term 'cattle' did not include the oxen used for ploughing), and 90 sheep.

The other manors were considerably smaller, and some also had pigs and goats. From the acreages and lists of livestock one can deduce that the contemporary agriculture was largely arable and sheep farming, showing that wool was already important in this locality.

Domesday was not designed as a census of the inhabitants, but the villagers and smallholders are assumed to have been male heads of household, and although no one really knows how big such households were, compared with other villages at the time, North Tawton was quite large.

Manorial History

This is not easy to unravel, and although the advowson (right to present the living, i.e. appoint the rector) usually went with the manorial rights, this was not always the case here. What follows may not be entirely correct, as documentary evidence is sparse.

As above, at Domesday the King held the manor of North Tawton, it was subsequently part of the honour of Plympton belonging to the Redvers family (later Earls of Devon), who granted it to Joel de Valletort, who also acquired Slade when Robert of Slade was hanged (see Chapter 3).

John de Valletort was granted a market at North Tawton in 1270. Other members of this family followed, and their arms can be seen in a stained-glass window in the north aisle of the church. According to Risdon writing in the 1600s, the moated site just east of the church was theirs.

Today this medieval earthwork is in the form of a mound surrounded by a ditch about five feet deep. It is crossed by a field boundary and is on private land. Such a structure would have been surmounted by a wooden palisade (stout fence) and a tower, of either wood or stone. Such mottes were built between the eleventh and thirteenth centuries, and ours may have been the residence of the Valletorts or their centre of administration, but nothing definite is known about its history. It is listed as a Scheduled Monument.

After several generations of Valletorts, Hugh de Valletort's daughter, Eglina, married Oliver Champernowne, who then owned the manor by right of his wife (in those days a married woman's inheritance always belonged to her husband), but the advowson had been previously sold by the Valletorts to Sir Richard Stapledon (brother of the Bishop of Exeter) about 1310.

There are various versions of what happened next, perhaps because the female line repeatedly inherited, with inevitable name change and confusion. The history of the advowson is probably as follows. Precise dates are not known.

A descendant of the Stapledons married Sir Richard Hankforth, and one of his two daughters, Thomasine, married Sir William Bouchier, later Lord Fitzwarren (hence Bouchiers Hill in the town). The other daughter, Ann, married Thomas Butler, 7th Earl of Ormonde. These families were patrons of the church consecutively. It then passed to the St Leger family through the female line, whose heirs sold it to the Cottles in the 1560s. The latter, represented by John Cottle, a cousin in London, when the North Tawton branch eventually died out, sold the advowson to the Hole family in 1716.

As regards the manor, in the Calendars of Enrolled Deeds in the Devon Record Office, dated 1543, the manor of North Tawton was at that time held in common by Sir Richard Eggecombe, bart., Alexander Wood (Joan Valletort had married Richard Wood or Atwood of Ashridge in the fourteenth century) and Otis Gilbert Esqs. On 4 December that year, Sir Richard sold to Alexander Wood his one-third share. Some of this property was in the Plymouth area but that recognisable as probably being in North Tawton included Bath(e), Newland, Ayscherygge (Ashridge), Lambertsweek, Stodden (Staddon), Brygge (Bridge), Slad(e), North Weke, Little Weke and Church Tawton. Sir Richard also sold his part of frankpledge, fairs, and markets (all of which would have provided income).

Risdon says the manor was divided among the co-heiresses of Oliver Champernowne whose daughter Joan married Richard Wood who had the manor for her share with Ashridge where the 'the family seated their dwelling'.

Dean Milles writing in about 1755 using information supplied by the then rector, Revd William Hole, says:

In this parish there are only two manors, North Tawton and Week. The former is said to have belonged anciently to the Valletorts. Since the Reformation it hath been possessed of the Cottrells (sic) of whose heirs it was purchased by Coulson Fellowes Esq., its present lord. There is no tradition or account given to whom Week belonged in ancient times, but its present proprietor is Walter Rolle Esq. in whose family it hath been some ages.

However, Lysons, whose book *Magna Britannica, Vol. IV* was published in 1822, does not mention the Cottles owning the manor, and in a somewhat complicated account says Fellowes bought the manor from Adam Pierce and others in 1718, 'trustees probably for the St Leger family'. This seems to be most likely.

All accounts agree that William Fellowes of Eggesford bought the manor in 1718. This family was connected by marriage with the Wallops of Hampshire, one of whose members, Charles, was created Earl of Portsmouth in 1720. The family names are somewhat confusing, as The Hon. Newton Wallop changed his name from Wallop to Fellowes, and then changed it back to Wallop on inheriting the earldom. Furthermore, the eldest son of Lord Portsmouth is always styled Lord Lymington. The Portsmouths lived at their newly built Eggesford House during the nineteenth and early-twentieth centuries, before preferring their Hampshire seat.

In 1904 the Portsmouth estate was broken up and with the Earl having disposed of his land, the titular manor of North Tawton was sold to the Shaws, the owners of the woollen mill in North Tawton at the time, who donated it to the Parish Council, which is an unusual state of affairs as very few parish councils are also the manorial lord.

There were a number of other sub-manors and estates, which are dealt with in Chapter 3.

There are two ancient bridges over the River Taw in the parish; one at the bottom of Fore Street, thought to date from the fifteenth century, and the other at Newland, also thought to date from the fifteenth century and widened in the eighteenth century. The former consists of five stone arches and has been widened on both sides. There is mention of it in 1647 when it was stated as being in decay and was later repaired or possibly rebuilt when Nicholas Arnold, a mason, was paid £110 by the 'treasurers of North Tawton' for his work on the bridge.

The old road to Torrington via Bondleigh crossed the river at Bailey's Ford in Yeo Lane. Flooding of the Taw obviously occurred as there is a note on Donne's 1765 map to 'turn in at the Bridge to avoid the river if water is high.'

Tarka Trail

This is a long-distance footpath based on the book *Tarka the Otter* by Henry Williamson, first published in 1927. It passes through the parish as it follows the River Taw to Barnstaple, passing through fields belonging to The Barton and then past Bridge Farm and through woods and farmland until it emerges on the continuation of Yeo Lane on the old road to Bondleigh.

It is well signposted throughout and a very pleasant walk in the North Tawton section, the town making a convenient stopping off point for refreshments.

There are a number of other footpaths in the parish and recently these have been regularly walked on Sunday afternoons by members of the general public, led by John Wright of the Environmental Trust.

Many villages have decayed over the years, partly because of the smaller numbers employed in agriculture but also because, with the coming of cars, people have been able to work and shop elsewhere, while supermarkets make shopping easier and often cheaper. The high price of existing housing for the young in many areas also contributes to the break up of families. Another factor is the ease with which people can seek entertainment further afield so the old community, as such, hardly exists any longer.

In North Tawton, which incidentally proudly regards itself as a town, albeit a small one, these trends have been discernible ever since the First World War and were exacerbated by the closure of the woollen mill in 1930. However, this has been offset by the arrival of new employment opportunities within the town, so we have not lost all our shops and pubs, nor our Post Office.

An ongoing problem is the lack of a car park and the dearth of garages attached to the mainly nineteenth-century houses. This results in the streets being choked at busy times. Since 1964 the Parish Council have been campaigning for a designated car park, which has not materialised to date.

The streets are as on the map *(see page 4)*, but were not always named thus. What is now Fore Street was formerly named Hatherleigh Street; High Street was known as Okehampton Street; while North Street was referred to as Lakeway and still is by the older inhabitants. What we now refer to as Essington, the continuation of Market Street, was called Eastington in times gone by. It originally contained the pound, near the church, where stray animals were impounded and held until their owners paid a fine for their release. At some time the pound was moved to the bottom of Lakeway. Further along the Essington road is an attractive row of houses named Park Terrace, built in the nineteenth century.

In The Square there was a post, thought to be the shaft of a cross, where proclamations were read and bargains sealed with a handshake. This was moved to the churchyard in 1887 to make way for the erection of the Jubilee Clock Tower.

As in so many places in Devon, where much of the building was of cob (a mixture of mud, straw, water and sometimes cow dung) with thatched roofs, the town has had many fires. Much rebuilding has therefore taken place over the years. As prosperity has increased many houses have been much remodelled and extended, so it is impossible to say how they appeared originally. In the case of farmhouses, sometimes the old house has been converted to an outhouse or abandoned and an entirely new house built, as happened at Halse Farm and Ashridge Court. Many farm workers' cottages have also ended up as outhouses.

In Fore Street there are several alleyways, once leading to cottages behind the main street, some of which still exist. There is also an attractive example of such buildings leading out of Exeter Street, known

The Square, 1875. Note the Town Post which was moved to make way for the Jubilee Clock Tower in 1887.

Fore Street, 1912.

High Street, 1935.

Top of the High Street, 1912. Note the cottages on right, which were demolished in 1933.

as Broad Park Terrace and thought to be Georgian.

In a few cases a whole row of cottages has been demolished, as at either end of the park. Originally there were cottages on the south side of Barton Street and the west side of High Street, where the park gates now stand. Gowman's Terrace at the lower end of town was demolished in the 1960s and new houses built on the site. Further down Fore Street there is another modern estate opposite the old woollen factory where the gas works once stood.

A substantial row of houses was built by Okehampton Rural District Council during the 1930s on Barton Hill, providing inhabitants with spectacular views of Dartmoor. Arundell Road in Essington, also commissioned by that same council, was built soon after the Second World War and named after one of Revd Hole's daughters, Mrs Arundell. This estate has recently been extended into Taylor's Field.

New houses have been built on the old barkyard site, but at least the name has been preserved in Barker's Way. Other developments include Moor View on what was known as Clotworthy's, south of the park, which took shape in the early 1970s.

At the bottom of North Street is a solidly built row of houses known as Victoria Terrace, dating from the 1890s. Nearby are the large Bouchiers Hill villas, which were built in the late-nineteenth and early-twentieth centuries, and on the opposite side of the road are the new houses and bungalows, built in the former grounds of Burton Hall.

Other big houses with large gardens or yards have had buildings erected therein, as for instance Melhuishes in The Square and Stoats in High Street. Again the name has been preserved in the latter case as Stoats Mews.

Butts Way is on a site where archery was once practised and this was extended into Gostwyck Close, built about 20 years ago on land once belonging to the family of that name.

The Square boasts the Town Hall, built in 1849 as the Market House, and the Jubilee Clock which was erected in 1887. An interesting old property, called Broadhall, is also situated here. All these are dealt with in Chapter 11.

A painting of Market Street looking towards the church, painted in 1894 by Kate Hole.

View over town from Bouchiers Hill, before the Second World War.

The Square. Note Gostwyck Garage which replaced the Gostwyck Arms in the 1920s.

Taw Bridge, c.1900.

Park Terrace, c.1914. Vera Knight is the child in the foreground.

Exeter Street. Note the old school playground on the left.

Market Street looking towards Melhuishes, The Square, 1935.

Lower Fore Street in the early-twentieth century.

St Peter's Church.

Donald Pridham and Revd Lane with the homemade 'bosun's chair', used for mending the steeple roof, 1972.

The interior of St Peter's Church, 2001.

The Revd Robert Hole, 1824–1916.

Detail of a window with medieval glass, showing angels bearing shields and carrying the arms of some of the manorial lords.

Chapter 2

CHURCH & CHAPELS

St Peter's Church

No one knows when the church of St Peter was built; perhaps it existed in Saxon times, but the first written record of the church that survives is dated 1257, when Amicia, Countess of Devon, appointed Oliver de Tracey as the rector.

As it now stands the church, largely composed of granite, lies adjacent to The Square. It consists of a nave, a fourteenth-century north aisle and a fifteenth-century south aisle, the latter being rebuilt at some time. There is a projecting chancel which was added in the 1840s at the expense of the then rector, Revd George Hole, and the tower, which is the oldest part, probably dates from the thirteenth century.

Originally the whole roof would have been covered with oak shingles, but today only the broach (octagonal) spire remains shingled. This has a somewhat curious appearance and appears to be too short, believed to be due to a lack of funds during its restoration following a fire in 1834 when 61 houses were destroyed and the spire caught alight. There is a south porch with roof bosses and an ancient south door with a sanctuary ring. The roof is a typical 'Devon wagon' roof with carved bosses. There is a west gallery which contains the organ and was added in around 1790. An 'old parishioner', writing in 1916, tells us that when he was young there was no lighting or heating in the church and music came from a barrel organ, which could play only 32 tunes, and the choir in the gallery were hidden from the view of the congregation by red curtains. He goes on to say that the service consisted mainly of a dialogue between the rector and the Parish Clerk who sat close to the pulpit. Revd Robert Hole wrote in the parish magazine, saying that when he was appointed in 1850 the music

Detail of a pew end carved with the Champernowne family arms.

in the church was provided by fiddles, bass viols, flutes and clarinets.

There has been a church choir for most of the past 150 years. In 1913, 19 choir members went on an outing to Bude and had a 'lovely day although the sea was obscured by mist.' Only two of the party had ever been to Bude before, which seems odd as there was a train service covering the 30 miles between Bude and North Tawton at the time.

According to Beatrix Cresswell, writing early in the twentieth century, the seats of the church rose in tiers beneath the gallery, enclosing the font. The present plain granite font dates from 1839 and cost £5. It was moved to its present position at the east end of the nave when the west end of the church was converted into the Mortimer Room, a meeting-room with kitchen and toilet facilities at the base of the tower. At the same time both doors were fitted with internal porches. This was made possible by the generous bequest of Walter Mortimer (1905–83), a former churchwarden, church treasurer, bell-ringer for over 60 years, Scout leader and choir master. He also printed the church magazine and was an eminent local historian. This conversion was not without controversy as some members of the congregation disagreed with the alterations.

Originally there was little or no seating in churches, but by 1600 most churches had seats, the more affluent of society renting their seats and keeping them in good repair, while there were free seats at the back. At St Peter's the north aisle was referred to as 'Mr Fellowes' aisle', where his tenants sat, and the south was 'Mr Skinner's' or the 'Ashridge aisle'. Elaborate seating plans still exist.

Inevitably disputes arose, as in 1791 when William Eastabrooke, the 16-year-old servant of Simon Starr of Court Green, was sent to sit in a pew which Starr deemed his but to which Thomas Prideaux, described as gentleman, and his son John, sergemaker, also laid claim. However, William was prevented from taking the pew by Thomas Prideaux's servant and a row broke out. Eastabrook returned home only to be sent back again with a female servant. This inflamed the situation, fighting ensued and the maid ended up on the floor shouting 'murder'. During all this confusion the psalms were still in progress. The case went to the ecclesiastical court, where the Registrar believed the Prideauxs to be in the wrong and awarded costs to Mr Starr. Thomas Prideaux made a counter claim for libel against Starr which he won and was awarded costs. The main beneficiaries were the lawyers, whose bills list 122 separate expenses, including journeys to Exeter, turnpike fees, and producing and copying documents. The total bills came to £105.11s.8d. plus witnesses' expenses (which included expenses at an inn) of £25.1s.9d. John Prideaux then appealed to the Court of Arches in London and in 1793 this court decreed that no action should be taken pending the result of the appeal. Finally, in July 1794 the judge sent the case back to Exeter for 'further consideration of the evidence'. There are no further documents relating to the case, perhaps after all the time and expense to both parties they agreed to bury their differences.

Like most churches there have been many restorations over the years. The screen was removed in about 1730, in the 1830s the seats were replaced by box pews, some of the bench ends were put at the east end of the new chancel and two further galleries were built but later taken down. The pews were replaced again in the 1930s and some of the bench ends were re-used, one in particular in the nave contains the arms of the Champernowne family, quartered with the Wood family. The Champernowne

The chancel window, erected in 1921 in memory of Revd Robert Hole.

arms are again depicted in a window in the north aisle, where four angels bearing shields also carrry the arms of other manorial lords. These are thought to be Valletort, possibly Stapledon and Butler, but opinion is divided on this. These shields together with the sunburst of York, which was the badge of Edward IV, and the Tudor Rose in the top of the same window are thought to be medieval glass. The rest of the windows are Victorian or later. The east window in the north aisle is dedicated to the memory of the Gostwyck family who were important in the town in the seventeenth and eighteenth centuries and are also commemorated on a tombstone, now badly eroded, just outside the north door.

The window in the chancel was erected by public subscription in memory of Revd Robert Hole who died in 1916 having served the parish for 66 years. This window depicts the Crucifixion, and the Hole coat of arms, on which owls are portrayed (a pun on the name Hole), can be seen in the bottom left corner.

The other stained-glass windows are in memory of John Kelland Durant, who died in 1887 aged 91, a member of the East India Company whose North Tawton connections stretch back to the 1500s, and Sarah Luccombe, his wife, whom he outlived by 51 years. The remainder of the windows in the south aisle commemorate various families from the parish: the Chapple family, who lived at Court Green next to the church; the Jackman family, who were in the leather and farming trades; John Henson Gibbings of Week Barton, JP and churchwarden from 1881–89; and the window nearest the south door is dedicated to the memory of John and Jane Durant, seed growers of Senderhills.

The altar rails are a memorial to the 11 men killed in the Second World War whose names are listed alongside. Just inside the south door is a copy of a vellum book in an oak case, beautifully inscribed with the names of all those men and women who served in the First World War, including the 52 men who lost their lives. The pulpit was erected in 1936 in memory of the Skinner family and the eagle lectern was presented in memory of John Francis Matthews of Nichols Nymett, who died in 1913, in addition to a commemorative brass tablet on the south wall which is also dedicated to him.

A list of the rectors from 1257 is displayed in the church porch. The Hole family held the advowson for many years and members of that family were rectors for 200 years, all named Hole except one, the Revd Starr, whose mother's maiden name was Hole. One of the most remarkable was probably the Revd Robert Hole who was the incumbent for 66 years and of whom there is a more detailed account in a later chapter.

North Tawton bell-ringers, winners of the eight-bell competition, 1953. Left to right: *Fred Harris, Bill Nicholls, Brian Drake, Walter Mortimer, Jim Bennett (captain), Clifford Westlake, Walter Axworthy, Cyril Matthews.*

There are currently eight bells at the church. Originally there were four which were first mentioned in 1535. These were recast into six bells in 1765 and two more were added in 1899. North Tawton bell-ringers have enjoyed much success over the years. In 1914 they rang 2,861 call changes in four hours under Captain William Fewings. This was claimed as a record at the time, although superseded since. They have won many competitions, including the Ross Shield on 20 occasions since 1928.

Bell-ringers with their trophies, 1974/5. Left to right, back row: *W. Folland, E.J. Cole, W. Axworthy, M.C. Way, S. Palmer, C.G. Westlake;* seated: *C. Pike, B. Drake, Revd B.A. Bailey (rector), W. Mortimer.*

A report of the Ringers Annual Dinner at the Ring of Bells pub in 1910 states that 'A short toast list is always observed as a musical programme is much preferred.' How very sensible!

The original clock is said to date from 1640, but was probably altered by Lewis Pridham in about 1710, and in 1968 a Smith's clock was installed. It strikes on an exterior sanctus bell inscribed 'TG', possibly Thomas Geffery, a bell-founder in around 1535. This bell hangs from a louvre towards the top of the spire. The old clock mechanism has been preserved but is not currently on view.

There is an ancient sundial on the south wall of the tower, bearing the inscription 'Life is like a shadow' and a niche where a statue probably once stood. There is a similar empty niche over the north door. Outside the tower is the shaft of an ancient cross which, until 1887, stood in The Square. It was moved to its present position when the clock tower was built to commemorate Queen Victoria's Golden Jubilee.

An avenue of lime trees was planted in 1979 to replace the original trees which dated from about 1740 and were diseased. Lime is said to denote Whig sympathies with William of Orange as distinct from the firs planted by the Jacobites. The cobbled path to the lych-gate is said to have been laid by the Napoleonic Prisoners of War quartered here in 1809/10, but as these are believed to have nearly all been officers this seems unlikely. The churchyard was closed for burials in 1902 after a new cemetery opened at the top of Exeter Street in 1901.

There was almost certainly a tithe barn, probably somewhere in the vicinity of the present Church Cottage near the Fountain Inn. A former local historian and parish clerk, Sam Howard, suggested that the tithe barn itself may have previously been the chapel of St Paul for which John Northmore, rector, was granted a licence in 1378 to hold services on the festivals of St Paul. Details are given with regard to the licence being for a newly built chapel in the burial ground of the Parish Church. No trace of this building survives. Howard further suggested that the tithe barn was subsequently located in what were then the grounds of the rectory, which is also quite possible as in a 1727 description of the parsonage there is mention of 'One large barn with house appendant, one little barn, one large linnie adjoining the great barn built by the present incumbent.'

Most villages had a church house built in the fifteenth or sixteenth century and North Tawton is no exception – there is reference to a church house in a deed dated 1688. It is likely that the house at North Tawton was subsequently converted into the poor-house with a 'school over', i.e. upstairs, in Exeter Street, which burnt down in 1834.

The monthly parish magazine was first published in 1910 and apart from a break in 1949/50 it seems to have been printed almost continuously since then. The original editor is not named, but it was not the rector. Usually the matters reported were strictly local, but occasionally national events were alluded to, including when a memorial service was held on the death of King Edward VII and 'all blinds were drawn and all amusements given up' and in 1912, when there

was an editorial tirade against the Suffragettes. The First World War was also reported on in the magazine. During the inter-war years the magazine became less informative and was padded out with articles on the Church worldwide, moralistic tales and cookery recipes, and for some years it was simply a folded sheet. A new look came to the magazine in September 1990, when Edna Eglinton took over, originally printing it with stencils and Gestetner but later with the aid of a computer. As the parishes of Sampford Courtenay, Bondleigh and Honeychurch had recently combined with North Tawton the magazine now became much more substantial and interesting.

Church-going was once compulsory and in 1678, under the heading 'Conviction Money' (a fine paid by those who did not attend church, which was distributed among the poor), it was reported in the overseers' account book 'From John Yeo, John Chigwell & Mark Burne Total 12s.0d.' (60p). The recipients' names then follow. On 5 November 1690:

... received of Robert Camp, 3s.0d. being convicted of 3 Sundays absence from church, and of Robert Crispin of South Tawton 5s.0d. being convicted of being distempered with drink, both of which monies were distributed as followeth to nine men and five women.

The lych-gate, North Tawton, early-twentieth century.

Church outing to Ilfracombe by charabanc, 1930s.

The Old Rectory.

Revd and Mrs Siviter (1939–43) in fancy dress.

The names of those to whom the monies were distributed were then recorded.

Some of the more affluent parishioners made bequests to the poor. An example of this was seen in 1690 when Ann Kelland, 'widow of this parish deceased' left £3 which was to be distributed to the poor of the parish 'to fifty men and twenty women (names given), so each had less than 1s.0d.', equal to around five pence today.

It is not known when the Sunday school was formed, but it met in the old schoolrooms in New Road, also known as Cackie Lane (a short pedestrian lane linking Market and North Streets). This was originally a thatched cob building with an outside staircase and could well have started life as a barn within the rectory walls. In 1912 improvements were made to the Sunday school when, among other things, new tortoise stoves were put in and 144 new chairs were purchased. By 1910 the Sunday-school children were having annual seaside outings, usually to Exmouth by train. In that year 150 went, including 23 parents and 12 teachers, who left North Tawton at 7.30a.m. and arrived home at 8p.m. Mr Attwell of the Gostwyck Arms and Mrs Heath of the Ring of Bells provided (presumably horse-drawn) transport to and from the station for the younger ones. Around this time the rector also provided a treat in the summer with tea in the rectory gardens followed by games and races in a field, the location of which is not specified.

Later in the 1920s and '30s the children also had a Christmas Party, which was provided by Mr Ernest May, one of the churchwardens, and Mrs May, of de Bathe, during which each child received a present. One of the May's granddaughters remembers as a child helping to choose the presents according to the age and sex of the child, and the excitement of wrapping them up and naming them.

The old Sunday school was demolished and the site sold for housing in the mid 1980s, in spite of a petition against the sale. The children then met at the primary school but later moved to the Mortimer Room in the church where, at the time of writing, the younger ones still meet, while members of the oldest class go to the Town Hall. Those of secondary-school age meet midweek with the Connect group of youth workers in the Mortimer Room.

In the early 1900s there was a Christian Endeavour group which was non-denominational and met in the Congregational Schoolroom.

The present rectory was built in 1962 in part of the garden of the former one, which was built in about 1832 and itself replaced an older parsonage on the same site (see Map 3). The latter, according to a description dated 1727 in the Devon Record Office, consisted of a kitchen paved with stone which had two chambers over, a pastry (sic), buttery, parlour floored with lime ashes, hall, two storehouses, a cellar, brewhouse and bunting (cider) house, all with rooms over and one chamber over the entry with a study adjoining, plus barns, stables, five gardens and 81 acres of glebeland. The house was built of cob and thatched with reed. Its successor was a grand stone building erected in the Tudor Gothic style, most likely to a design by Thomas Lee who was the architect of Eggesford House. As the Portsmouths and Holes are known to have been friends it seems logical that Lee should design the new rectory.

In 1939 the rector, Revd Siviter, installed electric lighting, central heating and completely renewed the plumbing with a new bathroom and basins providing hot and cold water to all the main bedrooms. Whether he carried out this work at his own expense or not the parish magazine does not divulge.

An amusing story is told of a mishap during the incumbency of Revd Siviter when Alfie Lias, sexton and former publican of the Globe, who lived next to the church, was in the habit of keeping the communion wine in his own larder. On one occasion when the rector took the sacrament he realised that there was something amiss, so he announced to the congregation that the wine was 'off' and they would have to make do with water. Alfie immediately realised he had picked up a bottle of rum by mistake and although the rector was understanding he said it could not be taken home or thrown out as it had been consecrated. Alfie quickly solved the problem by sitting down with the rector's warden, Sid Pike, and polishing off the rum before going home to Sunday dinner.

All manner of tithes in kind were due to the rector in addition to Easter offerings. In 1745 each person over 16 years of age had to pay 2d. Other fees included 1s.0d. (5p) for a marriage, 6d. (2½p) for churching, burials were free, and mortuaries cost 10s.0d., 6s.8d., or 3s.4d. 'according to their effects'. Mortuaries were payments due to the incumbent on the death of those with estates worth over a certain sum.

During this period repairs to the church and churchyard were financed by a church rate, except the north aisle which was repaired by Coulson Fellowes Esq., the lord of the manor, and the south aisle which was repaired by John Skinner Esq. of Ashridge. The clerk's wages were £5 annually and the sexton's were 10s.0d. (50p) annually; both were paid by the churchwardens.

Gleaned from the church magazine, a Church of England Men's Society was formed in 1911 and at the first meeting over 240 attended at the Town Hall, although numbers subsequently dropped, especially in the summer. There was also a Mothers' Union which was formed in 1957 and disbanded in about 1997, and a Women's Happy Hour which was formed in 1949 for the ladies of St Peter's Church. A church Scouts group was established in the early-twentieth century which undertook a camping trip to Taw Marsh on Dartmoor for the first time in 1912.

In recent years the benefice was merged with St

Happy Hour outing, 1950.
Left to right, back row:
Mrs Sanders, Lisa Arscott,
Jessie Knott, Elsie Densham,
Lucy Bird, Bessie Stoneman,
Mrs Luxton, Mary Harris;
front row: Fanny Knott,
Mrs Livesay.

The Revd Anthony Gibson at
St Peter's Church Fête in the
rectory garden, c.1990.

Revd Mark Butchers, c.1998.

Induction of Revd Brian Ardill in
2000 with Bishop Michael, and
the Very Revd Richard Gilpin.

James', Bondleigh in 1981, and the united benefice joined with St Andrew's, Sampford Courtenay and St Mary's, Honeychurch in 1988.

Since Revd Robert Hole's death in 1916 there have been seven incumbents at North Tawton, all of whom have contributed much to the community in their different ways. During the late 1980s and early 1990s, Revd Tony Gibson filled the post. Although he was only in the post for four years he will be remembered for his ecumenical work and his organising abilities. His successor, Revd Mark Butchers, inspired and encouraged all with his enthusiasm and was very concerned for the young of the parish. He was one of those instrumental in securing a grant for the purchase and conversion of the former Methodist Church to a youth and community centre. At the time of writing, Revd Dr Brian Ardill holds the post, having been appointed in November 2000.

It is believed that there were chapels at de Bathe, although this is not certain, and at Nichols Nymett, the latter believed to have been demolished before

1629. Within living memory there were the remains of a chapel at Crooke Burnell, which was part of a barn, but no trace remains.

The parish registers date from 1538, although they are incomplete in the early years. There are lists of officiating ministers, churchwardens and, for some years in the sixteenth and seventeenth centuries, of those parishioners responsible for the upkeep of the church wall, together with their holdings.

As a postscript, a little-known fact was reported in the *Exeter Flying Post* on 16 October 1897 when the late Admiral Benedictus Marwood Kelly left the whole of his property, amounting to £89,000, to trustees to build a college to be called Kelly College. This was to be built west of a line drawn north and south through the Parish Church of North Tawton and was to provide education for the sons of members of the Church of England, deceased officers of the Royal Navy and such other boys as the trustees may approve. As we now know this prestigious school was finally built at Tavistock.

Broadnymett Church

Broadnymett was once a distinct parish with its own tiny church dedicated to St Martin, which fell into decay many years ago and was used as an agricultural building. It was rescued and partially restored in recent years by a member of the Stanbury family who owns the adjoining farm. It no longer has any interior furnishings and dates from the 1200s. The rectors

date from at least 1332 to 1837, when it was merged with Bow and probably abandoned, although for at least 200 years before the merger it had no resident rector. It is now included within the North Tawton parish boundary and was visited by those who beat the bounds for the millennium celebrations, all of whom were fascinated by this charming little church.

St Martin's Church, Broadnymett.

Chapels

There is a long history of Nonconformism in North Tawton, with many chapels and meeting-houses in the town providing an alternative to Anglican worship. The *Billings Directory* of 1851 lists the meeting-houses of the Congregationalists, Bible Christians and Plymouth Brethren in the town. Also in 1851 a government census of church attendance reported that in North Tawton there were 26 Bible Christians, 153 Congregationalists and 164 Brethren attending services.

Two decades later *Kelly's Directory* records a Congregational chapel, one chapel for the Bible Christians and a meeting-room for the Plymouth Brethren. But these listings are relatively modern. Walter Mortimer records that a religious meeting was held at South Week during the reign of Charles II (1660–85) which was believed to be a meeting of the Congregationalists, one of the earliest recorded Nonconformist sects. Another Nonconformist sect that dates from this time was the Quakers.

Quakers

Quakerism, a form of worship avoiding all ritual and conducted in silence until participants are moved by the Holy Spirit to speak, was founded in the seventeenth century by George Fox. The Quakers' vociferous condemnation of 'steeple-houses' led to their nationwide persecution. In 1656 George Fox was in prison in Launceston and three Quakers travelling to visit him were arrested in North Tawton. They were duly fined under the provisions of a public order announcement calling for 'watch and ward to be tightened in order to apprehend vagrants and Quakers.'

In 1668 two men appeared at the Quarter Sessions charged with being the ringleaders of a religious assembly at North Tawton. It was alleged that over 60 people had attended this gathering at the house of John Yeo who 'sought the Lord in truth', a Quaker expression.

Following the Toleration Act of 1689 Gawin Holmes was granted a licence for a Quaker meeting-house in North Tawton but there is no indication of where this was and there are no further records of Quakerism in the town.

Congregationalists

The Congregationalists (or Independents) were founded by Robert Browne during the reign of Elizabeth I (1558–1603). It is a Congregationalist belief that each church should be independent of external ecclesiastical authority. Browne and his followers suffered much persecution; some were hanged at Tyburn while others sought refuge in Holland. It was not until the reign of William III (1689–1702) that Congregationalists were able to worship freely in England. In 1833 the Congregational Union of England and Wales was formed and it is from that date that written records begin in North Tawton. These records state that at the beginning of the eighteenth century there was no Nonconformist place of worship in North Tawton. At that time:

... some people who held Free Church principles, with Mr Thomas Durant as one of the leaders, met for worship in an old loft. A cause was established and before 1812 had a settled minister, the Revd George Moase.

Revd Moase was a former schoolteacher. The group were meeting in Dr Budd's yard (Melhuishes) and, later, when a better meeting-place was needed, a barn was 'secured and properly fitted as a House for God.'

This is recorded in 1878 as having been in the yard now occupied by Mr Samuel Day. The early leaders took a great interest in the chapel and established a Sunday school, the first public Sunday school in North Tawton and one of the first in Devon. Subsequently the chapel moved to 11 Fore Street, to premises occupied later by the Plymouth Brethren (see below). A chapel was built in 1816 by Mr Pedler near his residence at Merrymeet (location unknown), where Mr Moase often conducted services. This building became too small and it was decided that a larger one was required, and the 'spot whereon the present commodious structure stands was selected.' This building opened in 1833 and is still in use at the time of writing.

In 1859 Mrs Walker, the pastor's wife, formed a Dorcas Society, a women's organisation which made clothes for the poor and needy. It was later reported that:

... at least 340 garments have been given away to the poor and needy of all denominations and especially those belonging to the Independent Church and congregation.

In 1863 a new schoolroom with a classroom above was built and later enlarged in 1878 to meet the

Right: *Presentation to Revd Phyllis Ball on her retirement, 1999. Left to right: Vera Taylor, May Paddon, Shirley Turner, Greta Watkins, Violet Marsh, Bruce Freeman, Revd Phyllis Ball, Win Arscott, Rose Dadds, Olive Donovan, Nina Mills, Carole Dadds, Hannah Willcock.*

Left: *Reopening of the URC schoolroom, 1983. Left to right, back row: Phyllis Knott, Dorothy Stoneman, Greta Watkins, Les Knott, Revd Martin Ambler, John Avery, Revd Rosemary Humphrey, Rose Dadds, Norman and Janet Down; front row: Wendy Burns and Claire Quick.*

Right: *URC ceiling collapses, 1968. Les Knott among the ruins.*

Left: *URC annual garden party and barbeque at Pine Lodge, 1960s.*

requirements of the growing Sunday school. Unfortunately, nearly a 100 years later problems with this building led to extensive work being carried out to remove the top storey and lower the roof, relieving the foundations of tons of weight. The new slimline schoolroom was ceremoniously reopened in 1986. One former resident of the town remembers American troops being billeted in the schoolroom during the Second World War and recalls being given chocolate and 'candy' – a real luxury in those days of sweet and food rationing.

The Revd Thomas Taylor, probably the longest-serving pastor, completed 25 years of service in December 1902 and in 1904 he was summoned for non-payment of that part of the Education Rate which was to be used for sectarian purposes. On 23 March 1904 a lamp and stand (presumably belonging to him) which had been seized under a warrant were sold by public auction to enforce payment of the amount owed, plus costs. He retired in 1906 and died in 1925, aged 89 years. A brass plaque can be seen in the chapel, commemorating his long and faithful service.

The burial ground outside the chapel was closed in 1883 and the first burial in the parish churchyard, as required by a new Act of Parliament, was of Ethel Manning in February 1883, who died aged eight months. The first Nonconformist burial in the new cemetery in Exeter Street was that of Annie Skinner, aged 15, in June 1901. The occupations listed in the burial records of 1838–68 reflect the varied commercial activities of the town at the time when it was at its most populous and prosperous. Occupations included shoemaker, thatcher, carpenter, cordwainer, confectioner, basketmaker, woolcomber, miller, blacksmith, tanner, colt rider, weaver, farm labourer, policeman, clerk, mill worker, mason, labourer, engineer, servant, railway linesman, porter, gardener, sawyer, tailor, innkeeper, bag and rope maker, scavenger and minister.

During the early 1900s the church was re-roofed and much-needed improvements undertaken. The stained-glass window was installed in memory of Mr Henry Phillips, JP, the proprietor of the Devon Serge Warehouse (see Chapter 8) in appreciation of 50 years of faithful service. He died in 1920 and is remembered as a lovely old gentleman who always gave the first child to reach chapel an apple or an orange. Shortly after this the upstairs gallery was removed, the organ moved and choir stalls placed each side of the central pulpit. Oak panelling was placed across the front of the church. The organ was pumped by hand by volunteers, whose names can still be found scratched or written on the woodwork, the last one being Alfie Sealey before it was converted to run on electricity in the early 1960s.

In 1923 there was a major division within the congregation over an undisclosed matter which resulted in many members, including the secretary and treasurer, resigning and joining the Methodist Church instead. The ramifications of this schism went on for over three years but eventually the church Moderator appealed for Christian forbearance and unity and new officers were elected to fill the vacant posts. The loss of so many members and their wives had a devastating effect on the musical life of the chapel and caused real problems for the Tea Committee!

Ministers came and went and the Minister's house or Manse was at 46 Fore Street, now called Osborne House. This was maintained by several bequests, one of which was bestowed by the late Revd Taylor, one by Samuel Day and another by Philip Osborn, the latter two both being blacksmiths in Fore Street (see Chapter 8).

In 1965 the name of the Congregational Union was changed to the Congregational Church and in 1972 the Presbyterian and Congregational Churches combined to form the United Reformed Church.

In 1968 the congregation arrived for evening worship to find that most of the ceiling had collapsed. A major fund-raising effort began and the church was reopened in February 1969 by Mrs Susie Adams (the eldest member) and Miss Rachel Watkins (the youngest member) with a new suspended ceiling, electric heating and lighting, and other improvements. Latterly more changes have been made with the removal of the choir stalls and the organ and pulpit have been moved to their current locations.

Evelyn Bailey became the temporary secretary in 1961 and did not relinquish the post until 1978. She and her family lived at Pine Lodge and used to host an annual garden party and barbeque in the garden to raise funds. One of her brothers, Bob, owned the paper shop at the top of Fore Street and he and another brother, Eddie, were in turn Treasurers of the chapel. Her sister, Elsie, used to attend services at the Methodist church and her other sister, Nora, worshipped at St Peter's. This must have led to interesting debates around the dinner table!

Miss Bailey wrote in the minutes of a meeting held in 1969 that, 'there are few if any church meetings when the problems of £.s.d. crises or some part of the church structure does not need attention.' On this occasion the leaking kitchen roof and some guttering needed attention, but nothing has changed and the chapel once again needs a major refurbishment so it can continue to provide a facility for Nonconformist worship in North Tawton.

Methodists

Another early account of Nonconformism is that in the journal of John Wesley, the 'father' of Methodism, who visited North Tawton in 1765 and was not well received, commenting thus:

I rode on to North Tawton, a village where several of our preachers had preached occasionally. About six I went to the door of our inn; but I had hardly ended the psalm, when a clergyman came, with two or three (by the courtesy of England called) gentlemen. After I had named my text I said, 'There may be some truths which concern some men only; but this concerns all mankind.' The minister cried out, 'That is false doctrine, that is predestination.' Then the roar began, to second which they had brought an huntsman with his hounds. But the dogs were wiser than the men; for they could not bring them to make any noise at all. One of the gentlemen supplied their place. He assured us he was such, or none would have suspected it; for his language was as base, foul and porterly, as ever was heard at Billingsgate. Dog, rascal, puppy, and the like terms adorned almost every sentence. Finding there was no probability of a quiet hearing, I left him the field, and withdrew to my lodging [thought to have been 1 Barton Street, home until recently to Fred and Mary Harris, and possibly at the time it was the New Inn (see Chapter 8)].

The Bible Christians, or Bryanites, were formed in Devon in 1815 by William Bryant who broke away from the Wesleyan Methodists because he thought there were a lot of people, especially in rural areas, who were bypassed by religion. He started to hold meetings in the Thorne family home at Lake Farm, Shebbear. In 1829 Bryant's daughter Mary and her husband Samuel Thorne started a small boys' school at their home in Shebbear. By 1841 sufficient funding had been secured and it became the Bible Christian Proprietary College, later renamed Shebbear College.

The Bible Christian movement spread and in North Tawton a dwelling house in Barton Road (Barton Street has been variously called Barton Road, Lane or Street) was purchased in 1841 and converted into a Bible Christian chapel, known at that time as the Bethel Bible Christian Chapel. A larger building accommodating a church, school and classroom, which still exists today, opened in 1898 on the same site, presumably a sign of increased popularity.

In 1907 the Bible Christians amalgamated with the United Methodist Free Churches to form the United Methodists and in 1932 the Wesleyans and the Primitive Methodists joined to form the Methodist Church as we know it today. After the split in the Congregational Church in 1923 (see above) the Methodist attendance was considerably enlarged and Eleanor Manning ran a Bible class for teenagers on a weekday evening. Mr Arthur Knapman of The

Barton was a lay reader and he and Mrs Knapman were very active in church affairs and fund-raising fêtes were held at their home. Mrs Mondon played the organ, a role later performed by Miss Nancy Sampson. Elsie Bailey was one of the teachers at the Sunday school.

A Lancashire newspaper reported in 1947 that Mr W.E. Moss, a native of North Tawton, had just been appointed the new president of the British Temperance League. Mr Moss, aged 85 and now resident in Blackburn, still possessed the Band of Hope pledge card given to him in 1866 in the Barton Lane Bible Christian School, North Tawton!

Unfortunately the numbers attending the chapel slowly dwindled as the need for urgent repairs and renewals grew. The minutes record growing concern about the fabric of the building, including rotting floor boards, woodworm, problems with the gable end wall, and in 1981 it was reported that a large part of the ceiling had fallen down, narrowly missing Mrs Ranford who was badly shocked. The Sunday school closed in 1974, evening services were discontinued in 1982 and the last morning service was held in 1995. The remaining members joined with the United Reformed Church in North Street, which became the Lakeway United Church, and the building was closed and sold. After much renovation and refurbishment it now enjoys a new lease of life as the Youth and Community Centre.

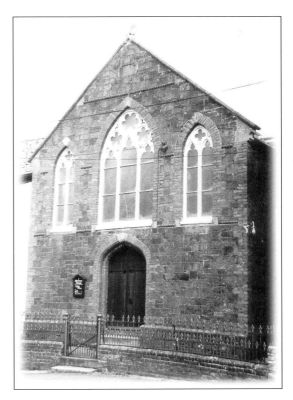

Methodist Church, Barton Street.

*Methodist Fête at The Barton, North Tawton, 1923/4. Pictured in the centre is George Lambert MP
(later Lord Lambert) with son George on his knee.*

Gospel Hall

The Brethren movement was begun in Dublin in 1827, as an alternative to Anglican worship, by John Nelson Darby, a minister of the Protestant Church of Ireland, and Edward Cronin, a former Roman Catholic. The movement spread due to Darby's extensive travels and writings and he eventually settled in Plymouth, hence the nickname the 'Plymouth Brethren'. Their presence in North Tawton is thought to date from 1839 when a preacher from Barnstaple visited the town. At first people would have worshipped together in each other's homes but as numbers grew a proper meeting-room was needed. The first chapel was opened in 1850 in premises in Fore Street, which had recently been vacated by the Congregationalists and latterly known for many years as 'The Pantry'. The chapel was closed during the First World War and not reopened for another ten years. In the interim the Brethren again met in each other's houses. Miss Ophelia Tamlin of 11 The Square organised the refurbishment of the chapel and it reopened for worship in 1928. Unfortunately, a short time later the building was found to be damp

and in need of further repair so a new chapel in Lakeway (North Street) was built in 1938 on land given by Mr Ernest Bragg of Bouchiers Hill. This building is still in use at the time of writing and many of the town's residents will remember the wonderful vegetables grown in the chapel garden by Mr Fred Crocker.

The Gospel Hall.

Chapter 3

FARMING

Northorth Tawton is fortunate in being largely situated on a tongue of fertile redland, which stretches from Crediton to Exbourne. This consists of Permian sandstones, part of the Bow Conglomerates, while at the periphery both north and south is a clay type of soil. Agriculture has always played a major part in the economy of North Tawton, although as elsewhere many of the agricultural holdings were quite small.

Throughout the Middle Ages and beyond, farming was carried out at a subsistence level. The Black Death in the fourteenth century took its toll on the population of Devon as elsewhere, but it meant that some of the survivors benefited by being able to move into larger holdings.

Sometimes there were harvest failures, such as in 1622 when corn was prohibited from use in brewing, and the Justices were directed to ensure that what was available was distributed fairly. In February 1623, the Justices of South Molton, North Tawton and elsewhere sent out constables to ascertain how much corn was available, meeting again ten days later to decree how much was to be sent to market (this was to prevent stockpiling), but they were able to report 'that our markets are plentifully supplied with grain at reasonable prices.' In those days wheat, barley and oats were the main crops with some rye, root crops and some green vegetables.

Over the years prosperity waxed and waned according to wars, climate, disease and taxes. Charles Vancouver, reporting for the Board of Agriculture in 1808, gives a snapshot of a farm in North Tawton, telling us that:

Mr Sweet keeps 160 new Leicester sheep, of which he lambs about 90 annually making his sheep stock between April and August about 250. He has four cows and some horses for his arable land. He cultivates annually ten acres of turnips... and has 65 acres of grassland. He sells his wethers at 18 months averaging 20lbs per quarter and 6lbs unwashed wool per fleece.

From the Land Tax returns it seems he owned several plots of land in the parish and he or members of his family were also engaged in the woollen trade as serge makers. It was common in those days to have more than one occupation.

An unsigned article in the parish magazine, dated 1911 but probably written by the Revd Robert Hole who came to North Tawton in 1850, stated:

A few reminiscences of North Tawton in the last 60 years. On first coming to North Tawton I remember seeing the wheat in the Home Barton being cut with reap hooks, and this method was soon replaced with scythes and a lath placed over the blades to keep the corn in place. Then came the wonderful reaping machine soon to be replaced by the present reaper and binder.

Today of course the combine harvester has replaced both reaper and binder, together with the threshing machine.

Reading old farming diaries there is a striking comparison between the scale of farming in days gone by and that practised today. Selling one or more bullocks each week to local butchers was commonplace. For example, in 1900 Ernest May of Crooke Burnell sold three fat heifers to Philip Madge the local butcher, for £12.5s.0d. each. After the railway arrived in 1865 some animals went by cattle truck to more distant markets such as Exeter, but many were driven by road to their destination.

Labour was cheap and plentiful then, those labourers on Crooke Burnell Farm were paid varying amounts, perhaps related to the hours worked, but they were never paid more than 10s.0d. (50p) per week. By 1939 this had risen to 34s.0d. (£1.70), although they may have received wages in kind as well, such as firewood, milk, etc. Before the advent of tractors a 100-acre farm could well employ three or four men and boys.

With regard to individual farms, many of these have been broken up in recent years as small farms are no longer viable. As mentioned in Chapter 1 there were six Domesday manors in North Tawton and a number of other farms can be deduced from the Lay Subsidy Rolls, which list the taxpayers. Those included are:

Addlehole

Meaning 'dirty place', this former smallholding was in Fore Street and is now a private house. In the 1960s it was a chicken farm owned by Mr Kilmartin.

Combining at de Bathe, early 1980s.

Baling hay on Station Hill, 2001.

Maurice Knott on the tractor at Chicken Farm, Addlehole, 1969.

Ashridge Court

This important estate was in the possession of the Champernowne family, who were lords of the manor, in the fourteenth century. They are commemorated with a carving of their coat of arms on a pew end and a portion of a stained-glass window in the church. Ashridge then passed by marriage to the Atwood (alias Wood) family in the fourteenth century.

It is mentioned in Chapter 9 that in 1549 one of the Justices who attempted to quell the Prayer Book Rebellion at Sampford Courtenay was Alexander Atwood of Ashridge. In the seventeenth century the Wood family name died out at Ashridge and the estate passed to the Skinner family through the female line, until their descendants sold it in 1902. Since then it has changed hands frequently.

The Revd Fulford Williams, who lived at Ashridge as a child, dates the present house to about 1800 and records that the carved beams from the old hall were placed in the kitchen roof of the new house. There is a site near the present house marked on old maps as 'former mansion' and a walled garden still exists there.

Some of the subsequent owners are remembered for their tea parties and treats to schoolchildren. Before the First World War, Mr E.C. Nicholls held an 'Open House' every Whit Monday, when everyone was invited for tea and games in the garden or in a marquee if the weather was poor. Colonel and Mrs Sharland continued the tradition in the 1920s and some of the older residents remember being entertained there when they were schoolchildren. Major Upton, Master of the Eggesford Foxhounds, lived there for a short time, followed by Sir Ashley and Lady Biggs in the 1930s. They came from Wiltshire bringing their staff with them, one of whom married the local ironmonger, Gilbert Avery. She recounts that they were very good employers, kind and considerate to their staff, and when they went on holiday they always brought back gifts for them.

During the Second World War Mr and Mrs Lawley, owners of a china firm, lived at Ashridge. They were a popular couple and supplied otherwise almost unobtainable crockery to Mrs Irene Sampson, who was struggling to stock her ironmonger's shop while her husband was on active service abroad. Several other owners of Ashridge came and went and at the time of writing it is a tree nursery.

de Bathe

This farm was split into two by the railway which arrived in 1865. The farm was first mentioned in the 1251 Assize Roll when it was held by the de Bathe family. Sir Henry de Bathe was a judge from 1245 to 1261, during the reign of Henry III. He was charged with corruption but taken back into favour and made Chief Justice of the King's Bench. The farm is said to have had a chapel in one of the smaller farm buildings, but this cannot be confirmed.

It has been suggested that John Bouchier, 1st Earl

Ashridge Court, 1927.

Left: *de Bathe Farm, 2001.*

Right: *de Bathe Pool, 1990.*

Above: *Cart horses in the yard at Great Beere, 1921.*

Right: *Mr James Ponsford with his sheep at Broadnymett, 1930s.*

of Bath, took his title from the farm in 1536, but this has never been substantiated. The ownership of the farm then passed through numerous families, many of whom did not actually live there but let it out to tenants. The old cob house at the far end of the farmyard is said to have burnt down in the nineteenth century. W.H. Kelland, a barrister from London whose family had owned it many years earlier, bought the farm and rebuilt the house in stone on a site nearer to the road in 1875. There is no record of him ever having lived there. Just two years later he sold it to Sir Henry P. de Bathe, a descendant of the original owners, who continued to let it out.

In 1919 Dame Charlotte de Bathe of London, Sir Henry's widow, sold 227 acres to her tenant Ernest May for £3,500 and Ernest May's great-grandson still farms there. Like so many small-scale farmers he has been obliged to diversify and combine farming with a woodwork business.

A fact not generally known is that Lily Langtree, an Edwardian actress born in Jersey as Emillie de Breton in 1852, first married Edward Langtree and later became the mistress of the Prince of Wales, the future King Edward VII. When she was widowed at the age of 46 she married Hugo de Bathe, who was the 28-year-old eldest son of Sir Henry P. de Bathe. She died in 1929 and her husband remarried but died childless, the title passing to his nephew.

de Bathe Pool

In one of the fields at de Bathe Farm there is a mysterious grassed-over depression in the ground which suddenly fills with water, irrespective of whether or not it has been raining. It is said that when it fills a member of the Royal family or other august personage will shortly die. It has been recorded that de Bathe Pool was 'out' on the deaths of the Prince Consort, Duke of Clarence, Queen Victoria, King Edward VII and King George V. Although dry at the time of Princess Diana's death in 1997, it filled just prior to Princess Margaret's death in 2002, but it has to be admitted that this was in the rainy season. There was no water in it at the time of the Queen Mother's death.

According to a newspaper report in 1936:

On one occasion a crop of barley had been cut and was stood in stooks. During the night the pool filled and the sheaves were floating next morning.

It is quite possible that the farm took its name Bath/Bathe from this phenomenon. At one time the Holmes in North Tawton always flooded at the same time but, presumably due to an alteration in the drainage, this no longer occurs.

Beere (known as Great Beere after 1836)

This Domesday manor was the site of a thirteenth-century development, which was excavated just before the Second World War. A typical Devon long-house (humans and animals under one roof, with a cross-passage between the two) was found with a central hearth and some pottery was excavated. A barn and two corn-drying kilns were also found, no doubt necessary because of the damp climate.

Under the contingency arrangements drawn up when Napoleon threatened invasion, Beere was to provide a wagon and horses to evacuate the old and infirm from the town, which was to be burnt.

In the tithe apportionments dated 1844 (when the whole country was surveyed and owners and occupiers of land listed) this 400-acre farm was owned by the Skinners of Westacott and farmed by Christopher Borne. A report in the *Exeter Flying Post* dated 8 August 1844 was headed 'Missing':

Whereas Robert Borne, son of Christopher Borne of Beer Farm, North Tawton has been missing from his home since Wednesday morning, 31st ult, should any person be able to afford information to his disconsolate parents it will be most gratefully acknowledged, and any attendant expenses readily discharged. He is 24 years of age, 5'8" high, round-shouldered, thin, pale and rather dejected features, and stoops a little on walking. Wore away fustian [hard-wearing material made of cotton and flax or wool] *jacket, dark stripe waistcoat and nailed shoes.*

Whether he was found is not known, but he was not listed as being at home with the rest of the family in the 1851 census. During the latter years most of the land has been sold off, as has happened to so many farms.

Bridge

This farm, as its name implies, is near Taw Bridge and there was mention of 'Walter at Bridge' in the Assize Roll of 1412. It was part of the manor of North Tawton and in the 1851 census amounted to 135 acres inhabited by the Snell family and employing four men. Bridge Quarries provided the hard green sandstone much used for buildings in North Tawton, such as the Market House, which was erected in 1849.

Broadnymett Barton

This Domesday manor was once a separate, but very small, parish of 450 acres. The tiny church of St Martin's was absorbed into Bow for ecclesiastical purposes in the 1800s, but for civil purposes it has always belonged to North Tawton and still does.

In the thirteenth and fourteenth centuries it was owned by Adam de Brodenymett and later on by the Lethbridges, who were considerable landowners in the district. In the 1851 census the farm was owned by Richard Dunning but was tenanted and consisted of 400 acres, plus 100 acres of moor, employing 13 men, four women and two boys, several of whom lived in cottages on the moor which have long since disappeared. Some years later, the Railway Cottages were built on the moor, but these too have gone.

Left: *Crooke Burnell.*

Right: *Cottles Barton, 1904.*

Left: *The plaster ceiling and coat of arms above the fireplace at Cottles Barton, 1904.*

Right: *Donald Drake of Essington Park Farm with Devon Longwool sheep.*

Today, only the farmhouse and the chapel survive. The former, which dates from the sixteenth century, was built of cob and began to deteriorate, requiring a partial rebuild during the last century.

In 1939 the farm comprised 479 acres and was sold for £6,750; nine years later in 1948 it changed hands again for £22,000.

Crooke Burnell

First mentioned as Cruk in the Domesday Book (1086), it had a chapel dedicated to St Mary, which was licensed in 1378, the remains of which were part of a barn until the middle of the twentieth century. The present house is largely seventeenth century. The suffix 'Burnell' was added in the fourteenth century when a family of that name owned it.

This has always been a large farm, which for many years has included the adjacent holding of Hollacrook (house now demolished), with grazing rights on Itton Moor in the neighbouring parish of South Tawton. There are extant deeds and complicated marriage settlements relating to the Wares who owned and farmed at Crooke in the eighteenth and nineteenth centuries, but by the date of the tithe apportionments it was in the hands of the Crootes.

The farm was about 400 acres when purchased from the Crootes by Richard May for £13,000 in 1884, which seems a huge sum for those days, and it has been in the same family since that time. Until recently part of the estate included a large quarry, known as Stone Quarry, which produced roadstone. This was used as a 'tip' for many years but has now been filled in.

Cottles Barton (The Barton)

The Cottle family are said to have come over with William the Conqueror and settled in Wiltshire, spreading westwards and giving their name to Cotehele in Cornwall, which they owned at one time. A branch of this family settled at North Tawton in about 1550, coming from Yeolmbridge near Launceston, when Thomas Cottle, gentleman, married Alice, daughter of Dunstan Heywood of North Tawton.

According to the date over the porch, which also bears the initials T.C., the present, attractive thatched house was built in 1567. The arms of the Cottle family are also engraved over one of the fireplaces with the letters M.C. and the date 1599. There is also a splendid plaster ceiling and fine oak panelling in one of the rooms. In Mark Cottle's marriage settlement of 1558 he gave as jointure to his second wife, Mary Yeo:

... the four mills, weirs, water courses, head waters, and mill leats appertaining to the said mills, lately builded and erected by my father Thomas Cottle, in and upon the said Barton, that is to say two gryst mills, one fulling mill and one edge mill, together with the pasture near the mill called New Meadow.

Although this has been interpreted by Revd Fulford Williams in his *History of North Tawton* as referring to Peckett's Ford, Newland, Town Mills and Bondleigh respectively, it seems more likely that all four mills were at Newland.

Mark Cottle died in 1622 and left a will bemoaning the fact that after payment of his debts there would not be much left and entreating his second wife to be 'kind to my poor grandchildren who are destitute and have no means to live by, and also to my old household servants.' Despite this, the family held on to their inheritance for nearly another 100 years, so things could not have been that bad.

In 1718 the estate was sold to William Fellowes (whose family later became Earls of Portsmouth). A North Tawton family named Durant became the tenants and remained for many years, followed by the Salters to whom they were related by marriage. New barns were erected in 1866 by the landlord and the farm of 428 acres was sold on the break-up of the Portsmouth estate for £10,200. It was shortly afterwards resold and bought by the Knapman family from Drewsteignton in 1907. The estate was sold again in the 1950s and then changed hands once more in 1966, when it was bought by Mr Ken Dunn who diversified, building large warehouses, which in the 1990s became the headquarters of the Vital Dog Company.

An interesting little-known fact is that in 1906 the North Tawton Parish Council wrote to the Seale Hayne Trustees suggesting that the new agricultural college about to be founded (now near Newton Abbot and part of Plymouth University) be established at The Barton. What a coup for the town that would have been!

Essington Park Farm

Little is known about the history of this farm. It is listed in the Land Tax Assessments for 1780 as belonging to the rector and farmed by tenant James Fewings, who also farmed Crispins, now a private house in Essington. Surprisingly, in the 1890s it was the home of two medical men, first Dr G.R.S. Banbury, followed by Dr Patrick Hislop, whose waiting room is reputed to have been up a stone flight of steps to a former granary. More recently, for many years it has been the home of the Drake family, who are renowned for the quality of their sheep, cattle and swedes.

Greenslade

This was one of the Domesday manors. Geoffrey of Greenslade, along with Robert of Slade and two others, was tried for the murder of William de Molis in 1234, who was killed with a knife 'evilly and in felony', but the accused all denied being involved. As Geoffrey and Robert were important people, a jury from a large area had to be empanelled. They found Geoffrey and Robert guilty and they were

The Queen Mother with Brian Drake and the Show President at the Royal Cornwall Show, 1985.

David Hampson at Greenslade Farm, 1996.

Greenslade farmyard, 2001.

hanged. One of the other defendants was fined and outlawed, while the other was found not guilty.

Moving on several hundred years, in the census of 1851, John Shillson of Greenslade is described as maltster and farmer of 205 acres, 'employing 10 labourers, and 16 moore Emp.' Presumably this should read '16 more employees', although in *White's Directory* of 1850 there is no reference to a brewhouse. The present owner confirms that there are the remains of such a building and he recalls seeing a reference to brewing in Elizabethan times, when of course most large houses would have brewed their own beer.

There was a brick-making enterprise at Greenslade, near Iron Bridge, in the nineteenth century where yellowish bricks were made, known as Greenslade bricks. It is said that these bricks were used locally but no one seems to know anything about this venture today. On the tithe map of 1844 there is a field on the farm named 'Brick Moor' close to Iron Bridge. There is also an old stone quarry on the farm in a field named 'Quarry Close', so Greenslade was well served with building materials.

The house is probably medieval in date although it has seemingly been extended in the seventeenth and eighteenth centuries. Little is known of its history. It was bought from the Daw family by Major and Mrs Hampson shortly after the Second World War. Their son, David, a noted breeder of Suffolk sheep, was the first president of that society from the South West and is a well-known judge at agricultural shows.

Halse Farm

This farm has a long history, being first mentioned in the Subsidy Rolls of 1333 and again in 1562, when the owner, Mark Slader, was required to pay his share for the upkeep of the churchyard wall. In 1844 at the time of the tithe apportionments, when it was owned by George Pike Sanders but tenanted, it was said to be 223 acres in extent. At the turn of the century

William Madge acquired it and built a new brick house in about 1906 at the opposite end of the farmyard from the old one. During the twentieth century it had a number of owners and is now the property of the Lennard family, who have lived there for nearly 50 years.

Nichols Nymett

Another of the Domesday manors, this estate was subsequently held by Simon de Lamprey. Adam Nichols Nymett and Roselynus of Nichols Nymett are each listed as paying tax in 1332. It was eventually bought by the Hole family of Zeal Monachorum. A member of this family, named Peter, mentioned among other bequests in his will, dated 19 February 1645, one acre of 'the very best rye', which is not a crop we hear of much in the parish today. It still belonged to the Hole family in 1780 but then seems to have been bought by John Wreford, who built the present handsome Georgian house which dates from about 1816 with later nineteenth-century additions. This may have been built on the site of a previous house, but the home farm is some distance away, nearer the road, and together with its barn conversions is no longer connected with active farming. The farmer of the surrounding land lives in a new house nearby.

An advertisement in the *Exeter Flying Post*, dated 29 July 1819, gives notice of 'A sale of 11 acres of very fine flax growing on the estate and the purchaser can be accommodated with convenient sheds for working.' Applications were to be addressed to Mr John Wreford of Nichols Nymett, proprietor. In view of the recent revival of flax-growing in the West Country, it is interesting to note that it is nothing new.

In 1900 the estate was bought by Mr Matthews of the Indian Civil Service whose wife headed the North Tawton Detachment of the Red Cross and held field practices and mock exercises in the grounds.

Halse Farmhouse, 2000.

Roger Lennard of Halse hand milking, 2000.

Left: *Nichols Nymett House in 1918.*

Below: *A wedding party at Slade in 1926, following the marriage of Andrew Ash and Rhoda Mary Davey.*

Left: *Stone Farm, 1998.*

Right: *Will Bale on the rick during haymaking at Wardens Farm, 1930s.*

Many years later, after several changes of ownership, the main house was successively a nursing home and a hotel, and at the time of writing is a guest-house.

A short distance away is Lower Nichols Nymett, formerly known as Wigwell, whose owners are dairy farmers and are well known for their excellent cream teas. In the tithe map of 1844 there are three rack fields and a mill pond near Lower Nichols Nymett, which suggests there was a fulling mill nearby and there is a mill mentioned in a law suit of 1628 (Hole v Snell).

Sandford Farm

This is an ancient holding which was first mentioned in the Subsidy Roll of 1332, when William of Sandford paid tax. It seems to have belonged to the Hole family from the mid-eighteenth to the mid-nineteenth centuries and in the tithe apportionments was stated to be a tenanted holding of 103 acres.

Slade Farm

As already mentioned under the entry for Greenslade, Robert of Slade was hanged in 1238 for murder and his lands became forfeit to the King. By 1563 Slade Farm was in the possession of Christopher Copplestone of Copplestone, who later sold it to Mark Slader of North Tawton.

Slade Farm has been very important as the source of the town's water from an early date (see Chapter 6) and there are many remains of reservoirs and pipes on the land.

A newspaper advertisement, dated 1857, is very informative as to some of the stock kept at that date on this 172-acre farm, when the owner was quitting his tenancy. These included:

5 fat heifers, 3 barren heifers, 2 Jersey heifers, 1 carthorse 7 years old, 2 cart mares and foals, 1 very powerful cart colt, 1 useful mare for saddle or harness, 2 sows in farrow, 5 large and 5 small slip pigs, 20 hogsheads cider, 1 prime Rick clover hay, several of straw, 2 wagons, 2 butt carts, sullies, iron drags and harrow, wood and stone rollers, turnip hoe and cutter, edit and other rakes, shaft and fore harness, 100 hurdles, bags, sacks, measures, pound Kiev's, stone pound trough and many other tools. Also very neat dogcart.

At the time of the 1851 census there were five labourers employed at Slade Farm, three of whom lived in at the farm, which was the norm for unmarried farm-hands. In 1919 Slade was sold for £2,650, the acreage at that time is not known. It was subsequently bought by Devon County Council to enable young landless farmers to set up in business. Shortly afterwards the front of the house fell out and had to be rebuilt. Andrew Ash, father of the tenant at the time of writing, who was the son of a Sampford Courtenay builder, was delivering stone to Slade for the rebuilding and there met his future wife, Rhoda Mary Davey. Marrying in 1923, they subsequently rented Slade and the family is still there.

Staddon Farm

This holding was part of the manor of North Tawton and one Robert of Staddon was a juror in the thirteenth century. One hundred years later John of Staddon paid 12d. (5p) tax. In the 1840s the farm consisted of 141 acres and was tenanted by George Bulleid. The present house is thought to date from the seventeenth century and in recent years much of the land has been sold off.

Stone Farm

There is a complex of multi-ditched enclosures visible as crop marks on the land belonging to Stone Farm, probably of a Bronze-Age date. In 1332 William at Stone is listed in the Subsidy Roll. The existing attractive farmhouse was originally called Lower Stone and there were also a Middle Stone, nearer to the road, and a Higher Stone. The latter farmhouse, said to date from the sixteenth century, was already demoted to a labourer's cottage at the time of the 1881 census. Today, Middle Stone and Higher Stone are barely discernible in the grass.

Upcott

This farm seems to have been part of the Nichols Nymett manor when Robert Uppecote paid 8d. tax in 1332. It was part of the endowment of the Charity School in the eighteenth century (see Chapter 5). By the time of the tithe apportionments 100 years later it belonged to the Skinner family and comprised 101 acres. At the time of writing it is still a working farm. The farmhouse has a medieval roof and a lower wing which is dated 1609.

Wardens

This farm was part of the glebe (land held by the clergyman) until the twentieth century, originally comprising some 80 acres. On this farm is a field called Blood Acre, named after a skirmish at the time of the Sampford Courtenay Rebellion (see Chapter 9). In the 1920s and '30s and for some years afterwards it was farmed by Will Bale and his son Arthur, but now it is a private house and some of the land has been sold off.

Week

This ancient holding is mentioned in the 1332 Subsidy Roll when Nicholas, Peter and William, all of Wyk (Week), paid varying amounts of tax for their respective parts of it. The hamlet of Week consisted of Underhill's Week, Hodge's Week, Reynold's Week and Pearce's Week, most of which was owned from at least the sixteenth century by the Rolle family of North Devon. The trustees of Lord Rolle sold off his portion of the estate some time after the compilation of the tithe apportionments in 1844.

In the 1851 census there were 14 households at Week, numbering 57 people. The Gibbings family bought some of it in 1889, including the farmhouse

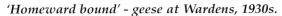

'Homeward bound' - geese at Wardens, 1930s.

South Week (top right), is now the site of a cheese factory, with Mill Lane cottages in the foreground.

Westacott.

Yeo Farm, 1914.

The plaster ceiling at Westacott.

Bill Dadds and Dora Way at Yeo Farm, 1971.

adjacent to the road, probably as sitting tenants. They had been there since at least 1866 and had lived in North Tawton during the previous 150 years. It is recorded that in 1816 the harvest was exceptionally late, Mr Gibbings not mowing (presumably his corn) until 6 September.

Subsequently the house and land were sold separately. Week House is no longer the family farmhouse it once was. During the Second World War a school was evacuated here (see Chapter 5).

South Week and Lamberts Week

These adjacent holdings were part of the North Tawton manor owned by the Portsmouth estate. Between the First and Second World Wars a family named Hobbs farmed there who also had a milk round. The house subsequently became derelict and was demolished to make way for the cheese factory.

Westacott

This farm was part of the Nichols Nymett manor in 1332, when Roger of Westcote paid 8d. tax for it. A most attractive former farmhouse, it lies some distance from the road. It is thought to have been a medieval hall house and smoke-blackened roof timbers survive. It is thatched and has two handsome seventeenth-century plaster ceilings, one upstairs and one downstairs, which were restored about 20 years ago. There is a ten-light oak window on the ground floor and a five-light window on the first floor. It is not known who owned the farm when the ornate ceilings were made. The Skinner family owned Ashridge and Westacott in the eighteenth century, at least since 1733, and at the same time rented Sandford and Staddon, so were probably successful yeomen and thus in a position to commission such fine work.

Previously a working farm with a large range of cob outbuildings, it is now a private house.

Yeo Farm

This was part of the manor of North Tawton. The house was built or rebuilt at some time by the Earl of Portsmouth, whose distinctive 'P' surmounted by a crown adorns the front of this attractive house. It was sold by the Earl at the break-up of his estate in 1904 and bought by the sitting tenant, George Webber. He paid £2,825 for the house and land of 311 acres and his family remained there until the 1990s, when the property was broken up and much of the land sold. The house and buildings are now in private occupation and some of the barns have been converted for holiday lets.

Market

The Market in The Square, pre First World War.

As already mentioned a market was granted by the lord of the manor, John de Valletort, in 1270, but lapsed in about 1720. It was resumed when the Market House was built in 1849, when market day was Thursday. Within living memory the cattle market was held in The Square, while the sheep were sold by the Old Rectory wall in Essington. Again the market lapsed, and was then restarted in the 1930s. There were iron railings protecting the windows in The Square and slots in the road which were used to fix hurdles on market days.

Traffic congestion eventually caused a change of venue, so it moved to the rear of the former Gostwyck Arms, then for a short while to a field near the railway station, followed by a move to the bottom of Fore Street, where Shipton's now stand, finally closing in 1986.

In the twentieth century there were a number of auctioneers, including May & Son, followed by Callaways, Kivells, and Harris & Co, represented by Sam Bassett. In the 1970s Roger Knapman ran the market, followed by Pyle and Ramsay until its closure as a cattle market in 1986, although furniture continued to be sold until the early 1990s.

From the erection of the pannier market in 1849 until the late 1930s consumer goods such as milk, eggs, butter, etc., were sold by local farmers' wives and traders from further afield. This building was open to the sky and had a cobbled floor, with trestle tables on which goods were displayed. At the great markets in April, October and December the cattle were led into the back of the building by a side door in Market Street where they were sold *(see page 45)*.

The Square with the Town Hall (the former Market House) on the left.

The Christmas Market in 1971, held at bottom of Fore Street. Left to right: Sam Bassett, Bill Webber, ?, Bill Dadds, Arthur Webber, Lew Quick.

Young Farmers Club

The Devon Federation of Young Farmers Clubs was formed in 1932 and the North Tawton club dates from at least as early as 1936. For a time in the 1940s it was combined with South Tawton and meetings were sometimes held in South Zeal. The club was part of the North Tawton group which comprised seven clubs and was always very active, meeting at various times in the school, in the Over 60s' Club and then in a room at the Fountain Inn.

Classes in various aspects of agriculture were held and competitions such as cattle judging, sheep shearing and poultry trussing were popular, as well as several well-attended social events.

The club also took part in fund-raising activities for good causes, such as the ram roast, which the club organised as part of the 'Old English Fayre' in 1955, in aid of the Town Hall Fund and the Brass Band. The YFC County Organiser, Tug Wilson, acted as chef and the event was opened by 'Jan Stewer' whom many will remember as a raconteur of tales in

the Devonshire dialect. The fire for the roast required two tons of wood, the band played and the children enjoyed rides on Mr Densham's miniature railway.

In 1979 a combined bonfire night and fireworks display, organised jointly by the YFC and the rugby club, was held at de Bathe Farm.

North Tawton took part in all the competitions over the years enjoying a considerable amount of success. In 1979 Norman Pyle was Champion Sheep Shearer of the group, while Philip Dennis took the junior title. In other years the club was successful at public speaking, swimming, darts and athletics, among other competitions.

Dances, discos, amateur dramatics, quizzes and various other social events were arranged, which no doubt were a boon to many otherwise somewhat isolated young people and it is sad to record the demise of this club in November 1992 following county restructuring, after so many successful years.

YFC members at North Tawton Market Hall, 1938.
Pictured left to right: *Mr Brock, ?,*
Walter Martin, Lawrence Sampson, Clarice Green,
Reg Dart, Fleetwood Green, George Dart
(leading bullock), *? Quick.*

YFC presentation of a silver tray by Alan Taylor
(president) to Norman Pyle at the Fountain Inn, 1978.
Others pictured include: *Kenny Jones, Carol Dennis,*
William Speak, Robert Pyle, Philip Dennis, Roger Bolt,
Alistair Stoneman, Jane Baulch, Christine Stacey.

Foot and Mouth Disease

Epidemics of various diseases have always blighted farming, but the scale of the foot and mouth outbreak in 2001 was enormous and unfortunately North Tawton did not escape unscathed. It was devastating for those whose animals contracted it and just as bad for those whose (healthy) animals were destroyed in the so-called 'contiguous cull'.

It is extremely difficult to describe the huge impact this had on a small community, with nearly all functions cancelled and footpaths closed. The holiday trade dried up and there was a feeling of being beleaguered and shunned by the public at large. Many people suffered financially because of the 'knock-on' effects. This, on top of the bovine spongiform encephalitis (BSE) epidemic a short time previously and the ever present threat of escalating bovine tuberculosis, has dealt a very severe blow to the entire farming community.

Slaughtered sheep in the 'contiguous cull'
at North Tawton.

Funeral pyre at North Tawton.

The Holmes, forerunner of the wool factory.

Part of the wool factory, 1989.

The wool factory with Dartmoor in the distance. Note the aqueduct carrying away the 'washings', top right.

Chapter 4

WOOL

Wool has always been of very great importance in the South West and the prosperity of North Tawton depended on this, and other branches of agriculture, until well into the twentieth century.

Of course wool was not only important in the South West. In medieval times English fleeces provided the ransom for Richard I (1189–99), who was imprisoned in Austria while returning from a Crusade, and the fact that the Chancellor of the Exchequer sits on a woolsack shows its importance in times gone by. Spinning, which could be done with the fingers, is said to have been introduced into this country in around 2500BC, along with weaving. By the twelfth century there was a flourishing cloth industry in England.

Many words and phrases we use even today are connected with cloth-making, such as 'spinning a yarn', 'on tenterhooks' and 'spinster'. Surnames, such as Webber (weaver) and Tucker (which is the Devonshire equivalent of 'fuller', one of the processes involved in making cloth), are widely distributed in Devon.

The first mechanisation of cloth-making came in the thirteenth century with the invention of the fulling mill powered by a water-wheel. This process required running water, of which there was plenty in North Tawton. The water in the area is also soft and there is a warm and humid climate, making processing easy. North Tawton also had sheep, but wool had to be imported as well to make up the shortfall. Before the development of the fulling or tucking mill, which used water-powered hammers to make the cloth thicker and heavier, this was done by hand, foot or club. The first known fulling mill in North Tawton was that at Cottles Barton in 1558, as mentioned in Chapter 3.

In order to support the woollen industry a law was passed in 1667 which required every person to be buried in wool, otherwise the family of the deceased would be subject to a fine. This law was repealed in 1814. Someone, usually a relative, had to swear on oath (an affidavit) that the body had been wrapped in a woollen shroud. In an extract from the North Tawton churchwardens' accounts for 28 October 1678 it states that a fine of £5 was levied because Mr John Wood of Ashridge was not buried in a woollen shroud; half of this went to the informer,

George Underhill, and the rest was divided among twelve named poor parishioners. Mr Wood was a gentleman and as such was probably buried in a silken shroud.

In an Overseers' Rate Book the seemingly expensive costs for the funeral of a pauper, Noah Welch, are recorded:

21 May 1744. To a coffin for Noah Welch – 6s.0d.
The lying of him forth – 3s.0d.
The making of his grave, bell and affidavit – 2s.0d.
A pound of wool to wrap him in – 1s.0d.

Until the Industrial Revolution, the making of woollen cloth was carried out at home and often the whole family played a part; children helping even when only a few years old – the boys carding (combing) the wool while mothers and girls did the spinning and fathers the weaving. Spinning-wheels and looms were a common sight in the cottages. An inventory of the goods of John Honichurch, alias Marten, of North Tawton whose will was dated 1587 includes '2 pairs of weaving looms'. Looms were often rented. Charity Lock rented one from Mr Sweet of North Tawton 'until Candlemas 1783', although generally weaving was considered to be men's work. Perhaps she had sons who were to do the weaving. It took about eight spinners to service one weaver. Often the men worked on farms at busy times such as harvest and in slacker periods did weaving at home. Master weavers employed men who worked round a courtyard under their master's eye and sometimes lived on the master's premises as well.

The Revd William Hole, while rector at North Tawton, when writing to Dean Milles (who was doing a survey of Devon) in about 1755, says that:

The woollen manufacture is the trade of the poor people, carried on by two or three masters and disposed of at Exeter.

In the seventeenth century, serge, which was a hard-wearing material, had come into fashion and it is apparent from insurance policies that there were a number of quite wealthy serge makers in North Tawton in the eighteenth century. For example, in 1747 Richard Sommers, John Brock and Thomas Day all insured their premises and goods against fire. An extract from the Sun Fire Office inventories shows:

25 August 1749. Thomas Day, sergemaker.
Dwelling house, workshop, combshop, sorting house, warehouse, dyehouse, stable and shippen adjoining forming a court – £100.
Household goods and stock in trade – £100.

Times must have been prosperous as by 1761 Thomas Day was insuring, in addition to the above, four tenements under one roof, probably for his workforce, with hanging linneys, insured altogether for £400.

Often times were hard too. Trade fluctuated, increasing when uniforms were needed in wartime, but there was also difficulty in exporting cloth at that time because the enemy captured or sunk many of our ships. Because of the uncertainty of the woollen trade many serge makers diversified and were farmers, brewers or shopkeepers as well. The Day family came into this category when, according to the Land Tax Assessments of 1794, Thomas Day, serge maker, also occupied the New Inn and later the George Inn.

Later on, competition, especially from the Lancashire cotton industry where coal was plentiful to run the new machinery, would have sounded the death knell of our woollen trade had it not been for the East India Company. For many years this company unloaded woollen goods to the Chinese at a loss and brought back tea, otherwise things would have been much worse for North Tawton. This trade ceased in the mid-nineteenth century when the East India Company's trade monopoly was abolished.

As the nineteenth and twentieth centuries progressed the Devonshire woollen mills failed, one by one, although North Tawton's was one of the last to go. Unemployment was a constant worry, particularly for the weavers who were outworking. They were badly paid and when they were superseded by machinery they often ended up in the workhouse. They were not eligible for relief until they had sold their loom, so were in a no-win situation.

In the *Exeter Flying Post*, dated 28 January 1799, there is reference to the bankruptcy of George Durant, serge maker. In 1801 by order of the Bankruptcy Commissioners, notice of a sale by auction of all his (considerable) property was published. Again in 1811 there is a Commission of Bankruptcy Order against a George Dicker of North Tawton, serge maker, shopkeeper, dealer and chapman (itinerant pedler).

It would seem that the Fulford family were the most successful woollen manufacturers in the town. According to the notes of Revd Fulford Williams, whose ancestors they were, and his writing in the *Transactions of the Devonshire Association* in 1954, which was later reprinted as a booklet, John Fulford came from a family who were serge makers, established in Crediton at 1 St Lawrence Green. He built

the Holmes in Fore Street, North Tawton in the mid-eighteenth century. Within living memory there has been a large cob barn (now demolished) in the garden at the Holmes and a number of other outbuildings, in which the wool and the finished cloth were stored.

With the coming of mechanisation at the end of the eighteenth century, factories were built to house the machinery. North Tawton's factory dates from this period, as in 1808 John Fulford leased the Manor Mills (or Town Mills), by the river at the bottom of the town, from the lord of the manor, the Hon. Newton Fellowes (who later became the Earl of Portsmouth). These would have been corn mills at that time and it is thought the original mill building is the one facing the road at the end of the yard. Over the next century other pieces of land were rented or purchased to extend the factory. Robert Fulford carried on the business, dying aged 36 years in 1821, leaving his widow Kitty and another Robert Fulford, serge maker of Crediton, as his executors. His will stated that he wished his body to be privately interred in a vault made by John Ellis, sexton, in ground which he had marked out for the purpose. He listed the bearers and left them each a pair of mourning gloves. He left all his household goods, plate, china and clocks (except his eight-day clock and silver teapot) to his widow, brother John and brother-in-law Anthony Loveband. The eight-day clock and teapot were to go to his son Robert and six marked silver spoons and an unmarked gravy spoon were to pass on to his son John Loveband Fulford. He left all his factory goods to his wife, brother and brother-in-law for life, then to his sons. His effects came to less than £600 and his widow continued to live at the Holmes.

Robert's brother, John, then took over until 1837, when the deeds show that he gave the mill to his son-in-law, Gilbert Doke Vicary, who had married his daughter Emma. Gilbert was born at Newton Bushell near Newton Abbot, where the family were fellmongers (dealers in skins) and tanners, and were probably related to the Vicarys who owned the tannery in North Tawton and lived at Park House nearby. Gilbert built the large handsome listed building on the right of the original corn mill in the early 1840s. A map dated 1883 shows that this building was originally three storeys high and was subsequently converted to four. Here, wool was sorted downstairs and on the third floor blankets were hung to dry on tenterhooks, where there were special louvered windows to assist the drying process. If the weather was fine the blankets were hung in the rack field. So now the changeover from cottage industry to factory was almost complete.

In a letter dated 1 July 1820, in response to Lysons, who was compiling a book on Devon, Revd Thomas Hole states that, 'The woollen trade does not flourish as formerly, it is now in the hands of Mr Fulford who has a spinning mill by the river.' So although the main building is said to have been erected in the 1840s, the Fulfords had clearly established a woollen mill on the site earlier, probably following their negotiations in 1808.

On the site there were two water-wheels, a mill pond and a leat to bring the water, which was taken off the River Taw at the weir in the Hams. There was a rack field and a small garden where teasels still grow, which would perhaps have been used on the finished cloth.

When Gilbert Vicary retired his son, John Fulford Vicary, took over and he is listed in directories from 1857 onwards. In the 1861 census John Fulford Vicary, aged 28 and born in North Tawton, is described as woollen manufacturer and attorney-at-law, living at Park House with his wife and children. It was he who built Burton Hall in 1872 (see Chapter 11), but prior to moving into his new house he was living at Nichols Nymett House with his wife and seven children and was described as employing 600 workers in the 1871 census, and 503 ten years later. Earlier accounts differ as to the number of employees at the factory, as the 1851 census quotes 412. Perhaps many were outworkers as it is certain there were never such large numbers employed in the factory itself. The *Billings Directory* of 1857 gives a figure of 250, which seems more likely.

When John Fulford Vicary died in 1887 the mill was closed. The Board of Guardians, meeting in Okehampton at that time, agreed that those thrown out of work should have relief, but only as a temporary measure, and should be advised to seek alternative employment – the Victorian equivalent of 'get on your bike', perhaps. However, help was at hand in the shape of the Shaw family, who bought the mill and five acres for £6,000 from John's widow. The Shaws were mill owners from Halifax who proceeded to modernise the mill and enlarge it.

A first-hand account of the mill during the Victorian era is given in an anonymous article by a writer in the parish magazine, dated 1910, with his recollections of the past 60 years. He stated that:

The woollen factory was owned in my youth by Mr Gilbert Fulford Vicary, with John Pinn as foreman. Nearly all the trade then was with China and government orders for the Navy. The Chinese mandarins walked about in North Tawton in scarlet serge and our sailors in their wooden ships wore the blue. There were looms in the front rooms of nearly every cottage, and my great delight was to go around with Mr Charles Manning in a donkey cart to collect the pieces. All pieces were finished here, then dyed scarlet and blue and sent out fit for the market. The wool was all combed by hand and I used to watch the process with great delight.

Note that the writer has muddled Gilbert Vicary with his son, John Fulford Vicary.

The Shaws who followed the Vicarys had a reputation for being good employers. They provided treats for their staff such as at Christmas 1913 when there is an account of a party for 180 employees at the Town Hall with a meal, dancing and entertainment. They gave wedding presents to those getting married, giving two blankets to Daisy Pope, who was a spinner, when she married Roland Moore in the early 1920s and she was still using them on her bed in 1990.

In 1919 it was reported in the *Western Times* that the proprietors proposed giving £5 to each employee for every three months they had served in HM Forces, to be invested in the company at five per cent until 1923 when it became theirs absolutely. They reinstated all those who had been in the Forces in the war and gave grants to the families of those who had not returned.

A typical day for factory workers was as follows:

Terms of Employment 1927
56 hour week

6a.m. start	*(factory hooter at 5.30a.m.)*
Breakfast	*8 to 8.30a.m.*
Dinner	*1 to 2p.m.*
Leave work	*6p.m.*
Saturdays	*8 to 12 noon*
Wages	
Starting pay	*4s.0d. to 6s.0d. per week*
Men's wages	*36s.0d.*
Christmas bonus	*2s.6d.*

The workers mostly went home for meals and it was said to be a 'lovely sight with everyone streaming out of the factory, the girls with coloured shawls.' Others, particularly children, found it rather frightening as 'they seemed to walk in lines, and woe betide anyone who got in their way.'

The workers seem to have been a happy bunch and the girls liked to sing as they worked and enjoyed the camaraderie of the factory, according to some of those interviewed years later.

Clearing out the factory leat, 1950s.
Left to right: *Will Bolt, Clifford Bolt, Harry Kelly, Will Pollard, Will Cann, Will Page, Dick Anstey.*

Sidney Palmer, who came to North Tawton in about 1905, lived behind the Globe (Copper Key). His mother worked at the factory and caught her arm in the machinery, necessitating amputation just above the elbow (this seems to have been one of the few accidents anyone could remember). As a consequence of this he was allowed to leave school at thirteen and went to work in the factory doing various jobs. He stayed there for ten years, only leaving because they went on to a three-day week. By the time he left the factory he was working in the sorting shop where Thomas Mortimer, father of Walter who later wrote a history of the town, was the foreman. Leonard Lias remembered how noisy the combing shop was and he blamed this for his loss of hearing in later years.

The processes carried out in the factory included sorting, washing, drying, combing, spinning and weaving. Washing the raw wool made the men's hands very soft because of the oil it contained and enabled one man to get a part-time job kneading the dough at Attwells, the bakers. There were numerous sheds and workshops for all the different processes. The men were not allowed in the spinning shed where the girls were employed, but of course they disregarded this. Leonard Lias told a story of being about to be caught there by the foreman, Phineas Knapton, so the girls quickly bundled him into a skip until danger was past.

The finished product was taken in Paddon's, Lewis' or Gregory's wagons to the station and sent to Bradford to be dyed. There were plans to install a dyeing plant at North Tawton but, because of the recession in the 1920s and the death of Captain Shaw, the plans were shelved.

Flooding at the mill was common and often the water from the floor had to be swept out before work could begin.

After the 1914–18 war, the woollen trade was depressed and the factory only carried out spinning and producing 'tops' (large balls of wool) for Bradford, employing scarcely 80 people.

In 1919 a report in the *Western Times* stated:

The present woollen factory needs extending, because of the cost of brick it was decided to use concrete blocks and make them on the spot, 25 are employed. There is contemplated an entire re-organisation, old machinery to be brought up to date, and old buildings to be replaced, and then eventually to erect dwellings made of concrete blocks made on site.

As well as being cheaper to manufacture their own blocks, they sold the excess to the public and a few houses in North Tawton are constructed from these.

The foundation stone of what became known as New Shed was laid by Master Anthony Shaw, the four-year-old son of the managing director, Captain Shaw, and a representative of the sixth generation of the family firm which started in 1770 in Yorkshire.

Captain Shaw, the owner's son, died from pneumonia in 1924, aged 39 years, although he had not been well for some time following a motor accident. He had also been wounded in the war and his left arm was practically useless. This kindly man was involved in many of the town's activities and was also known for being a good shot, golfer and fly fisherman. His death could not have come at a worse time. Things went from bad to worse, culminating in the voluntary liquidation of the company in 1930.

Staff were employed on a short-term basis as orders were scarce and machinery old-fashioned, compared with the parent company at Halifax. Nevertheless, the closure was a great shock and the impact on the town was immense. For example, the Adams family, consisting of four brothers and four sisters, all worked at the mill and were thrown out of work. There was also a tremendous knock-on effect. The wage bill at the time was £150 per week, nearly all of which would have been spent locally.

According to Arthur Adams:

... unemployment benefit was 15s.0d. a week but after a few months you were out of benefit. The Employment Officer suggested my sisters should get work at Lapford Milk Factory but the cost of getting there was more than the wages.

What did folk do? Some did farm work, much of it casual. A few of the men found work at Meldon Quarry in Okehampton, but for the women there was not much alternative to domestic service. The Devon Serge Warehouse also closed in the early 1930s, compounding the problem.

Leonard Sanders started working at the wool factory on leaving school and returned after service in the First World War. When he was in his nineties, Leonard commented:

... that was a bad job for North Tawton. I had to try different things but eventually my father worked on the railway (he did 44½ years at North Tawton Station) and he got me on the permanent way. I stayed till I was 65.

Eventually the Shaws paid off 19s.11d. in the pound (99½p) to their creditors but it took several years to do so.

A local man remembers his father taking machinery to the station in the 1930s when it was (allegedly) sold to German and UK manufacturers and used for war equipment. Another remembers the machines standing idle with the wool still in them. Subsequently, much valuable archival material was burnt during a clear out, so a very important part of North Tawton's history will never be known.

Right: *Wool factory workers, c.1919.*

Left: *Wool factory workers. Left to right, back row: Will Cann, Joe Towell, Will Pollard, Will Gage, Walter Woods; front row: Will Bolt, Charlie Pollard, Edward Butt.*

Right: *The wool factory showing the chimney.*

Left: *Laying the foundation stone of the New Shed, 1919. Note the concrete blocks, which were made on site.*

Laying the foundation stone of the New Shed, 3 August 1919. Pictured in the foreground: the Hon. Mrs Shaw, Anthony Shaw, Capt. Shaw.

A building, thought to be the original corn mill, 1990.

Below: *Rice sorters for Ambrosia at the wool factory, c.1960. Left to right, back row: Alice Day, Amy Kelly, Vera Knott, Emily Sillifant, Hilda Long; front row: Edna Yeo, Myrtle Dart, Doreen Cook, Albina Hoare, Edith Crocker.*

Above: *Wool sorters, Terry Cook and David Hoare, 1989.*

A Brief History Since 1930

The mill was subsequently bought by Hosken Trevithick & Polkinghorne, trading as Farm Industries, for use as a store and wool-grading centre.

1939–51. The New Shed was requisitioned by the Ministry of Works and was a major centre for storing Government wool.

1948. The North Devon Water Board abstracted water from the leat. Two pumps were built to extract water and the mains water was augmented by the factory supply.

1950. Ambrosia of Lapford rented a building for the storage of milk and rice where ten women were employed sorting grain in the old tea room.

1957. The North Devon Water Board leased the yard and a shed for storage at £25 per annum.

1964. The British Wool Marketing Board took over the premises and it became an important wool-grading centre. Wool buyers came from all over the country to view the Board's samples. The sales based on the samples took place regularly at Exeter.

The Wool Board made their own electricity until 1991 and sold the surplus to the Electricity Board.

1992. Wool stores were closed at Buckfastleigh, Launceston and North Tawton and the business was concentrated at South Molton. Two of the remaining employees were transferred there. A sad end to what was once a great enterprise. In the *Okehampton Times* of 17 December 1992 it was reported that:

West Devon Council issued a development brief for the wool factory, which, it is suggested, could be put to leisure use, e.g. a public sports hall, the mill leat could be developed for water sports, and buildings converted to a restaurant and/or museum connected with the former wool industry.

In 1994 the premises were bought by Mr K. Dunn of The Barton and at the time of writing lay empty.

North Tawton Infants School, 1920s. Left to right, back row: *Lizzie Glover, Daphne Woolfe, Dorothy Arscott, Vera Knott, Sybil Norman, Minnie Arscott, Nellie Way, Enid Tolley, Enid Taylor, Irene Madge, Winnie Bolt;* second row: *Fred Bolt, Donald Francis, Sybil Pope, Winnie Adams, Jack Delve, Jack Stoneman;* sitting on the bench: *Mary Bolt, Roy Lee, Doreen Anstey, ?, N. Edworthy, K. Edworthy, ?;* sitting on the floor: *George Coventon, Jim Coventon, ?, Bill Hoare, Buster Woolacott, Jim Woolacott, Jack Bolt.*

North Tawton Primary School, 1932/3. Left to right, back row: *Winnie Heyward, Phyllis Dart, Frank Day, Joan Bolt, Edna Bolt;* third row: *Bernard Bale, Cyril Heyward, Gerald Day, Eric Stoneman, Sylvia Heyward, Edith Jones, Hilda Way, Sarah Way, Mabel Bolt, ?, Alf Bolt, Alfie Jones;* second row: *? Heyward, Hazel Bale, Margaret Way, Vera Heyward, Ruth Vanstone, Leonard Lee, Les Finch, Edward Palfrey;* front row: *Dudley Heyward, Colin Heyward, Laurence Finch, Norman Bolt, Clifford Bolt, Cecil Vanstone, Charlie Bolt, Wallace Palfrey.*

Chapter 5

SCHOOLS

The Charity School

There has been a school in North Tawton since before 1746, when a charity school was endowed by Revd Richard Hole, along with land at Upcott. He stated that the school was to be:

... for the better education of poor children of the parish of North Tawton in reading English, writing and arithmetic, and for the better support of a charity school there and in order to make some provision for the then master...

This school is shown on a map, circa 1780 *(see Map 3)*, as being in Exeter Street where the Church Cottage and its garden stand at the time of writing. This building was originally the church house and there was obviously a school there before 1746. It may even date from 1688, when one Christopher Rowe, described as a weaver, was granted a 21-year lease of the upstairs room of the church house by the churchwardens, and mention is made of his 'schollars' who were to have liberty to come and go at all times. Interestingly he was responsible for the hearth tax on one chimney and also for any broken window glass. It seems slightly odd that a weaver should double as a schoolmaster, but he signed his name very clearly on the document and other documents imply the Rowes were quite a prosperous family, suggesting that he himself had probably received some education.

The later Charity School was almost certainly in the same location, the church house having been converted to other uses at some time. It was over the poorhouse and was reached by an external flight of stone steps. The schoolmaster's salary, paid by the trustees, was £8 per year. He was paid to teach ten poor scholars, boys and girls, who were nominated by the trustees and the rector. They generally stayed about three years and the schoolmaster was also allowed to take fee-paying pupils, of whom it seems there were quite a number. It is known from his will, dated 1758, that Christopher Kelland also left £20 to endow the school and various small bequests were added. This charity, now known as the School Lands Charity, still exists and makes small grants annually to promote the education of the children of North Tawton.

In 1834 the school and poorhouse burnt down, together with much other property in North Tawton. According to tradition a cob building was acquired from the rector and converted into a school; he also gave some land for access (New Road or Cackie Lane) beside the Old Rectory. It is said that Hannah and Elizabeth Pyke taught about 100 pupils, but this must have been later, as they would have been too young to be teachers when the school burnt down. This school was later (and perhaps at the time also) the Sunday school which was sold in 1983 and demolished, after which a house was built on the site. In the churchyard is a gravestone with the following inscription:

Upcott Farm, the rent from which endowed the original Charity School in 1746.

Mary wife of the above [William Bickel] *who was schoolmistress in this parish for a period of 50 years and was a respected and useful member of society. She died March 28th 1848 aged 66 years.*

From this one gathers that she was teaching before and after the fire of 1834.

However, from a press report of the Charity Commissioners enquiry it seems the school moved to a house belonging to the rector, which R. Bovett says, in his *Historical Notes on Devon Schools* of 1989, has been identified as Broad Park House, now known as the White House at the top of Exeter Street. Hugh Pyke, the schoolmaster, certainly lived at this house for most of his life and next door to his father-in-law, John Ellis, who is also described as a schoolmaster in the census of 1881. Perhaps both versions are true and following the fire in 1834 the children went to New Road and, subsequently in the time of Hugh Pyke, to Broad Park House.

Hugh Pyke was renowned for his copperplate writing and documents in the archives bear witness to this. He died in 1893 aged 73 years, when a 'cold turned to influenza'. A newspaper account of his funeral states that from 1850 until 1874 he was the master of the National School. He was also an assistant overseer for 47 years, superintendent of the Sunday school, Parish Clerk for 40 years, connected with the Water and Market Committees and, for a short time, a member of the School Board. For 37 years he was the Registrar and head of Messrs Pyke Horne & Powlesland, auctioneers. One of his granddaughters, Miss Emily Heath, followed him in the teaching profession, becoming headmistress of Atherington School in North Devon.

In a deed dated 1857, the Earl of Portsmouth, who was the lord of the manor, gave land in Exeter Street to the rector, churchwardens and overseers for the children or adults of 'the labouring, manufacturing and other poorer classes in the parish of North Tawton.' The school was to be open to inspection as per the Act of 10 August 1840. The principal minister (rector) for the time being was to be in charge of religious instruction and he was allowed to use the buildings for a Sunday school. The subjects to be taught were the 'three Rs' (reading, (w)riting, and (a)rithmetic), geography, scripture and history, plus needlework for the girls. The Bible was to be read daily.

The building began with an infants' school and school house for the master or mistress. The conveyance is dated 23 October 1857, but the school was not completed until 1864. The original accounts, dated 31 March, are held in the Devon Record Office and show the builder to have been Mr Samuel Hooper, who carried out the work for a total cost of £937.9s.11d. (£937.50 approximately).

Later, in 1870, the building was enlarged with the addition of a schoolroom for boys and one for girls on either side of the original building. An entry in *White's Directory* of 1878 states that 'the School Board was formed in 1872 and schools accommodating 260 children built in 1874 at a cost of £1,800.' A number of Education Acts around this time decreed that all children must be instructed in the 'three Rs' by a certificated teacher. Unfortunately Hugh Pyke, in spite of his many accomplishments, was not allowed to teach in the new school because he was not certificated. The attractive stone school building remained in use until the children were transferred to the former

senior school in 1962, after which it was sold and converted into five private dwellings in the 1980s.

The school managers' minute-books from 1883 onwards show that there were five or six managers who dealt with repairs to school buildings, with frequent reference to the state of the toilets, the appointment and payment of staff, reports on school attendance, and inspectors' reports (which seem mainly to concentrate on religious teaching). Managers fixed the holidays and closed the school during epidemics of infectious diseases. School attendance was rigorously enforced and those who repeatedly kept their children at home were prosecuted. Indeed the managers' meetings seemed chiefly concerned with absenteeism.

In 1883 the headmaster's salary was £55 yearly and there were always four or five monitors (older children who helped instruct the younger ones) who were paid about £3 a year, for which post there was a waiting list. The minute-books show that around the turn of the twentieth century the teachers repeatedly requested salary increases, with variable results.

In 1914 an application was received to use the school for a temporary wartime hospital if required. After discussion, Mr Phillips, the owner of Devonshire House, which was previously the Middle Class School (see later in this chapter), offered it as an alternative and the offer was gratefully accepted. In 1917 the first woman governor, Mrs James Tavener of Kerri House, was appointed.

By 1919 inflation had set in and the new headmaster, Mr Shopland, was appointed at a salary of £250 annually. (There were 32 applications for the post and four candidates were shortlisted.)

A newspaper reported on 3 September of the same year that:

... there was a school strike when the school managers declined to accede to the King's request to give children an extra week's holiday in recognition of the conclusion of Peace. Both parents and children have displayed much feeling as they think it reflects on their loyalty, and the patriotic work done by their scholars. The Honours include 1 MC (Military Cross), 2 DCMs (Distinguished Conduct Medals) and 2 MMs (Military Medals). Last week a petition was drawn up with one hundred names and presented to the Chairman Mr H Phillips, who declined to call a meeting. When school opened on Monday morning there were only forty nine out of one hundred and thirty two children in the mixed school and twenty two out of sixty four in the Infants. A number of parents assembled and sang the National Anthem, while several children paraded the town. In the afternoon the attendance was considerably less, and less still next day. The parents await the result with interest as the Managers have threatened to take proceedings.

There is no record of any such proceedings being carried out.

In 1928 Mrs Sharland of Ashridge, who was one of the managers, provided shoes for the children. There was no reference as to why or how many shoes she provided, but times were hard with the wool mill workers on short time (see Chapter 4).

A more momentous event was a fire, which destroyed two rooms in the school and badly damaged a third. Unfortunately this destroyed all the school records housed therein, but the only reference in the managers' minute-book (which survived because it was kept in the Parish Council office) is the docking of the caretaker's salary because the school was closed for a time. She complained as she had a lot of extra work cleaning up and the decision was rescinded.

The fire occurred on the night of 28 February 1929, after which two classes were taught in the Sunday school. The school was closed again for a week in the same year due to a diphtheria outbreak. This was quite a common occurrence in those days; every time there was an epidemic of any of the infectious fevers the school was closed. In February 1938 it was closed for three weeks on account of measles.

On 20 April 1929 a religious inspection showed that:

... instruction is used as a basis for character training, including development of self reliance, initiative and individuality of thought. There is an atmosphere of enthusiasm in school and the results of teaching are real and deep.

In the following year it was reported that 'this large and important school possesses no piano.' Following this report Devon County Council agreed to contribute £7.10s.0d. (£7.50) towards the cost of purchasing one, but they had to wait until 1937 to get a radio and until 1941 for a telephone to be installed, and then it was only installed in the senior school which had come into being in 1932. Earlier that year it was recorded that 'this school is very cold. At 9a.m. this morning it was 32°F', i.e. freezing point. At this time the school was still heated with coke burning stoves, although gas had been laid on for lighting

with incandescent burners in 1903, to be succeeded by electricity in the 1920s.

In 1938 the outbreak of the Second World War loomed and the school was hired out one evening per week for ARP (Air Raid Precautions) training. A year later the senior school was permitted to be used as a reception centre for evacuees, while it was agreed that because of blackout restrictions the school needed to be closed at 3.15p.m. This was because it would be too dark inside to see without lights and the managers did not want the expense of purchasing blackout curtains. Around that time wire netting was bought for £5 to cover the windows (to prevent flying glass in case of air raids).

In the summer holidays the children had collected 1,974lb of firewood (sold for £1.10s.6d. i.e. £1.52½p), 23lbs of fir cones, 8½ hundredweight of cardboard and 1,201lbs of bones. They had picked 103lbs of blackberries and 35 hundredweight of peas, and 526 cabbage white butterflies had been destroyed as part of the war effort. This salvaging was repeated the following summer. It seems the children were now drinking powdered milk as Miss Olive Priest was appointed milk mixer and the County Education Committee were asked to install an electric or gas stove to heat the water for mixing, thus implying there were no electric kettles in the school. Miss Priest was duly appointed at 7s.6d. (37½p), presumably per week. Liquid milk was restored in 1948.

In September 1939 a number of evacuees were admitted to the school, most of whom were living with relatives. In June 1940 more arrived with their teachers and had to share classrooms with the local children, taking it in turns to be indoors or out doing games, going for walks and so on. It is uncertain how long they stayed as there is no further reference to them in the log-book and although a number went home some stayed throughout the war.

By November 1950 there were 106 junior and infant pupils in the junior school and the premises were described as 'old fashioned and inconvenient', which was unsurprising in a school built in mid-Victorian times.

Turning to the reminiscences of former pupils, memorable teachers include Mr and Mrs James Pierce, the former a very long-serving headmaster from 1883 to 1920. He is remembered as strict but fair and one of his pupils, writing many years later, remembers him ruling the school with a rod of iron. He recalls:

After roll call and prayers the whole senior school (aged seven years and upwards) remained standing and recited their tables, multiplication, square measure, decimal, the lot, and at a stab of his finger the room fell silent and one hapless individual was asked to continue solo to see if he knew his tables or was miming, and if the latter it was a painful experience for the soloist.

Schoolchildren in fancy dress in Exeter Street, c.1930.

This informant was even more in awe of Mrs Pierce, although he goes on to say how on social occasions she was the life and soul of the party and that her husband was much in demand at concerts, where he sang light, humorous songs. Mr Pierce was involved in practically every organisation in the town at one time or another and must have left a huge gap when he retired. They both took part in evening classes which were started in 1903. As well as academic subjects there were classes in agricultural subjects such as sheep shearing, fungoid and insect pests, and there is reference to a Dairy School in the 1930s which Hilda Powlesland, née Dart, remembers attending. Lace-making was popular and a Honiton lace class started before the First World War, as an entry in the parish magazine of May 1914 shows, and many people remember learning 'pillow lace' from Olive Priest who was an accomplished lacemaker.

In the parish magazine in 1911 there is an account of an:

Devon County Council Dairy Class, on the Town Hall steps, 1931. Those pictured include: *Emma and Hilda Dart, Nellie Sanders, Gwen Bale and Miss Bray (instructress).*

... Evening Scholars Outing when a little band of women with Mr and Mrs Pierce went to Exeter Cathedral, the Guildhall, the Museum and Northernhay Gardens, then to St David's Station and took the train to Dawlish, lunched on the beach and paddled, took a walk on the cliffs to Teignmouth and a boating trip. Boarding the train back to Exeter they then visited the Lower Market and at 10p.m. left Queen Street for North Tawton.

This must certainly have been a day to remember, not least because of its length. At their retirement Mr and Mrs Pierce were presented with a case of notes (£50) and an album containing a list of subscribers.

The school is remembered in the 1920s as gloomy with high windows and very cold in winter. Former pupil, Bill Baker, described the school about this time as a grim structure, where they 'mostly scratched away on slates copying the alphabet, doing simple sums, or standing in a circle reading aloud.'

The lavatories come in for hefty criticism, with graphic accounts of visits there. In 1897 a load of ashes was ordered for 'the closets' and things did not improve until well past 1930. Even in 1953 the County Medical Officer was complaining about the same lavatories, although by this time flushes had been installed but were not satisfactory because they were not connected to the mains water supply. Over the years there were several discussions on the inad-

equate water supply to the school, right up to 1955. By the 1930s there were wash basins in the lavatories and there was drinking-water in the school. Previously drinking-water had to be obtained from a tap in the street, in a recess in the school wall, with a lead cup on a chain.

The infant teachers, according to one former pupil, were:

... kind though strict, Miss Bowden, tall and imposing with high necked blouse, cameo brooch, and a watch pinned to her bosom, and her deputy Miss Eva Pike, a small dapper lady, with gold pince nez who warmed the milk in winter on top of the tortoise stove.

According to Hilda Dart, who walked nearly three miles to school from Itton Farm and back with her brothers and sisters in all weathers, Miss Bowden dried their wet clothes.

A former pupil in the 1930s who was left-handed was forced to write with her right hand and although this seems wrong today, it was accepted practice at the time.

As well as conventional lessons, there was modelling in coloured plasticine, 'which by the time we got it was all coffee covered', plaiting of raffia and unpicking threads of old pieces of material for some unknown purpose. This last named activity has been mentioned by several former pupils, as was the presence of a model butcher's shop in a glass-fronted cupboard in the classroom, at which the pupils gazed longingly but were never allowed to touch, nor was it referred to in any way.

When Miss Eva Pike retired in 1949, aged 65 years, she had been at the school throughout her life as pupil, monitor and teacher and was known and loved by several generations of children. She was succeeded by Miss Vera Olding, who proved equally popular with parents and children alike. Another teacher at this time was Dorothy Attwell, said to be always happy and smartly dressed; sadly she later died in childbirth. Mrs Pyne, who was appointed to the junior school in 1932 with a salary of £140 annually, made lessons really interesting and could have earned her living as an actress, according to one of her pupils. She retired in 1950, to be succeeded by Miss Westcott.

A girl who joined the school in 1923 remembers singing lessons with Mr Shopland (while headmaster at the junior school) but she, having recently come from Wales, found the singing very poor compared with her native valleys. Mr Shopland was also very keen on football and North Tawton won many matches. He gave the school team new football boots, so was popular with the boys.

Mrs Howard, the wife of the Parish Clerk, succeeded Mr Shopland as the head of the junior school when he moved to the newly built senior school in 1932. She organised concerts to fund PE equipment, such as mats, hoops, colours, etc. She also kept spare plimsolls for those who arrived with wet feet. She had the happy thought of arranging families to be in the same school photograph, regardless of age, so that parents need only buy one copy, however many children they had in the school.

At this time, Mrs Madge, the former Ena Paddon (previously a monitor), who lived next door to the school with her husband, Acland Madge, taught needlework. One lady still has a nightdress she made at school in the 1920s. Another former pupil remembers that there was only one wash basin and the tap could only be turned on by Mrs Madge who had a key. She rationed the water very strictly, but as previously mentioned there often seemed to be a water shortage in that part of the town. After the school was partly demolished by fire in 1929, Mr and Mrs Madge were nervous about sleeping next door in the school house and so Leonard Lias, a boy at the time, slept in their house for several months afterwards.

A daily highlight was the coming of Mr Attwell the baker, who rang his bell and sold halfpenny buns, which were 'hot and delicious'. Games played at that time were spinning tops, hoops, hopscotch and skipping. There were few cars on the roads so these games could be played in the streets after school, where collecting car numbers was also popular.

In 1932 the senior school was built and opened on 7 March by Sir Francis Dyke Acland, chairman of the Education Committee. Those who did not go to the Grammar School in Okehampton progressed to the new senior school from the junior school. Mr Shopland transferred to the new school as headmaster, with Mrs Madge as his deputy, while Mrs Howard took his place as head of the junior school. At that time the school-leaving age was 14 years.

Mr J.O. Heard succeeded Mr Shopland in 1938. He was an officer in the Home Guard during the war and fortunately, for posterity, kept a very detailed account of their activities. Mr Blight was another master at this time who had moved with the children up from the junior school and was also an officer in the Home Guard.

There was a great fear of air raids in the months leading up to the Second World War and the Government had made contingency plans for mass evacuation from the cities to the countryside. Many of these children, who had been sent to North Tawton from the Battersea area of London, were at first billeted at the senior school before they were found family homes. One North Tawton girl who was an only child vividly remembers seeing one of the mothers, who had accompanied her children, breast feeding her baby at the school and was transfixed with amazement. Some evacuees returned home quite soon, as the enemy had not bombed London as feared, but others came at various times during the war, such as in 1940 when invasion fears were at their greatest and again in 1944, when the raids by V1 flying bombs (known as 'doodlebugs') and the V2 supersonic missiles started.

Some children were homesick and never became integrated in North Tawton, but those who stayed seem to have 'bonded' very closely with their adopted town. These of course are the ones who have kept in touch and re-visit from time to time, so the picture we get is inevitably a distorted one and we can only guess about those with unhappy memories of North Tawton.

Those who were at the school at the time and still remember the evacuees say they fitted in quite well and joined the local 'gangs', although one or two girls found them slightly intimidating at first. One girl remembers playing in the fields and the newcomers getting covered in blisters which they got from playing in stinging nettles, a plant they had not

The senior school which opened in 1932.

The cookery class at the senior school with Mr Blight, 1934. Left to right, back row: *Greta Down, Edna Winslow;* middle row: *Joan Raby, Winnie Stoneman;* front row: *Edith Knott and Esmee Raby.*

North Tawton Primary School, 1954/5. Left to right, back row: Iris Griffiths, Carol Blight, Angela Mills, Rosemary Burns, Anna Crang; third row: Barbara Bowden, David Johnson, Shirley Stapleton, Ann Taylor, Janet Matthews, Marlene Johnson, Mary Harris, Margaret Dennis, Jennifer Venton, Valerie Knott, ? Heyward, Leonora Jones; second row: Susan Lake, Janet Ford, Jane Arscott, Elizabeth Stapleton, Rosemary Lambourne, Sally Edwards, June Tremlett, ? Bailey, Victor Heyward; front row: Keith Phillips, Owen Jacobs, Roger Long, John Bennett, Trevor Ayrton, Arthur Brookes, Roger Bailey.

Mr Thompson and Miss Olding planting a chestnut tree on the occasion of her retirement, 1969.

previously encountered (see Chapter 9 for evacuees' memories of North Tawton).

In 1957 Mr Denzil Mortimore from Okehampton was appointed as headmaster, to succeed Mr Heard, and he returned there with his pupils in 1962 when the senior school was merged with Okehampton Secondary Modern. The senior school building at North Tawton became the primary school, to which the 142 children and their teachers transferred, and the old Victorian building is now five attractive private dwellings, as mentioned earlier in this chapter.

Miss Ninnis was the headmistress of the primary school at this time, having taken over on Mrs Howard's death in 1941, and it was during her tenure that this transfer occurred. In 1959 Miss Ninnis told the managers that, 'the general intelligence of the children was declining due to over fatigue' from watching television and a few months later the managers agreed that television was not having a good effect on children's education.

The winter of 1963 brought with it blizzards and the school buses were unable to run for at least two months. Miss Ninnis recalled that the school had to be heated by oil heaters and the many uncommon birds that came looking for food turned a lot of the pupils into keen bird-watchers. It was during this year that oil-fired central heating was installed in the school and the swimming pool was opened. Much attention was paid in subsequent years to teaching swimming, particularly by Mr George, one of the teachers at the time.

Miss Ninnis retired in 1968, to be followed by Mr Jack Thompson, when the total number of children on the roll was 133, arranged in five classes in the morning session and four in the afternoon. The following year Miss Olding retired and to mark the occasion a horse chestnut tree which had been growing in a syrup tin in her classroom for over nine years was planted outside. It is now a resplendent specimen growing at the bottom of the school grounds.

In 1970 Mr Thompson was taken ill and his deputy, Mr Mayfield, took over the running of the school for a time. An interesting entry in the school log-book for that year reads 'a reserve team of children took decimal coinage shopping with the Over Sixties Club in North Tawton.'

The school numbers fluctuated somewhat over the years and in the summer term of 1972 the total number of pupils was 157. During that same term the first North Tawton football tournament was held at the school and the A.J. Gregory Cup was presented by Mr Gregory to Okehampton Primary School.

Also that year North Tawton had a visit from Richard Adamson, one of the original team who discovered the tomb of Tutankhamen, and he gave a talk to parents and pupils in the Town Hall. Mr Thompson, also a keen Egyptologist, then involved the children in the construction of a replica of the tomb, a venture so successful that other schools brought their pupils to see it.

Mr Mayfield left for a headteacher's post at Clyst Honiton at that time and his name is remembered by the Mayfield Cup, which is presented every year on the school open day to the child who has shown the most school spirit. Mrs Vera Smidmore took his place.

In 1974 Christopher Milne, son of A.A. Milne (the creator of *Winnie the Pooh*) and the original Christopher Robin in these classic children's stories, visited the school.

Miss Ninnis with Nina Wilkinson, 1983.

Two years later, a name now well known appears in the school log-book, which records that Mrs Clare Morpurgo (now of Nethercott House, Iddesleigh, where she and her husband give farm holidays to city children), carried out her final teaching practice at North Tawton. The following year, 1977, was a difficult one, when Mr Thompson was seriously ill and later resigned. There were also several staff changes, including the retirement of Miss Ball, who had been on the staff for 50 years, first at Sampford Courtenay and then North Tawton, following a merger.

Neil Hallam was now appointed headmaster and took up his post in the summer of 1978. A memorable event the following year was the planting of wild-flower seeds by the children on the newly widened section of the North Tawton to Whiddon Down road, followed by the planting of daffodil bulbs. These still flower every spring.

The 1980s started with an opportunity for the children to see HRH Prince of Wales at close quarters when he came to the cheese factory and was presented with a bouquet of flowers by Sara Brady. Several 'firsts' took place in this decade, during which some of the juniors spent a week under canvas at the

*The primary school, c.1963.
Left to right, back row:
John Eyke, Trevor May, Sylvia
Huxtable, Rachel Watkins,
Beverly Crawford, Holly Webb,
Carol Griffiths, Tim Smidmore,
Simon Gregory; middle row:
Paul Aldred, Jean Gibbons,
Carol Bolt, Sandra Crang,
Janet Jones, Christine Whiteley,
Jane Furneaux, Nigel
Stapleton; seated: Anthony
Vanstone, David Piper,
Paul Gerry, Terry Stapleton.*

Above: *Class Two of the primary school, February 1979. Left to right, back row: Mr Hardiman,
William Hosegood, Jonathan Hayman, Darren Westlake; middle row: Roger Dennis, Sean Brady,
Anthony Down, Christopher Whiteley, Giles Dunkers, Richard Armstrong, Martin Horn, Nigel Ware,
Dickon Higgins, Michael
Wyatt; front (seated):
Gordon Matthews, Stephen
Turner, Valerie Davey,
Elaine Shapland, Kim
Russell, Marie Taylor, Tara
Field, Naomi Leaworthy,
Bridget Dennis, Barry
Coles, David Bragg.*

*Planting seeds near Whiddon
Down, 1979. Pictured in
the centre is Neil Hallam,
headmaster.*

Devon Schools camp at Loxhore on the fringes of Exmoor. In 1982 the school had a visit from North Tawton's twin town of Blangy-le-Chateau. The following year a return trip was made by children from North Tawton, when the highlight was a trip to Paris. These exchange visits have been repeated since. It was noted in the school log, dated 3 June 1985, that 'A party of twenty four children visited our Twin Town, ... it was rather hectic at times and quite tiring for the adults.'

In 1983 the first micro-computer appeared in school and then in 1987 the new swimming pool building was opened, as the result of a lot of hard work by all concerned, following a decision taken by the Friends of the School to raise money for this purpose.

Of course during these years there were a number of staff changes, none more regretted than the retirement in 1983 of the school caretaker, Mr Les Knott, after 27 years' service. There were other changes too, such as the introduction of the National Curriculum in 1987, and the following year saw the first full inspection which took four days and four inspectors, a precursor of OFSTED (Office for Standards in Education). Inspectors again visited the school in 1995 and found it provided a good education and good value for money. In the same year the older children took the newly introduced Standard Assessment Tests (SATs).

Meanwhile numbers waxed and waned, until by 1989 a double mobile classroom was installed to cope with the extra numbers, which had now risen to 160, and another mobile classroom followed in 1991. By 1998 the school had increased to 186, the highest it had ever been. At the time of writing, numbers stand at 137.

The late Poet Laureate, Ted Hughes, visited the school to open the newly refurbished library in 1993

Planting the 'Millennium Oak', presented by Capt Jamie Miller, RN. Left to right: Lois Garwood, ?, Carl Poynton, David Simmons, Simon Fear, RFA, Louise Brown.

North Tawton Primary School (Top Class 1), 1992. Left to right, back row: Amy Hocking, Christopher Mearing, Claire Quick, Lucy Cleave, Brian Milford, Alison Brown; middle row: Sean Sandercock, Geoffrey Lee, Craig Huntley, Rebecca Maxwell, Ben Thwaites, Heidi Brown, Ashley Arscott, Ian Crisp, Katie Pratt, Mrs Jarvis, Timmy Williams; front row: Christopher Bedford, Robert Murrin, Katie Andrews, Tristan Richards, Simon Green, Kate Burrows, Josie Thorne, Michael Keast, Daniel Hoare.

and delighted the children by reading them stories from one of his books, *How the Whale Became*.

The summer term of 2000 saw the official opening of the 'Millennium Garden' by John Kinsey, the chairman of North Tawton Town Council. As well as being a natural amphitheatre this garden forms a huge sundial which tells the time by casting a shadow of a child. A Millennium Oak was also planted. Now plans are afoot to build a new assembly hall together with kitchen and dining facilities. Neil Hallam, who has been headmaster for nearly 25 years, sadly retires at Christmas 2002 and will be very much missed.

Education has come a long way since that charity school was endowed in 1746 and although the basic purpose remains one wonders what the next 250 years will bring.

The Playgroup

North Tawton pre-school (play group) was started in September 1969 by the then district nurse, Winifred Davies, at her home Long Meadow in Exeter Street. She was helped by Connie Evans and Mary Webber and all of them put in a small sum of money. After two terms they moved to the old primary school and some time after this the staff received a small honorarium of about 50p per week.

Inevitably staff changed as their children moved on. Shirley Armstrong then took over, helped by Anne Moore and Monica Simons. Another move took place to the Town Hall where it stayed until September 1999, before moving again to the Old Chapel, Barton Street.

The pre-school is now inspected by OFSTED and has to provide a foundation-stage curriculum, but it is still run as a non-profit-making organisation with parents forming a committee. The most important thing that has stayed the same throughout its 30 years is that children have fun and learn through play.

Mother & Toddler Group

This group caters for children from birth to three years of age who come with a parent to the Town Hall on a Friday morning to interact and learn social skills.

Other Schools

Another school, about which very little is known, was at Bridge Cottage, where children who worked at the wool factory had lessons for part of the day in the nineteenth century.

There have always been numerous private schools, the largest of which was the Middle Class School for boys, which ran from 1867 to 1896 and was built on land in Essington given by the Earl of Portsmouth. Built to take 150 to 200 scholars and costing £2,000, by 1868 the school was doing so well it had to be enlarged. An investigation carried out by a Mr Goode in 1874 reported that the subjects studied, apart from the usual ones, were bookkeeping, land surveying and agricultural chemistry. There were 50 pupils, of whom 30 were boarders. However, financial problems dogged the enterprise and the governors constantly put their hands in their pockets to help pay the bills.

Among the pupils was Viscount Lambert of Spreyton, MP for this division (South Molton), 1891–1945, who, when unveiling the North Tawton War Memorial in 1921, recalled how he and other boys always raided the rectory pear tree, the garden of which adjoined the school playground. With the coming of free schooling for all in 1894, numbers dwindled until it was closed and sold for £1,000 to Mr Phillips, who started a tailoring business on the premises.

The earliest private school known in the area is mentioned in the reminiscences of Thomas Durant, born 1776 at North Tawton, the son of Roger and Susanna of The Barton. He writes:

... when in petticoats I went to Aunt Dinah's School at the Furze near The Barton, when five or six I went to the school of Miss Croote at North Tawton and at eight or nine I went to the writing school of Philip Holmes.

There is a reference in the Portsmouth Papers, dated 1792, to 'Philip Holmes for Charity School three-guineas', but almost certainly Thomas Durant would have been fee-paying. He continues:

Aged ten I went on horseback to Topsham, with my father's servant, Richard Hawkins. There I learnt French, as my brother William, a large manufacturer of serges, intended to send me to a Counting House in Bordeaux.

It seems that not all schools taught writing, only reading, but we know the Charity School was somewhat superior in that it taught the 'three Rs' and there was certainly a Philip Holmes signing documents and witnessing signatures in North Tawton in a flourishing hand around this time.

Right: *Play School Christmas Party, 1978.* Left to right, back row: *Mrs Erica Beglin and Julian, Mrs Jo Diffey and Thomas, Mrs Celia Boughton and Alex, ?, Mrs Jill Vanstone and Graham;* third row: *Sally Turner, Sara Brady, Vicky Boughton, Michelle Iles, Karen Burns, ?, Matthew Diffey, Tracey and Lisa Nicholls;* second row: *David Burns, Rachel James, Kevin Bridgeman, Rachel Squires, ?, Phillippa Beglin, Ann Ware, Gill Hoggins;*

Above: *Play School Christmas Party, 1978 continued,* front row: *Amy Thwaites, Cassie Brady, Hazel Richards, Claire Trick, David Ware, Darren Nicholls, Paul King, Jamie Hoggins.*

Left: *Mrs Taylor's School for Young Ladies at 38 Fore Street, c.1900.*

Right: *Week School, 1940s.* Left to right, back row: *Valerie Stoneman, Michael Partridge;* front row: *Shirley Ridd, ?, Anthony Ellacott.*

Left: *Tawcroft School on an outing, 1963.* Left to right: *Mrs Jane Cox with Frieda Hughes on her knee, Tim Playford, Sarah Cox, John Gregory, ?, ?, Mrs Dorothy de Leysin with Tim Cox on her knee, the rest unknown.*

Also in the eighteenth century, an extract from the *Exeter Flying Post*, dated 13 June 1799, reads:

North Tawton Academy. T. Halse respectfully informs his friends and the Public that he intends to open his school on 15 July for the reception of boarders, who will be genteelly boarded, kindly treated and carefully instructed in Reading, Writing, English Grammar, Arithmetic, Vulgar and Decimal Fractions, Square and Cube Roots, Logarithms, Trigonometry and Geometry, Mensuration, Gauging, Land Surveying, Booke keeping etc., according to the man of business, on the following terms:- Board Lodging washing and instruction £16.16s.0d. Music and Dancing Masters will attend if required.

There are several other advertisements in the same vein. In the 1890s, 100 years later, Mrs Elizabeth Taylor had a school for young ladies at 38 Fore Street where she was assisted by her sister and niece. Four of these girls were boarders aged 11 to 15 years.

Moving on to those within living memory, in the first decade of the twentieth century, the Misses Florence and Emily Goss ran a school for girls in The Square, thought to have been behind what is, at the time of writing, the Post Office. By 1910 Miss Florence Ellis had a day school for both boys and girls. She lived at Grove House in Fore Street and had her school next door at number 34 where there were about 20 pupils. Her sister, Mrs Hoyle (wife of the manager of the wool factory, who lived at Roseberry), taught English literature and poetry and children attending this school received an excellent grounding, according to Herbert Sampson who attended it.

Mrs Bevan, the Congregational minister's wife, ran a school at the Manse in Fore Street for a time while her husband, as well as his ministerial duties, was a keen cricketer who did much for the cricket club.

In the 1930s Miss Joyce Woodgates ran a small infants' school (mornings only) at 21 Park Terrace, holding six children at most. They used slates to write on and were well taught, but this school was not very safety conscious. They had a coal fire in the schoolroom, without a guard, and when it was cold the children moved their chairs to sit in a semi-circle around the fire. Inevitably they started to rock forward and back on their chairs and one child fell in and burnt her hands. Another pupil, David Tucker, used to ride his pony to and from school, putting it in Mr Knight's shed nearby during his lessons.

During this period there were still some families who employed a governess, such as Captain and Mrs Shuter at Nichols Nymett, who also took in a friend's child as a boarder.

Another pre-Second World War school was run by Mrs Northam, originally at South Week and later, when she and her husband moved to a bungalow in Station Road, in a specially built schoolroom alongside. She is mostly remembered as a clever producer of concerts and plays, which gave much pleasure to the participants and the spectators. Her husband owned the adjoining field in Station Road where sports were held.

A school opened at Week in the 1940s, run by Miss Willis, a member of the Plymouth Brethren, whose school, named Hill Crest, had been bombed in Exeter. She renamed her North Tawton school the 'Homestead' and had about 25 pupils, divided into two classes housed upstairs. Miss Willis herself did most of the teaching, including piano lessons, while Miss Stocker, who always wore a gown, taught Latin, and Mrs Tucker taught needlework and botany; the latter consisted of walking round the lanes in summer. There were some boarders and a school matron, Miss Marriott, who was Miss Willis' aunt. Domestic Science involved helping cook the lunch (which was not a great success), after which the whole school lined up to 'do' 20 pumps each at the water pump to fill the cistern. The playground was the adjoining farmyard and if the weather was wet the pupils played in the barn, where dangerous pastimes were indulged in, including climbing ladders and jumping out of the loft. Miss Willis is remembered with great affection and her pupils really enjoyed their schooldays, although they sometimes needed extra coaching when they transferred to other schools.

After the fall of France in June 1940 invasion was expected on the South Coast. In response to this, a mixed boarding school from Rustington, Sussex, called Chawton School, was evacuated to de Bathe House where overcrowding must have been a problem, since most of the staff were resident as well. With no mains water, the supply drying up in summer, and merely a generator producing just enough electricity for lighting, added to all the other difficulties of wartime, running this school must have been no easy task. At the end of the war the school closed and some years later Miss Barbara Lee of Wylands, North Tawton, started a day school at de Bathe which functioned from 1960–2 with about 20 pupils. By this time there were mains water and electricity but the large Victorian farmhouse was still cold and spartan, with two classrooms, in one of which presided Mrs Dorothy de Leysin and in the other Barbara herself.

Lunch was served in the farmhouse kitchen. According to a former pupil, 'the teaching was good and discipline quite strict.' Unfortunately it was not financially viable, so when this school closed Mrs de Leysin started a school of her own at her home at Tawcroft in September 1962, which ran for several years and also had a good reputation.

The church organist, Mr Abbott, ran a school at St Peter's Sunday School in New Road for a short time in the 1950s, and 'Professor' Sedgewick ran a 'crammers' at the White House at that time, taking in Roman Catholic boys and coaching them for university entrance.

At the time of writing in 2002 there are no private schools in the town.

Chapter 6

PUBLIC SERVICES

In former times the whole well-being of the town depended on the efforts of our forebears in the shape of the lord of the manor and his officers, later on the Vestry (which consisted of a meeting of the male ratepayers), and, after 1894, the Parish Council. It would seem we have been well served by all these mostly nameless people who have laboured on our behalf.

Poor Relief

In medieval times everyone was provided for by the manor, augmented by the monasteries and private charities for those who fell through the net. Later we had our benefactors who left money for charity, including Edmond Rowlands and John Hoyle in 1636, Christopher Kelland in 1758, William Clapp in 1827, the Kelland de Bathe charity (set up in 1887 in memory of Richard Kelland who died in 1603) and John Letheren in 1873. These have now been amalgamated to form the Consolidated Charity. Judicious investment has meant that this fund, which was the subject of a windfall payment in 2000, now has a balance of £700.

When Henry VIII dissolved the monasteries and the old manorial system began to change, the village became governed by the Vestry, which was formed by the ratepayers but overseen by the Justices. It appointed the constables, overseers of the poor and all the other officers necessary for the efficient management of the community's affairs. North Tawton's Vestry met in the schoolroom in 1779 and, presumably, continued to meet there until it was burnt down in 1834. Subsequently, it met at the George Inn until the Vestry room was built in Market Street in the early 1850s.

The overseers had a particularly demanding job, not only relieving those in want but also complying with the notorious 'Settlement Acts', begun in Elizabethan times and lasting until well into the nine-

The Vestry, Market Street, which once housed the fire engine.

teenth century, which required everyone to have a 'parish of settlement' before their needs could be supplied. Because many of the labouring poor moved about in search of work, unless they had a certificate from their own parish agreeing to take them back, deciding which parish was responsible for any particular person was very difficult. Much time and money was spent in returning people who had fallen on hard times back to their 'place of settlement', i.e. where they were born, had served an apprenticeship or had other claims to 'belong'. The overseers also had to collect the rates. Most hated their task; they were untrained, unpaid until 1819, unpopular and some were barely literate, although this last criticism does not seem to have applied in this parish. The account books of the overseers of North Tawton contain much detail on how they went about their tasks:

1653. Paid for a paire of stockings for Maire's Maide 1s.0d. and paid for a paire of shoes for her 2s.0d.
1663. Paid 1s.0d. for attendance on Stephen Hill in his sicknesse and £1.2s.8d. for 34 weeks at 8d.
17 March 1745. To searching the Register at Plimouth (35 miles distant) for Anne Luxton's marriage 3s.0d.

(A woman took the settlement of her husband so it made a difference whether she was married, and to whom, as this proved which parish was responsible for her and her children.)

There are no less than 15 consecutive entries for 31 March 1746, concerning the settlement of John Bray. These include three journeys to Chittlehampton, which is 17 miles from North Tawton as the crow flies but longer by road, to obtain sworn evidence from his wife, also 'meat and drink for the gardsmen and John Bray', before finally he was taken to his place of settlement which turned out to be Crediton, 11 miles distant. The bill for all this came to £8.1s.1d. which was equivalent to five per cent of the annual income from the rates. The entries continue:

27 March 1748. To Mr Edward Gostwycke for clothes for the Poor £20.1s.1d.
21 January 1750. To a poor sailor 6d.
24 December 1750. To Peter Luxton for the lent of his horse to carry Mark Hawkins to Exeter Hospital. 2s.0d.
12 April 1754. To William Western for killing a badger and one night's watching 1s.6d.

But times were changing; the Industrial Revolution meant people flocked to the towns from the country-side seeking work and wages were low. There were bread riots and machine breaking, even in Devon, and eventually this system of amateurs administering the Poor Law broke down. With the idea of containing costs the Government passed the Poor Law Amendment Act in 1834, which provided for parishes to be grouped into Unions. Each parish elected Guardians to oversee the building of a work-house, where the conditions would be spartan in the extreme, thus discouraging people from going there.

Paid officials, called relieving officers, were appointed to administer the scheme and North Tawton's nearest workhouse was opened in Okehampton in 1838. The idea was to do away with 'outdoor relief', that is paying benefits, but allowing the recipients to stay at home, but in fact it was left to the discretion of the relieving officers and outdoor relief continued, although on a reduced scale. In 1881 there were 14 people from North Tawton in the Okehampton workhouse, six of whom were children, two of these newly born.

Central Government was still not shouldering the burden and all the collecting of rates and disbursements was done at local level. It was not until the early years of the twentieth century that this was reversed with the coming of the Insurance Acts.

As far as the other functions of the overseers were concerned these were relatively unchanged until the end of the nineteenth century, when local government was completely overhauled and the parish and other councils came into being, taking over the civil functions of the Vestries, which survived as ecclesiastical bodies until 1922.

The Parish Council

In December 1894 a parish meeting was called to elect a Parish Council. There were 22 candidates and a poll was demanded, 12 men being duly elected. The new council met in the Boys Board School Room, then in 1899 it moved to the Vestry room belonging to the church, where it still meets. At first they met quarterly, but for many years since they have met monthly to cope with the increasing workload.

One of the first acts of this new body was to purchase a field, Great Broadpark, for use as a cemetery. It was bought for £650 from the Earl of Portsmouth using a loan from the Loyal Morning Star Lodge of Oddfellows. The capital was repaid over 40 years. Recently an additional piece of land has been purchased to extend the burial-ground. The Parish Councl became the Town Council in 1974.

Clerks to the Council	
1894–1908	Mr J.E. Pyke
1908–26	Mr W.D. Gibbings
1926–36	Mr A. Goss
1936–37	Mr C. Pyke
1937–66	Mr S. Howard
1966–73	Mrs H. Lane
1973–81	Mrs M.A. Bloor
1981–88	Mrs B.C. Earwaker
1988–	Mrs A.J. Baker

The Town Council, 2000. Left to right, back row: Steve Whiteley, David Tucker, Robin Squires, Mike Thwaites, Ron Iles, Pat Ward, Derrick Field, Alison Baker, (Town Clerk); front row: Janet Morgan, Gill Hoggins, John Kinsey, Frances Brookes, Claire Weller.

Chairmen of the Council			
1894–1907	Revd R. Hole	1962–3	Mr R.J. Bennett
1907–13	Mr H. Phillips	1963–71	Mr D.C. Philip
1913–22	Mr S. Hoyle	1971–7	Mr C. Westlake
1922–8	Mr R. Way	1977–92	Mr J. Avery
1928–9	Mr W. Beer	1992–6	Mr N. Ruby
1929–40	Mr E. May	1996–9	Mrs A. Brereton
1940–6	Mr J.G. Durant	1999–2001	Mr J. Kinsey
1946–62	Mr D.C. Philip	2001–	Mrs G. Hoggins

Water Supply

Water, and clean water at that, was of course vital to the health of the inhabitants and the first reference to a water supply found so far is in 1738. A deed of this date states:

Edward Gostwyck, mercer, has at his own expense conveyed a certain stream or watercourse arising in lands of John Durant called East Lake and has at his own charge dug a well and erected a pump in the waste-land belonging to Coulson Fellowes, Lord of the Manor of North Tawton.

There is another reference to this supply in a deed dated 1783. The eighteenth-century map *(3)* shows the pump in North Street, just below where the NatWest Bank stands at the time of writing. It seems that Durant and others paid a peppercorn rent for this pump and perhaps sold the water, as an entry in the 1770s in Pillman's diary reads 'paid Mr Francis Cole for watter' (Francis Cole was the brother-in-law of Edward Gostwyck and subsequently his executor). Again in 1827 when the Gostwyck family were selling several lots of property, a newspaper advertisement refers to 'the public pump' as lot number 21.

Undated evidence from Dean Milles, c.1755, states that in North Tawton 'there are many wells over 50ft in depth, one of which is supplied by a conduit 200ft in length.' Possibly this was connected to the well and pump described above.

From a scrapbook, there is a note in the hand of Sam Howard (Parish Clerk in the mid-twentieth century), as follows:

The minute book of the Water Company has come into the writer's hands. It is written in copperplate by Hugh Pyke junior. The supply in use prior to 1851 was from the Essington Reservoir at the head of Great Tree Meadow (the latter now no longer identifiable), but this supply failed owing to Mr Bickham draining a field above Slade Farm, and another [reservoir] just past Essington Park, visible in the hedge as a piece of stone walling, but this was never successful as a water supply.

In May 1851 work started on a new supply from Slade, piped in iron pipes, at a cost of £600 with ownership divided into £5 shares. Among those who carried out the work were F. Ford, James White, T. Rattenbury, W. Tamlin, Samuel Day and Mr Banbery. When it was finished on 15 January 1852 a public dinner was held at the Gostwyck Arms to celebrate completion, presided over by Revd Robert Hole.

In the late 1890s the new Parish Council then handed over their interest in the water company to the Okehampton Rural District Council, who augmented the supply in the early 1900s at a cost of about £4,000. Although a great improvement, not everyone was satisfied. A newspaper report, dated 18 January 1912 and headed 'Water Question', reported that a meeting of local people was called because the Local Government Board were forcing ratepayers to provide a covering for the reservoir without affording an opportunity for them to express an opinion. The cost was estimated at £1,000, plus £1,300 already spent in excess of the original loan of £3,000. Water often did not get to the top of the town and a green growth was often present. The meeting wanted the covering delayed for 12 months and it was resolved to write to the local MP to express their dissatisfaction. In fact the delay was 15 years as the tank was not covered until 1927.

Richard Ash, the present occupant of Slade, knows of a number of water systems on the farm, but they are difficult to date and complicated to describe. The 1851 reservoir, and possibly an earlier one, was fed by a network of underground pipes connecting up with the land drains, which supplied part of the town by gravity. This is the lower reservoir, now disused, where people used to swim. The area where it is situated is fenced off with iron railings and there is a little brick-built pumphouse in one corner of the plot. This pump was installed in 1932 and water was lifted out of a borehole, 120ft deep and 15 inches in diameter, and a higher reservoir was built opposite Staddon Lane which held 50,000 gallons. This top reservoir is still in use and is 33ft across and 13ft deep. It is now augmented by a supply of water from Meldon Reservoir near Okehampton.

There were numerous other water supplies and wells for groups of houses and individual dwellings, such as Bouchiers Hill, Burton Hall and the farms adjacent to Slade. There was a further supply for Mill Lane, which was located at South Week, where the cricket field is now. Even then not every house in the town had piped water; many still used wells, as the pump at Gowman's Terrace shows, and there were permanent standpipes in nearly all the streets. It was not until after the advent of the North Devon Water Board (NDWB) in the late 1940s that the dream of universal piped water became possible for the people of North Tawton, and even this could fail, as in 1976 when a drought again caused the need for standpipes.

The Act which brought the establishment of NDWB was passed in 1945, although the idea had been mooted before the Second World War. Charged with the provision of public water supplies over an area of 1,664 square miles, the region was divided into a northern section based at Barnstaple and a southern one based at Devonshire House, North Tawton. The latter was acquired shortly after the war and used for offices, stores and staff accommodation.

The old Rectory was then bought and renamed Essington House. This housed more staff while the coach-house and stables became a vehicle and plant maintenance unit. Later acquisitions included 'Inglebank' in Exeter Street and the rental of part of the old woollen factory for further storage and parking. The area administered by the southern division stretched from Tiverton to Bude, Launceston and Tavistock. The total population of this area was 200,000, of which 180,000 received mains supplies – a truly gigantic undertaking. At the peak of activities in 1964, staffing levels at North Tawton included 14 management staff, 6 supervisors, and 67 manual workers, thus it was the largest employer in the town at the time.

In 1974 the NDWB merged with other water boards to form the South West Water Authority and is still in operation under that name. At that time the run-down of staff at Devonshire House and relocation to Barnstaple began, Devonshire House finally closing in 1978.

D.C. Philip of North Tawton, a board member since its inception and later vice-chairman, is credited with bringing NDWB to North Tawton in order to promote employment to the town post-war.

Above: *Mr Lund outside his house in Gowmans Terrace in the 1960s. Note the pump.*

Above left: *Rose Dadds collecting water from a standpipe during the drought of 1976.*

Left: *NDWB workers. Left to right: Jack Bailey, Peter Arscott, Aubrey Brock, Dipper Lee, ?, Les Skinner.*

Drainage

An early possible reference to drains is in 1827, when sale particulars of the Gostwyck family house in The Square (almost certainly where Cowley Café stands at the time of writing) states:

At the bottom of the garden is a very large pit, which by underdrains receives the wash of the town, and in which is deposited annually a great quantity of soil valued at from £6 to £8 a year.

Recently, a large tunnel, seemingly blind at both ends, has been discovered at the rear of the premises and is possibly part of this drain.

Dr William Budd, writing of his experiences in North Tawton in about 1839, has this to say about the sanitation:

In the first place, there was no general system of sewers. A few houses occupied by the more opulent, were provided with covered drains, but all these might be counted on the fingers... each cottage or group of three or four cottages had its common privy to which a simple excavation in the ground served as cesspool.

Most people kept a pig and he goes on to say, 'Thus, often, hard by the cottage door, there was not only a privy, but a dung heap also.' Clearly this was an undesirable state of affairs.

From the *Exeter Flying Post*, dated 27 October 1880, Dr Ash (presumably the Medical Officer of Health) reported to the 'Rural Sanitary Authority on the Sanitary State of North Tawton' and stated that:

... having visited 50 houses where he found the houses were not generally drained into the sewers, and the outfall in its present state was most undesirable. He strongly condemned cess pits which caused an abominable nuisance.

Again in a report by Dr Blaxall, dated 1882, it is stated that:

... there is no means of filtration and after rain the water is delivered thick and of a reddish colour... [also] the water mains are in direct communication with the water closets.

He was very critical of the drains, the joints of which were often not cemented at all. He also refers back to a report of Dr Blyth in 1879, who found seven out of eleven wells polluted with sewage.

However, it was not until 1894/5 that a complete drainage system was installed for £700, although many houses not in the town still have cesspits today. The public toilets in Market Street were erected on land sold to the Parish Council in the 1940s for £27.

Scavenging

It is not known when the first street cleaner was appointed but in 1899 the Parish Council appointed Jack Ford for £10.8s.0d. (£10.40) yearly. In May 1913 they advertised for a scavenger and had 11 applicants who tendered for sums between 17s.0d. (85p) and £1.3s.0d. (£1.15) per week. Mr G. Taylor was appointed and he and his successors cleaned the streets of horse dung and rubbish with a donkey cart, dumping it in Yeo Lane where it became overrun with rats. Much sport was had in shooting them.

It was many years later, in the late 1930s, that there was a regular rubbish collection; until this time many people disposed of rubbish by burying it in a corner of the garden, although there was then nothing like the plastic containers or excessive packaging and tin cans we have today.

Gas

From a newspaper report dated 30 December 1868, it is recorded that the:

Erection of new gasworks has been determined upon, Mr Willey, gas engineer from Exeter attended a Public Meeting and presented plans which were accepted, and he has been entrusted with the work.

One year later the works were completed by the Devon Gas Association, subsequently taken over by the Parish Council in 1899 so that they could extend the area of the town covered.

The gas works was situated at the bottom of Fore Street, almost opposite the entrance to the wool factory, and Mr Densham was the manager in the early 1900s, followed by Mr Hughes. During the First World War they burnt sawdust among other things, as there was insufficient coal. The fumes were thought to be beneficial to those with whooping cough and within living memory many a child was taken there. Until 1922 the street lamps were lit by Jack Arscott, using a long pole to reach them. He also cleaned the streets.

The church was first lit by gas in 1873 and incandescent burners were installed in about 1910.

Left: *Jack Arscott, official scavenger, in Exeter Street, 1920s.*

Middle left: *Mr Densham, manager of the gas works, c.1915.*

Middle right: *Gaslight in the churchyard.*

Bottom: *The Square, early-twentieth century. Note the cobbled pavements and the drain in the middle of the street.*

Electricity

North Tawton was not as forward with its electricity as its neighbours, Chagford and Okehampton, since it was not until 1922 that the houses were supplied by the Madge Brothers of Cocktree and Halse, together with Freddy Ford. The electricity was supplied from an area that is now occupied by Gostwyck Close. From a newspaper report dated 1922 it is recorded that:

The power station is at Mr Ford's steam saw works on the site of the old Gostwyck Arms, burnt down a few years since (1917). Mr Ford designed the whole of the work and private consumers will pay 10d. per unit.

Freddy Ford, who lived in Exeter Street, had only two fingers on one hand; legend had it that as a baby a pig 'chawed off his fingers' when he hung his hand over the side of his pram. However, it made no difference to his mechanical expertise. The Christy Brothers took over the works in 1930 and then the South Western Electricity Board (SWEB) took charge.

Private consumers were slow to change to gas or electricity and even when their houses were connected many people only had it supplied downstairs and still went to bed with candles. Such was the case in the Gibbings household at The Nook in about 1930, when Trixie, their daughter, remembers that there was also no hot water system.

Outside the town everyone would have been without electricity or gas except a few of the better off who had their own generator, but these engines were seldom powerful enough to run cookers or any other household appliance. Many people in those days sent their washing to washerwomen, such as Kate Pillman in North Street and Mrs Taylor in Exeter Street, while others employed one to come to the house on Mondays to do the washing. Many houses had a 'copper' boiler which had to be lit with sticks and coal, and various processes followed the washing, such as the 'blueing' of some items and starching of others, mangling and then hanging them out to dry. Some of these ladies came again on Tuesday to do the ironing.

Street Improvements

On 15 May 1892 the ratepayers held a meeting regarding the state of the pavements, when it was reported that:

At present nearly the whole of the pathways are covered in small stones taken from the river, and are anything but pleasant to walk upon, and it is suggested that cement, asphalt or paving brick should be substituted, the cost being spread over several years.

The Chairman of the meeting was Mr F.N. Budd, JP. Presumably the work went forward but it was not until 1919/20 that large-scale street improvements were carried out in memory of those who lost their lives in the First World War.

Within living memory there was a stone breaker named Arscott who sat in a lay-by near de Bathe Cross. He cracked stones by hand, which were then used for mending the roads. According to the late Arthur Adams, who worked as a quarryman for some years, these would have been brought from Stone Quarry (opposite Crooke Burnell but recently closed), Bridge Farm or Baron's Wood (in Bondleigh parish).

Fire Fighting

Like many other towns and villages, North Tawton was plagued with recurrent fires. The combination of open fires in the thatched houses huddled together, plus the difficulty of obtaining water and lack of equipment all contributing. In order to stop the flames spreading, people went ahead of the fire tearing off the thatched roofs of neighbouring houses, making 'fire breaks' which must have been terrible for the inhabitants.

The first fire we know of was in August 1676 when ten houses were destroyed. A 'brief' (either a collection taken in church or door-to-door, known as a 'walking brief') was organised to which surrounding parishes also contributed. This resulted in approximately £18 being paid out to named parishioners for rebuilding. The following January these victims petitioned the county authorities saying that with help from the other parishioners they had rebuilt the walls and put timbers in place, but had no money for the roofs and asked for help. Their request was granted and they were allowed £5 out of 'county stocke so they may lie dry this winter.'

Incidentally, North Tawton itself collected nearly £4 towards the relief of the victims of the Great Fire of London in 1666.

In 1832 there was another serious fire while townsfolk were preparing for a revel to celebrate the passing of the Reform Act. No lives were lost but 40

Left: 'Neptune', the original fire engine. Left to right: Charlie Knott, Charlie Setter, Fred Skinner, Reg Letheren, Wilf Stoneman, George Bird, Harry Cann, Harry Densham, Fred Axworthy, Levi Down, Fred Moore (Capt).

Right: Lakeway (North Street) before the fire in 1891, after which the porches were removed.

Left: Fire fighters at the old wool factory in 2001.

Right: Mill Cottages during the floods of October 2000.

Left: The Fire Service, 1981. Left to right: Tony Vanstone, Norman Lidster, Barry Ware, Anthony Burns, Twiggy Lake, Lindsey Field, Peter Fewings, John King, Peter Stocker.

families were rendered homeless. Fire engines attended from Okehampton and Crediton.

Only two years later in July 1834 there was yet another catastrophic fire when 70 houses were destroyed, the church steeple was damaged, and the charity school, poorhouse and parish stables in Exeter Street, together with the Fountain and George Inns also sustained substantial damage. The total cost of the conflagration was estimated at £10,000 and the properties were mostly uninsured. There was an interesting sequel to this when Richard Taylor, with his wife and son, all from North Tawton, were charged with arson but found 'not guilty'. A full account of this can be found in *Take Care of your Fire and Candle* by F.D. Gentry.

There is a scathing reference in the newspaper to North Tawton's failure to acquire a fire engine following the 1832 fire and it has not been possible to find the date at which one was obtained, but by 1843 the North Tawton fire engine attended a fire in Winkleigh, and in 1852 tenders were invited for building an 'Engien House and Vestry Room' and receipt for 'new key for Ingin House' 1s.2d. This building would be the one in Market Street. The horse-drawn fire appliance was always referred to as 'Neptune'.

A bill from Thomas Banbury to the church feoffees (trustees) dated 1851 'for measuring and making an estimate for making a vestry room etc. in the parish stables' implies that the stables, having been burnt down in Exeter Street in the fire of 1834, were re-sited in Market Street. At some point the parish ceased to have stables. Then the horses used to pull Neptune were farm horses, which had to be unhitched from the plough, have their loads dumped, or be caught if grazing in a field when they were required. Most of the firemen liked a drop of cider as fire fighting was hot work, so it is said the horses always turned automatically into the Globe before proceeding to a fire. It was also said that if the property was known to be insured there was less haste to get to it. Fire insurance started in the seventeenth century, and certainly by 1749 some houses in North Tawton were insured, but many were not.

Another fire occurred in 1875 following the April cattle fair, which started at Mr Woodrow's grocer's shop, spread to Mrs Tamlin's drapery and grocery, then to Mr Skinner, druggist and postmaster, where the Post Office telegraph was destroyed. All these properties were in The Square. The fire extended to Mr Durant's premises on the corner of Exeter Street. He was a seed grower and also a wine and spirit merchant (see Chapter 8).

Twelve years later there was a fire at the lower end of the town when the former residence of Mr Vicary, which was divided into dwellings for the 'humbler classes', was destroyed. Fortunately, on this occasion there were two or three houses unoccupied, so the homeless were able to shelter in them or in the back room of the Market House (Town Hall).

Yet another fire involved North Street which occurred in about 1891. Following this fire the porches, which jutted into the street and had a room over the top, were demolished, thus enabling the street to be widened, and at the same time the thatched roofs, which were severely damaged, were replaced with slate. This row of cottages probably contains some of the oldest buildings in the town. One of the houses has a plate over the door reading 'John Loveday Durent 1711.' (John Durant, alias Wolfe, had married Loveday Gostwyck in 1705.) It was removed fairly recently from lower down the street and re-sited. The whole row probably belonged to John and Loveday.

A fire occurred within living memory on 24 March 1917, when the Gostwyck Arms in The Square burned down. Although there were no casualties this was a great loss to the town and it was never rebuilt. Neptune attended, as did the Crediton and Exeter brigades, but the water pressure was poor. All and sundry helped to save the furniture and belongings and the late Daisy Moore (née Pope) recalled that the boys were rewarded for their efforts but the girls were not. Again, arson was rumoured but no one was ever charged.

When the fire service was taken over by the Parish Council in 1897, it had 11 men and a captain. Three practices were held annually, for which the men were paid 2s.0d. (10p) and the captain twice this amount on each occasion. Costs included one old penny to be paid yearly to Messrs Fisher Brothers for the right to rest fire ladders against their wall. The last fire for which Neptune was used was at a cottage near Iron Bridge in 1939, but even in 1926 the engine was described at a Parish Council meeting as 'an antiquated old tub'.

During the First World War the engine was moved from Market Street to the bottom of Muller's garage in The Square. It was then moved to what had previously been Paddon's garage, next to Farwells, Fore Street, in a building which can still be seen and is dated 1919.

By the time of the outbreak of war in 1939, the fire brigade had been equipped with a trailer pump, towed by a K2 Austin with bench seating inside and a ladder on top. The captain and one fireman were instructed how to use the new apparatus. Not until 1941 were they equipped with special clothing. Although the new engine was said to be satisfactory, the mains water supply was not, and due to a mix up North Tawton were without a hose for at least six months that year. Fire fighting must have been a nightmare. As by now it was superseded, Neptune was parked in Essington in the war years, presumably to deter German invaders by blocking the road, and was ignominiously sold for a song after the war.

A new fire station was built in Barton Street in the 1960s, which at the time of writing is being enlarged and modernised.

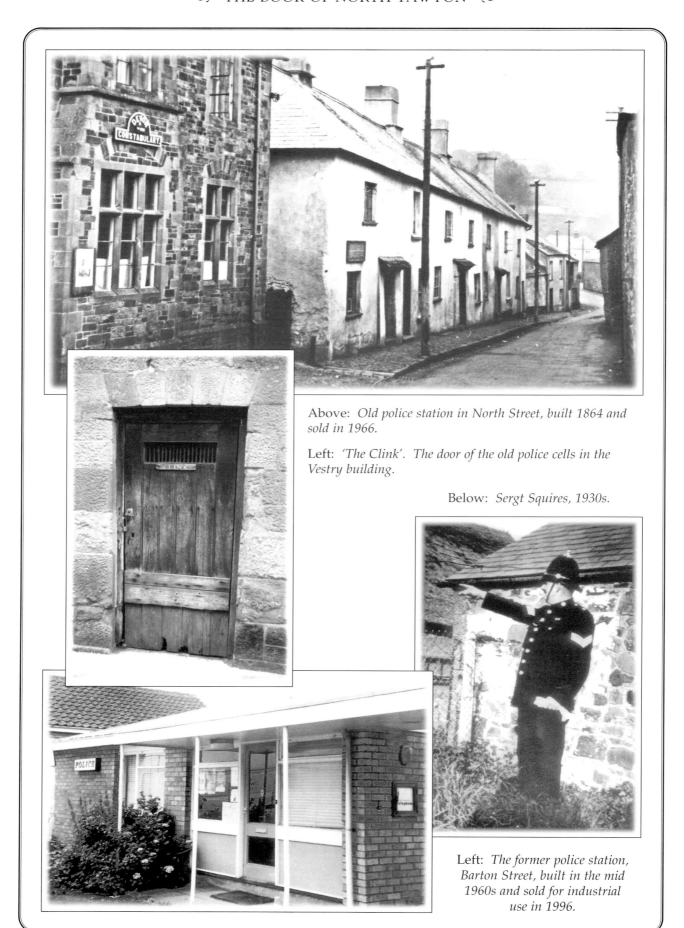

Above: *Old police station in North Street, built 1864 and sold in 1966.*

Left: *'The Clink'. The door of the old police cells in the Vestry building.*

Below: *Sergt Squires, 1930s.*

Left: *The former police station, Barton Street, built in the mid 1960s and sold for industrial use in 1996.*

Originally the church bells summoned the parishioners at the time of a fire and after this the factory hooter was sounded, but when the factory closed in 1930 the church bells were again rung, until in 1936 a maroon was fired for the first time when a fire broke out in a row of cottages opposite the White Hart.

As well as fire fighting the brigade also helped with floods, to which North Tawton has always been prone. In a newspaper report, dated 1874, it is stated that:

Never in living memory has such a flood taken place in North Tawton, rain had fallen incessantly for 30 hours. From the White Hart to the factory the roads were impassable, and all the houses in the vicinity were flooded. In some instances as much as 3ft of water were in the lower rooms. Furniture had to be carried upstairs and people were imprisoned in their houses. At the woollen factory the whole of the work had to be stopped, many of the sheds being under water...

Again, in November 1894, it was reported that:

... the woollen factory had to be again stopped ... the River Taw close to the weir and leat burst through the bank and cut off all supplies to the leat ... fortunately the mills are supplied with a very powerful steam engine.

In recent times, Mill Cottages, the White Hart and the bottom of North Street have been flooded repeatedly, their occupants having to be evacuated and housed in the Town Hall, roads closed, and major disruption being caused. The town is currently awaiting a flood relief scheme, at an estimated cost of £750,000.

North Tawton Brigade is now in the Eastern Division under Exeter. The crew consists of 12 part-time firemen and the first six to arrive at the Fire Station ride to the fire. In recent years the North Tawton crew have been very successful in competitions under their Station Commander, Twiggy Lake.

Justice

In earlier times justice was dispensed at the Manor Courts and the Ecclesiastical Courts, while the constables were responsible for apprehending those breaking the civil law. Although there was a 'clink' in Market Street, which still stands so named under the old Vestry room, prisoners must have been held somewhere long before this was built. In 1587, which was a year of above average deaths, five named prisoners were buried during four weeks in January and February.

The first county police station was built in 1860 in Lakeway (North Street) where, as well as living accommodation for the sergeant (the constable lived elsewhere in the town), there were two cells. This old police station is a handsome building, which is more than can be said for its successor, a typical 1960s construction. As the first police station built in North Tawton was before Okehampton acquired its county police station, those in custody there were brought either to North Tawton or Hatherleigh. No doubt Okehampton police found this humiliating.

In 1964 a new police station and two police houses were built in Barton Street, but these were sold off in 1996, as was their predecessor in North Street. Today, there is no police station or resident police officer in the town.

On 30 October 1939 a presentation of a silver cigarette case was made to Sergt James Squires who retired after 11 years in North Tawton. He had previously received a Royal Humane Society Award for saving two people from the River Yeo while in Barnstaple. He embodied most people's idea of a country bobby and some of his descendants still live in the town.

North Tawton was in the South Molton Petty Sessions Division and the magistrates heard cases from surrounding villages as well as North Tawton, meeting alternately in North Tawton and in South Molton. Usually two or three justices (occasionally only one) sat in the Market House, but sometimes in the vestry.

The rector, doctor, managers of the wool factory and of Newland Mill, and prosperous farmers were the local magistrates. Extracts from the Justice's minute-books of 1886 to 1912 show the cases were predominantly paternity suits (often dismissed for lack of proof, all the magistrates being male), cattle straying, drunkenness, failure to send children to school, failure to have children vaccinated, non-payment of rates, common assault and cruelty to animals. Nearly all of these were fined between 1s.0d. (5p) and £1 or were bound over. Those convicted of vagrancy and begging were usually sentenced to seven or fourteen days' hard labour.

More important cases went to the Assizes, as in 1883 when, on Whit Monday, a fatal fight occurred in the town. Reported in the *Exeter Flying Post*, it seems that Robert Arscott offered to fight or wrestle with anyone in the alley of the Globe (Copper Key). He and the deceased, Robert Northcott, stripped off and blows were struck, resulting in the latter receiving injuries from which he died. Various witnesses gave conflicting evidence; one suggestion put forward at the trial was that Northcott had a rupture for which he wore a truss and it was because he fell on the truss that his fatal injuries were caused. The jury found the prisoner 'not guilty' of the manslaughter of which he had been accused and he was discharged.

Medical Matters

Healers of one sort or another have always been with us, many of them doing more harm than good, but at least most of them were trying to be helpful according to the tenets of the time. The medical treatment of paupers by the overseers showed that the sick were not neglected, as the following entries show.

15 April 1744. To Doctor Clapp for physic for Richard Taylor and Ann Kentisbeere 4s.0d.

Another entry, dated 26 November 1750, suggests that some homely remedy was tried before summoning a medical man.

To Abraham Smith for curing Arminel Allers leg by his own receipt £4.14s.6d.

This was a huge sum then, but shortly afterwards:

To Mr William Skinner and Mr George Durant for their journey to Cruys Morchard [a distance of about 20 miles] *to get a chirurgeon* [surgeon] *to sett Armenel Allers leg 5s.0d.*

Another folk remedy we know of is recounted by Jonas Pillman, a cooper by trade, writing in his diary on 31 August 1813:

I was to Clapps Beer, and split a small ash tree in the west side of Broad Park and drew thro it Matthew Hicks to cure him of rupture. A spike was put in it and a bolt is to be put thro. He was 17 months old.

Other medical references in the diary include:

Sept. 7 177? [illegible] *James the son of James and Elizabeth Pillman ennockalated by Mr Star, the apothecary.*

Assuming this was for smallpox (later entries specify smallpox), Mr Starr (who has been mentioned previously in connection with a pew dispute) would have used material from an actual smallpox pustule which was kept in a bottle for one and half years. This was later superseded by Dr Jenner's practice of using material from a cowpox lesion, which was very much safer, accounts of which he published in 1796.

The Devon and Exeter Hospital was opened in 1743 by public subscription for the sick and lame poor, with the doctors giving their services free and the Matron receiving £10 annually. To gain admission as either an in-patient or an out-patient, the sick person had to have a 'recommend' from a Governor (someone who subscribed not less than £2 a year). A typical entry in the hospital's casebook reads:

Dr Isard returning from his 'rounds' in the winter of 1947, with Gordon Mondon at the wheel.

16 August 1759. Samuel Shilston, No. 9813, aged 43, address North Tawton, recommended by Revd Thomas Hole, ill six weeks with vomiting and pain in stomach, security for burial or removal Mr Hole. Under care of Dr Andrew and Mr Pillett. Discharged cured 1 November 1759.

As late as 1910 there was an appeal because the town was two recommends short of requirements and Messrs Shaw of the wool factory made up the deficit.

Hospital Sunday was an annual event when money was raised for the Exeter hospitals. It is not known when it started, but in the early days was under the auspices of the Loyal Morning Star Lodge of the Oddfellows Society. In 1891 it was decided to broaden the organisation of this event and officers were appointed. An account dated 3 July 1934 describes how £31.11s.9d. (£31.58) was collected in the street and churches when the annual Sunday parade was held. A procession formed at the bridge, composed of the Oddfellows Lodge in full regalia, the British Legion, the Boy Scouts, Cubs, Girl Guides and Brownies. The parish magazine tells us, 'for over 40 years this Sunday had been observed and interest never waned.'

Many medical men came and went over the years but none so extraordinary as the Budd family, an account of which is in a later chapter. Dr Samuel Budd, after serving in the Royal Navy, came to North Tawton in the late 1790s and almost a century later his son Christian, who had also practised in North Tawton, died. The family lived at Melhuishes, in The Square, and it is said that the surgery was on the higher side of the house. In 1809/10 Napoleonic prisoners of war (PoWs) arrived and Dr Budd was appointed Medical Officer. He was allowed to charge the Government agency for attending them as follows:

10s.0d. for each cure when the patient is ill more than 5 days, and

Dr Hugh Webb with Hugh Spence (pharmacist), 1970s.

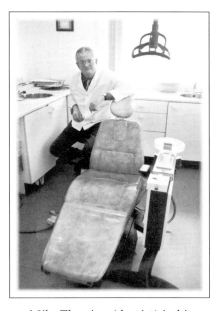

Mike Thwaites (dentist) in his surgery, 2002.

Dr and Mrs John Warre at a wedding, 2001.

5s.0d. if ill for less than 5 days. 1s.0d. for drawing a tooth, and the same for bleeding.

Dr Budd must have found the added income welcome.

Turning to doctors within living memory, there was Dr Deprez, who seems to have taken a very active part in the community and lived at the Holmes in Fore Street, while his partner Dr Langdon lived opposite at Hillside.

Their successor, Dr Clifford Isard, came out of the Royal Navy and settled in North Tawton in 1919, also living at the Holmes. He is remembered as an immaculately dressed man who carried kid gloves and was always very kind and courteous. David Bale remembers being carried from home in his father's arms across the street to the surgery, where he had his tonsils removed by Dr Isard, whose partner Dr Sharp from Sticklepath gave the anaesthetic. This would have been in the 1930s.

Dr Isard's charges before the Second World War are said to have been 7s.6d. (37½p) for visits in the town and 10s.0d. (50p) for those in the country.

Dr James Boyd was in North Tawton briefly in the 1930s, practising from Devonshire House where the surgery is situated at the time of writing.

In 1958 Dr Hugh Webb took over from Dr Isard, building a new surgery in Essington. He continued to practise here for over 25 years and conveyed great benefit to the visual amenity of the town in 1972 by planting a huge number of daffodil bulbs, brought from the Scilly Isles, in the hedges of all the approach roads. These have since multiplied and give much pleasure every year. He was followed by Dr John Warre who came in 1985, converting part of the old Devonshire House into a surgery.

With regard to dentistry, longer ago this was performed by anyone who was handy with a pair of pincers, as was Mr Henry Phillips, owner of the Devon Serge Warehouse, who pulled teeth in the early 1900s for 3d. (1p). This sum was put in the missionary box. Doctors practised dentistry too, as mentioned above.

By 1910 there was a visiting dentist from Okehampton, Mr H.J. Weighell, and later Mr Watson Field who was not fully qualified but had a large following. They were followed by Mr Smallbones who practised from Senderhills on the corner of Exeter Street and High Street, and then after a lengthy gap came Mike Thwaites in 1986, who set up his practice in The Square and is still there at the time of writing.

Nursing

Little is known about nursing in earlier times, although there was a Nurse Gill living in High Street at the time of the 1881 census and in 1934 the death was announced of Mrs Joanna Bolt, who was one of the oldest residents at 84 years of age and had been a midwife for many years. The photograph shows a German nurse, about whom very little is known except that she lived in North Tawton and attended a lady with quinsy in about 1914.

In 1908 and again in 1910, meetings were held regarding the formation of a Nursing Association, although on the latter occasion it was decided not to proceed because a canvass of the town the year before had found the people to be against the idea.

However, in 1919 such an association was formed with a local committee who raised money for part of the nurse's salary. Nurse Barratt was the first to be appointed. Many of the minute-books are missing but in 1928 the Devon Nursing Association rented a cottage, which they then equipped, and Nurse Robinson was appointed. She was followed by Nurse Burrows and then in 1932 by Nurse Biggs,

A German nurse who attended a local lady in 1914.

who lived in what is now 49 High Street. Her salary in 1938 was £150 annually and the records show that during that year she made 2,021 home visits. She stayed for a number of years until Nurse Winifred Davies replaced her in the early 1940s. The latter remained for over 30 years, long after nursing services had become part of the National Health Service, and did much for the town besides nursing. Today no nurse lives in the town but a team based at Okehampton provides full cover.

On 24 February 1978 North Tawton held its first blood donor session at the Town Hall, organised by Mrs Grace Lawrence who reported an extremely good attendance with 84 pints being given. This service continues today, now being run by Mrs Rose Dadds.

A great benefit to the town is the Meals-on-Wheels service, started by the Women's Royal Voluntary Service but now run by Social Services, whereby hot meals, cooked at the school, are delivered by volunteers to the old and the sick. To some extent this has now been super-seded by the delivery of frozen meals.

Chapter 7

TRANSPORT

Horsepower and 'shanks' pony' were obviously the only means of land transport until the coming of steam trains. In 1346 Bishop de Grandisson of Exeter responded to the Black Prince's request for horses and carts by writing:

... as your people who know this country are well aware, there are but few chariots and nor such horses in this country, for all the transporting we do here is by packhorses or bullock carts because of the mountains and valleys and bad ways which are here.

Originally each parish was responsible for its own roads and travelling by wheeled vehicle in the sixteenth and seventeenth centuries was very uncomfortable, many people preferring horseback. But when springs were invented matters improved and in the mid-eighteenth century the Turnpike Trusts came to Devon. From the overseers' account book we read, '17 March 1745. To James Croote for making the turnpikes 7s.4d.' With the payment of tolls at the turnpike the roads should have paid for themselves, but few did. They started to improve following McAdam's invention in 1815 of a wear-resistant surface, after which coaching became much easier.

In 1830 about 70 coaches left Exeter each day and some of these called at North Tawton on the way to Stratton, changing horses every ten miles or so and travelling about ten miles per hour. An old lady, Mrs Susanna Tamlin who died in 1940 aged 97, remembered the coaches stopping at the Gostwyck Arms to change horses and hearing the horn blowing as they came up Fore Street. Revd Robert Hole, who was the rector of North Tawton from 1860 to 1916, tells of a journey to Lifton in the 'Quicksilver Mail' when the coach hit a carrier's van, somewhere near Bridestowe, catapulting the passengers into the road, one of whom broke his leg. He had to be carried back to Okehampton on a hurdle for treatment. This was a compound fracture (the bones were apparently sticking out through the skin) but he recovered although 'was never the same man again.' At this time Mr Hole used to go to Exeter in a tandem (a two-wheeled vehicle drawn by two horses harnessed one behind the other), the journey taking two hours. Subsequently when the train reached Crediton he was driven to catch it there and later still at Copplestone.

An advertisement in 1857 is for 'The Queen Four Horse Coach' which went from Copplestone, through Bow, North Tawton, Hatherleigh, Highampton, Holsworthy, Stratton and Bude. It ran three days a week in each direction, leaving Bude at 6.30a.m. and arriving at Copplestone in time for the 1.24p.m. to Exeter.

Many people owned a horse and trap or similar vehicle, especially farmers and tradesmen, the latter taking orders and delivering to those outside the town. This explains why nearly all the shopkeepers owned or rented one or two fields in days gone by. The inns all had stables and yards for keeping a pony and trap while the occupants did their shopping.

The coming of the railways, although ending the main coaching routes, still left a number of country coach services, which often linked up with the trains. The railway was first brought here by the London and South Western Railway, later the Southern, and it was possible to board the train at North Tawton and travel to Waterloo without changing trains. The official opening was 1 November 1865 and was suitably celebrated with a lunch in the Town Hall when the wool-mill hands had the day off. Originally there had been plans to build a branch line from North Tawton to Bude, which is why the station platform is somewhat longer than might be expected. These plans were dropped and the branch line was built from Okehampton instead.

To reach the 'down' platform there was a footbridge over the double track reached by flights of steps which was originally covered over, the cover being removed between the First and Second World Wars. The station is over a mile from the town, probably because the land, being of poorer quality, was cheaper. However, in those days everyone was accustomed to walking so this would have been of little consequence. It must have been a boon to the wool factory as they were able to bring in new machinery via the trains.

An account in the parish magazine of 1910, referring to the woollen mill, probably after the Shaws bought it in 1887, states that:

The arrival of the first boiler and the erection of the first steam engine was a great event in the annals of the town. The boiler was drawn by 12 or 14 horses. Coming down

Left: *The Gostwyck Arms, before 1917.*

Right: *Mrs Gibbings and her family near Week Farm, 1905.*

Left: *The goods train at the 'up' platform, 1960s.*

Right: *The footbridge at the station, c.1920s.*

the hill it in some way slipped on the trolley and the back of the poor horse in the shafts was broken.

As well as bringing in coal, both to work the machinery and for domestic use, the railway also meant the factory was now able to send the finished cloth away by train.

Many years later, when the mill was owned by the Devon Woolcombers, at certain times of the year there was much inward and outward traffic in wool bales. Newland Mill sent away flour and animal feed, local farmers sent sundry other goods including crates of rabbits and churns of milk. The mail and the newspapers also used the rail service.

A lot of cattle and sheep were transported by train and the coming of the railway opened up markets, hitherto unavailable. Many farmers sent their stock to Exeter's Friday market by train, bringing new stock back. At least one local farmer, Ernest May, went to Kent annually to buy breeding ewes which arrived by train. For a short time there was a cattle market near the station, which made transport even easier. Horses went in special horse boxes and at the outbreak of both the wars many were commandeered for the Army and left from North Tawton station for a very uncertain fate. A horse was also kept at the station to help with the shunting of trucks.

Children attending the grammar schools in Okehampton and Crediton went to school by train, getting up to mischief in the process. A story is told by a lady, who was born in 1904, that the girls tried to avoid travelling with the boys, but sometimes the latter would climb along the running board while the train was moving to get in with them (there were no corridors on local trains then). Two girls, who worked in Exeter in the 1950s and cycled daily to the station, remember that if it was wet when they returned home in the evening, the postman would put their bikes in the van and give the girls a lift back to North Tawton.

Originally a wagonette, owned by the Ring of Bells and possibly another run from the Gostwyck Arms, met the trains, to be replaced in due course by taxis, but many people preferred to walk or cycle.

The railway also provided employment and people were very proud of working for the railway. The Sanders brothers who lived in Exeter Street were immensely proud of their father being a signalman at North Tawton station. Another signalman was Andrew Gregory, father of Archie who started the haulage firm described below. As well as tending the flower beds on the platform, Andrew was very proud of his vegetable growing. There were perks too. The late Sid Palmer was also a signalman there from 1947 to 1967 and had this to say:

While working for the railway I got free train passes and had holidays all over the place, I even went to the Channel Islands. The other signalmen were Arthur Tonkin who lived in High Street and Billy Bowden who

Horses being assembled to be sent to the Front, 1914.

Left: *Charlie Baker, signalman, with Jim the shunting horse, c.1920.*

Below: *The Ring of Bells wagonette at the top of High Street.*

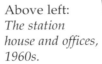

Above: *Andrew Gregory with prize-winning potatoes in front of his signal-box.*

Above left: *The station house and offices, 1960s.*

Above right: *Leonard Corney, stationmaster, 1933–38.*

Left: *S.J. Taylor on his motor bike, early 1900s.*

lived at Bow. It was shift work and when I was on the early shift, I started at 3.30a.m. and had seven trains before daylight, all these were goods trains except the Mail Train and one passenger train. Then one day on getting to work at 3.30a.m. I found a note saying I was stopped as North Tawton signal box was no longer going to be manned and I never worked there again.

This was said with great sadness and occurred in September 1967. The station did not close to passengers until the summer of 1972, when the Phillips family were granted a licence to run a bus from North Tawton to Exeter. The single fare was 20p and return 28p, compared with the current price of £2.25. Today we have regular bus services to Exeter, Okehampton and North Devon.

The station house occupied by the stationmaster was a handsome building although primitive in the early days. Water had to be pumped from a well into a tank and there was no bathroom or electricity provided until the late 1940s. North Tawton was well served by all its stationmasters and their staff. Before the Second World War there was a competition between the stations for the best-kept station and North Tawton won this on more than one occasion. In winter there was always a fire in the waiting room, the whole station was spick and span and the stationmaster usually had a flower in his buttonhole. Sadly one stationmaster, Mr Videan, met with an accident and was killed in 1959 while trying to save his small son who had somehow strayed on to the line.

Phillips Garage in Exeter Street, with Keith Phillips, RAF.

Bill Martin with his taxi in the 1920s.

Minnie Underhill, manager's wife at Powlesland's Garage, Fore Street, 1930s.

Blue Line coaches, Pine Lodge.

A.J. Gregory at the wheel of his first lorry, 1921.

Gregory's cattle lorry, c.1964, which cost £600.

Arthur Lee at the wheel of his father's lorry, 1930s.

Trains always seemed punctual and farm workers within earshot often told the time by trains. Today there is still the occasional goods train using the line, carrying stone from Meldon Quarry near Okehampton and, from time to time, a special train, sometimes steam, carrying railway 'buffs'. Some of those living nearby still run out to watch these trains, which are a splendid nostalgic sight, especially if lit up in the dark.

At the time of writing the station complex is owned by Mr Bill Speak who, renting it from its closure, finally bought it in the 1980s, and the house and station offices have been turned into flats.

With the coming of motor transport, North Tawton was well to the fore. Fred Muller's garage was in The Square for some years, then in 1948 he sold it to Bob Carter. After several more owners it was bought by John Blogg and in spite of subsequent changes in ownership it remains as Bloggs to date. Powlesland's, later Melhuish's Garage, was at the bottom of Fore Street, opposite the White Hart, which was managed by Fred Underhill (there are now houses on this site). There was also Beer's in Exeter Street, which ran charabancs, succeeded by Thomas of

A.J. Gregory, 1896–1976.

W.J. Gregory, 1924–.

J.K. Gregory, 1957–.

Chagford and then Phillips, who also ran coach trips. This garage, until 1999, was owned by Ken Wills from Bow and was recently demolished, leaving a site awaiting housing development. There remains a coach company in the town, called Blue Line and operating from Pine Lodge near Taw Bridge.

The town had taxis, notably Paddon's, who were also coal merchants and hauliers, one of whose drivers was the popular Reg Parsons. Other well-known taxi drivers were Reg Lias, who was a keen rugby supporter, Frank Day, who with his wife also ran a grocer's shop, and Bill Martin. These taxis met all trains and ferried people to and from the station and elsewhere. One old inhabitant remembers that at her wedding, to keep things fair and business evenly distributed, the taxi drivers drew lots for the privilege of driving the bride to church and afterwards to the reception. After many years without a taxi, there is now a magnificent 'people carrier', owned by Jim Brereton, which is a boon to those without a car and those who do not want to drink and drive. As well as Paddon's there was another haulier, Archibald John Gregory, known as Archie. Founding his business in 1919, he first used a horse and cart to haul coal from the railway station to the wool factory. He then purchased an ex-War Department Model T Ford and as well as hauling coal and wool carried agricultural goods. On high days and holidays he transported the rugby team and others, having swept out the lorry and added a canvas tilt. Sometimes 'Tin Lizzie' had to ascend hills backwards (reverse gear being lower than bottom gear) and at others the passengers had to get out

Gregory's yard, 2001, during the foot and mouth epidemic. Note the straw soaked with disinfectant.

and walk, when their combined weight was too much for the vehicle. From the early days when the lorry was housed in Barton Street, just below the park gates, to 1933 when the firm moved to new premises in Fore Street, where the veterinary practice now stands, business increased and by the late 1930s the company had seven vehicles. The war years were difficult with the garages taken over for Army vehicles and the problem of ageing lorries. In 1947, when William Paddon died, Archie bought Paddon's business and was joined by his only son, Jack. The firm continued to enlarge until 1962, when it moved to its present site. It was in 1985 that the third generation, in the person of John Kennedy Gregory, returned from Australia where he had been general manager of Transamerica, and joined the firm. There was now a fleet of 36 lorries, some warehousing and 41 employees, but with the business still firmly rooted in agriculture. Since then the business has greatly expanded, changed its name to Gregory Distribution and has additional depots in Cullompton, Avonmouth and recently Amesbury. At the time of writing it employs about 1,000 people, of which 300 work from North Tawton, which remains the head office. The company operates 400 vehicles, 100 of which are based in North Tawton on a 13-acre site in Fore Street – a real success story from small beginnings.

Arthur Lee's father was another who started a haulage business between the First and Second World Wars, keeping his lorries at The Barton. At the time of writing the business is being run by his grandson Richard, who houses his vehicles in the station yard.

Left: *Newland Mills, 1912.
The water-wheel was on the
left (obscured).*

*James Camble Tavener, JP, the
owner of Newland Mills, died
in 1909.*

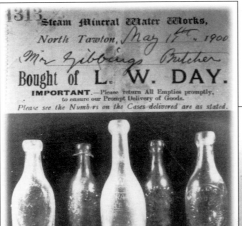

*An assortment of Day's
bottles.*

Above: *The workforce at Newland
Mills. Left to right:* Stanley Hole,
Roland Moore, Jim Pope, with Jack
Tolley on top of the
steam wagon.

Left: *The workforce outside the
Devon Serge Warehouse, early 1900s.*

Chapter 8

BUSINESS

The early businesses in North Tawton of which we have much knowledge centred around the woollen industry and agriculture, which are described separately. Other important enterprises in the past included milling and tanning, while today a cheese factory, a pet food distributors and Gregory's Distribution are the largest employers. The latter is described separately in the previous chapter.

Newland Mills

The first mention of Newland is in 1242, in a Feet of Fines (a legal document concerned with ownership of land). As well as the town mill, which was converted to a wool mill in the mid-nineteenth century, there has been a corn mill in the vicinity of Newland from the earliest times, although the present mill was built in 1814. It had a water-wheel fed by a leat taken off the River Taw south of the railway line, although within living memory this has been filled in. In 1883 it is described as being powered by water and steam and in a directory of 1906 it is said to be lit by electricity.

This would not have been mains electricity at that date, but probably produced by a water turbine. It was owned by the lord of the manor at the time of the tithe apportionments in 1844 and was managed for three generations by the Tavener family. They originally lived at the mill house, but subsequently bought Dr Budd's house, Melhuishes, in The Square. The Taveners were succeeded by Kenneth Sampson at the mill, but on his retirement it lay empty for many years and became derelict. At the time of writing it is being renovated to provide dwellings.

Tanning/Bark Stripping

No records exist of when tanning started in North Tawton; there is reference to John Skinner, tanner, in a deed of 1775, and the tanyard appears to have been erected by Charles Sweet, serge maker, according to a deed dated 1806. Charles Sweet junr of Farwells is listed as tanner in the apprenticeship records of 1784. In the nineteenth century it was owned and worked by the Vicary family, who intermarried with the Fulford family, who were serge makers. William Vicary came from the Newton Abbot area where his family were both tanners and

woollen staplers. The tannery was in the vicinity of Barkers Way, known before development as Barkyard. The Vicarys lived at Park House nearby. The directories show that the tannery was still in existence in 1857, but according to Walter Mortimer, in his book on North Tawton, it was bark stripping that was carried out here and the bark was then taken to the tannery at Bow. In its heyday it employed 100 men and together with the wool factory and agriculture must have provided major employment in the area.

Mineral Water Manufacture

According to an advertisement this enterprise was started in 1866 by Lewis Day. This seems a little odd as he would only have been 18 years of age at the time. However, since his father was a blacksmith by trade it is quite likely that they started it together, as the father would have had the expertise to set up the machinery required. The Day family have been established in North Tawton since the early 1700s and many of them were blacksmiths. Several of their

descendants still live in the town. Lewis Day's premises were at the bottom of Essington Lane. He is credited in North Tawton with having developed the closing of the bottles, known as Codd's bottles, with a marble, but he failed to take out a patent. However, he probably did patent a type of closure, as some of his bottles with a different kind of 'cork' are stamped 'patent stopper'. In the early days of aerated drinks much difficulty was encountered in

"Necessity is the mother of invention."

BY ROYAL LETTERS PATENT,

STOPPERS FOR BOTTL ETC.

L. W. DAY'S
Crystal Mineral Waters

In Syphons and Patent Stopper and Corked Bottles.

Certificate of Analysis.

Analytical Laboratory,
11 & 12, Great Tower Street,
London, 8th April, 1899.

I hereby certify that I have submitted to very careful Chemical Analysis samples of the Aerated Beverages manufactured by Mr. L. W. Day, North Tawton, and from the results arrived at I am in a position to express a very favourable opinion as to the skill and judgment that have been exercised in the process of their preparation.

They are admirably flavoured drinks, of excellent composition and quality, well aerated with purified Carbonic Acid Gas, and free from turbidity or deposit.

Granville H. Sharpe, F.C.S., &c.,
ANALYST,
Late Principal of the Liverpool College of Chemistry.

Southwood & Co., Exeter.

Extract from the "**Western Times**" Jan. 22, 1897

A visit to a local inventor's establishment (The North Devon Ginger Beer Factory, Mineral and Aerated Water Works.)

Mr. Lewis W. Day's mineral and aerated waters are well known throughout the whole of the North Devon district, and having heard of the numerous inventions of the ingenious proprietor, I applied for and was readily accorded the privilege of inspecting the works, under his courteous guidance. First I was shown how some hundreds of dozens of bottles were in a short time put soaking before being brushed by revolving brushes, by which means two bottles are cleaned both outside and inside at one time. (This is one of Mr. Day's many inventions.) They are then rinsed on the outside and on the inside with jets of crystal clear water and placed in special cases to drain. The bottles are then taken to a revolving table, where they receive their different flavours, such as lemonade, ginger beer, every kind of fruits, soda water, potass, lithia, seltzer and salts to represent the constituents of the different foreign and mineral springs. I found four different filling apparatuses in use, one for syphons for the mineral and saline waters, one for corked bottles, and two for the different patent stoppers. Here the worthy proprietor's inventive genius has again been applied, and for this he holds letters patent. The machine for making the mineral waters was constructed by Mr. Day himself, who has taken every precaution to thoroughly aerate the waters, in course of which the latter come in contact only with the purest tin to prevent metallic contamination. There is also a machine for marking bottles and syphons or other glass-ware in an artistic and indelible manner, being driven by a steam engine, the boiler also supplying water for all the requirements of the factory. The same precaution is taken in preparing the different flavours and fruit syrups, thereby ensuring perfect purity and cleanliness. I had the still further privilege of entering the laboratory connected with the establishment. Here the many labelled bottles and processes of extracting the flavours and extracts in their different stages made one feel as if this was indeed a veritable chemist's laboratory; lemons, oranges, raspberries and ginger were being treated so that the extracts might freely mix with the different syrups and become perfectly soluble in water. One process particularly interested me, viz., that of separating the resin in ginger root. By other processes oil was being separated from the lemon, the orange, in fact, almost from every substance that flavours are extracted from were undergoing similar processes. Mr. Day, who has conducted the business with much success during the past 30 years, informed me that he is about to remove shortly to larger and more convenient premises, which the state of his business necessitates. From the many ingenious contrivances—not a few being the direct result of Mr. Day's lengthy experience and inventive brain—for securing perfect cleanliness and freedom from metallic contamination, I was not surprised to find that the above-mentioned removal is about to take place. Anyone interested in the process of the manufacture of aerated and mineral waters would, I believe, be readily escorted over the works by making application to Mr. Day. THE CHIEL.

Equalled by few, excelled by none.

"Perseverance overcomes all difficulties."

Steam Factory, North Tawton

ESTABLISHED 1866.

An advertisement for Day's mineral water.

closing the bottles because of the gas produced, which blew out the 'cork', so many makers patented their own designs. Lewis Day also invented some machinery connected with bottling. There are a number of bottles in private ownership with his name on, from early amateurish examples where the lettering is seemingly scratched in freehand, to those obviously factory-made elsewhere. He traded until at least 1906 and died in 1914. None of his family followed in his footsteps, although one of his sons, Percy, was a watchmaker and radio engineer, whose shop was in Barton Street.

The Devon Serge Warehouse

As previously mentioned in Chapter 5 the Middle Class School was sold in the 1890s to Mr Henry Phillips, who had previously been associated with the wool factory, and he started a tailoring business there called the Devon Serge Warehouse. The family moved across the road from Court Green, their previous home, and were very successful, employing over 40 tailors and sending high-class clothing to many parts of the world. The Phillips family lived in the main building with their drawing-room to the right of the main door and dining-room to the left. John Saunders remembers his mother giving or lending them a piano and when the removal men got it

Tailors outside the Devon Serge Warehouse, c.1902. Left to right: ?, Bert Martin, Ern Mann.

into the drawing-room it sank through the floorboards. He also remembers seeing the tailors sitting cross-legged at their work in the smaller building on the right of the main one. There was a shop at the front where material was sold by the yard (metre).

The Phillips' tailoring business closed in 1930 in the wake of the wool factory closure and for a time the building was the home and also the surgery of Dr James Boyd. Shortly after the outbreak of war, a firm of London stockbrokers came with their staff and families and in 1949 it became the offices of the newly formed North Devon Water Board (see Chapter 6).

Inns

The Gostwyck family gave their name to a large coaching inn of the nineteenth century, which may have been converted from a private house belonging to Lady Gostwyck, sister of Edward Gostwyck senr. She had married her kinsman, Sir William Gostwyck, and died a childless widow in 1786. Shortly afterwards the following advertisement appeared in the *Exeter Flying Post*, dated 7 September:

To be let by private contract at North Tawton from Michaelmas next, an elegant new built dwelling house, late the residence of Lady Gostwyck deceased, consisting of two exceedingly good parlours, very good kitchen, seven lodging rooms, a brew house, cellar, and pantry with all other conveniences belonging to a good house with exceedingly good walled garden. For particulars apply Mr Cole, Witheridge or Mr John Cole, North Tawton.

One wonders if this house later became the Gostwyck Arms, which first appears in an advertisement in 1810. The Gostwyck Arms was certainly the premier inn in the town, where the coaches changed horses and many important meetings, sales and dinners were held. Sadly it burnt down in 1917.

At least from 1780 there was a New Inn in the town, which seems to have ceased trading in about 1820, but its whereabouts are uncertain. It was part of the Gostwyck estate and may possibly have been on the corner between High Street and Barton Sreet, now known as the Corner House. To add to the confusion, another inn at Newland was sometimes called the Bridge Inn and sometimes called the New Inn, appearing in the 1841 census as the former but in the tithe apportionments a few years later as the latter. It was situated immediately west of the bridge, in what is now Newland Cottage garden, and perhaps started when the existing mill was built in 1814. There is no further reference to it after 1878.

The Fountain Inn deeds go back at least to 1818, although it has been burnt down twice since; in 1834 and again in the mid 1860s. Likewise the George Inn (sometimes called the Commercial Inn), which once stood on the corner of High Street and Exeter Street, was also burnt down in 1834 and rebuilt. The George Inn belonged for very many years to the Durants and in around 1900 ceased to be an inn, when it is said one of the family became teetotal and poured all the alcoholic liquor down the drain.

Above: *The bar at the Ring of Bells, the day it closed in 1997.*

Below: *An advertisement for the Gostwyck Arms, dated 1900.*

July 24 1900
Mr Gibbings

GOSTWYCK ARMS HOTEL & POSTING HOUSE
NORTH TAWTON
W. WARE, PROPRIETOR

GOOD FISHING & SHOOTING DISTRICTS.
CHEAPEST POSTING HOUSE IN THE WEST OF ENGLAND.
DOG CARTS, BREAKS, CLOSED CARRIAGES, WAGGONETTES & WEDDING CARRIAGES SUPPLIED.
FUNERALS CONDUCTED TO ANY PART OF THE COUNTRY, NEWEST DESCRIPTION OF GLASS HEARSE.

HIGHEST CLASS BRANDS OF WINES & SPIRITS STOCKED.
BEER SUPPLIED IN SMALL CASK FOR PRIVATE FAMILIES.
BUS MEETS ALL TRAINS.   GOOD STABLING.
TERMS MODERATE

N.B. GOOD HOME COMFORTS FOR COMMERCIALS OR VISITORS.
APPOINTED CYCLISTS' TOURING CLUB HOTEL.

Above: *The Fountain Inn on the left, 1930s.*

Above: *The Globe Inn (Copper Key), 1961.*

At the White Hart, a sponsored 'Beard Growing', c.1980. Left to right, back row: Gill Hoggins, Bill Clarke, Alan King, Ray Vaggers, Rod Stoddart, Steven Crawford, Chris Fear; front row: Stuart Girling, Charlie Wilkins, Steven Stoneman, Alan Boughton.

The Ring of Bells was built in about 1832 and until recently had remarkably few landlords. The first was the Fisher family who brewed beer there and had a smallholding. It then passed to their relatives, the Harveys, and then to the Heath family, also relatives, in 1895. The Ring of Bells also ran a car hire service. The Heaths finally sold it in 1956, after which there were a number of changes in ownership, including a couple of years when it remained closed. Eventually it was closed in 1997 and converted into private dwellings. So ended 165 years of innkeeping, where many dinners, weddings and other functions were celebrated.

The White Hart, first mentioned in a directory in 1873, and the Copper Key (Globe), first mentioned in 1866, probably also have a long history, but it is unknown when they first opened. The Globe is said to have been the scene of cockfighting in earlier days.

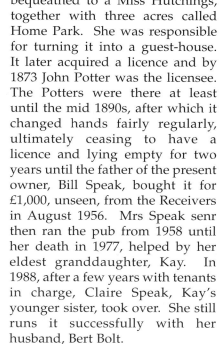

The Railway Hotel, early-twentieth century.

The Railway Hotel was opened as such a few years after the railway came to North Tawton in 1865. Built originally as a private house, it was bequeathed to a Miss Hutchings, together with three acres called Home Park. She was responsible for turning it into a guest-house. It later acquired a licence and by 1873 John Potter was the licensee. The Potters were there at least until the mid 1890s, after which it changed hands fairly regularly, ultimately ceasing to have a licence and lying empty for two years until the father of the present owner, Bill Speak, bought it for £1,000, unseen, from the Receivers in August 1956. Mrs Speak senr then ran the pub from 1958 until her death in 1977, helped by her eldest granddaughter, Kay. In 1988, after a few years with tenants in charge, Claire Speak, Kay's younger sister, took over. She still runs it successfully with her husband, Bert Bolt.

Blacksmiths

Before the coming of the motor car there was a great demand for blacksmiths, who of course also shod the shire-horses before the tractor era. The Day family, ancestors of the Lewis Day previously discussed, were blacksmiths in North Tawton in the eighteenth and nineteenth centuries, one branch of the family subsequently moving into the motor trade at Okehampton where they set up a very prosperous business which ran for many years. It is not known where they had their original forge, but in the last century one branch of the family ran what is now known as the Old Forge, in Fore Street, and another

Ivydale, known as Osborn's Forge, in Fore Street, early-twentieth century.

William Jones with son Clifford at the smithy at 1 The Square, c.1933.

operated from High Street, where people took their pots and pans to be mended in the 1920s and '30s. Yet another member of the family was blacksmith at the wool factory.

There were two other smithies in the town; one at Ivydale in Fore Street, otherwise known as Osborn's Forge, which burnt down early in the twentieth century, and another in North Street run by the Bradley family. The latter is now a garage run by Alec Ranford. There was another smithy out of town at Paffords, known to locals as 'Paradise', on the road to Bow. Today a private house, the last blacksmith there was a man named Lovell, who was born in 1869. He learned his trade from the Days of North Tawton and was said by his son-in-law to be one of the last blacksmiths who had shod cattle – the oxen used for ploughing. There were blacksmiths at Paffords at least since 1803 when Barnabas Hooper paid Land Tax for the property. He was followed by a member of the Osborn family who later moved into town and whose forge burnt down early in the twentieth century, but not before William Jones senr had started business there in 1902, moving to The Square soon afterwards. His son, also William, joined the Army in the First World War, serving as farrier and driver (horses) in the Royal Engineers attached to the Royal Artillery, based on the Gaza Strip, Suez and Palestine; places which are well known today but at that time must have seemed like going to the moon. He obtained early release after three and a half years due to a severe outbreak of influenza in Devon, where his services were urgently required. Succeeded by his son Clifford, the business now is entirely one of a general smith rather than a shoesmith. It seems that those with horses now rely on a travelling farrier, thus missing out on all the lovely smells of a blacksmith's shop and the cosy warmth in winter.

Blogg's Garage, 2002.

Builders

Obviously there have always been builders in North Tawton; the family of Ellis were certainly such by 1835 as they are mentioned in deeds of this date and, according to a contemporary rate book, by 1878 they owned 29 houses between the various members of the family. The Banberys owned even more houses which they presumably built themselves, numbering 37 during the same period. Both the Ellises and the Banberys were still in business at the outbreak of the Second World War. Another firm of builders were the Fishers, whose workshop was in North Street, and it was they who built the houses on Bouchiers Hill.

These old established businesses were followed by the Delve brothers, whose premises were in Exeter Street, and the Bennetts, who came from North Devon in about 1850 and were builders for four generations, operating from their workshop at 23/25 High Street

Ellis's workmen, c.1940. Left to right: Tom Adams, Tom Medland, William Adams, Ern Arscott.

Mr Bennett's men outside the (old) Primary School. Left to right, back row: Harry Densham, Wilf Stoneman, Jim Bennett, Charlie Stapleton, ?; seated: ? Willcocks, Jim Browning, ? Coombes, John Mark Bennett.

while living at number 29. At the time of writing among others there are Barry Ware and his sons, one of whom has a decorating business, the Rice family, Phil Squires, Ron Iles and a house decorator, Twiggy Lake.

Thatchers were always in demand and Stanley Coles, who was still thatching in his eighties, lived at Westacott. His son Archie carried on the tradition, himself retiring only recently. Thomas Taylor who lived in Exeter Street was another.

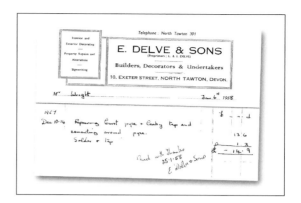

Delve's billhead.

Seed Merchants

This business started by the Durant family was in the former premises of the George Inn, which has already been mentioned, and flourished in the first half of the twentieth century. The earliest reference to this family in the North Tawton Parish Register is in 1586, when Margaret Durant was baptised. Trading variously as butchers, serge makers, drapers, saddlers, silversmiths, carriers and chapmen (itinerant pedlars) the family name continued in North Tawton until John Grendon Durant died childless in 1947 leaving a large legacy to the town. His will directed that this money be invested. His housekeeper, Miss

Maude Discombe, was to have a life interest and after her death the money was to go to the Parish Council as sole trustees 'for the benefit of the inhabitants of the parish of North Tawton or some part thereof.' Miss Discombe died over 40 years later in 1990. The trust fund was deemed to be a charity and by the time it had been set up was worth £135,000. The Trustees resolved to invest £100,000 in income bonds and spend the rest for the immediate benefit of the town. Initial disbursements were made to all the organisations in 1991, the largest amount going to St Peter's Church for its steeple restoration appeal.

Durant's workforce with the Smallbones children who lived next door, c.1950.
Left to right: *Lynette, Charlie Setter, Jill, Bill Martin, Fergus, Allan Stapleton, Fred Skinner and Deidre.*

Administering this fund has been beset with problems, in spite of taking much legal advice. Whether or not this is a 'benefit trust' has been disputed, as this makes a difference to the type of project which can be helped. Thus some donations have been made which subsequently proved unacceptable to the Charity Commission, meaning several clubs are having to repay the Trust at £1 per week in arrears for 38 years! However, the Trustees continue to meet quarterly and support various local organisations, having made donations to a large number of projects during the last ten years.

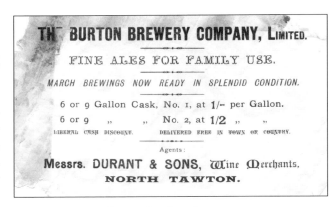

Durant's advertisement.

Threshing Machine Proprietors

There were threshing machines in the pre-combine harvester era, worked by steam engines. These were hired, pre-war, either from the Heyward family or from Alfred Potter, who lived about half a mile from the railway station on the road to Whiddon Down in a home-made mobile home. This was there so long that everyone forgot it was on wheels until one day it disappeared, having been hauled away by one of his steam engines. Anyone working with a threshing machine had to take it to the farm, position it close to the corn rick and get up very early in the morning in order to 'get up steam' next day.

Avery and Merchant were also threshers. Threshing was extremely hot and exhausting work, requiring many extra hands, so casual labour was in much demand.

Banks

The National Provincial Bank (later renamed NatWest) came to North Tawton in the early years of the twentieth century and was always situated, as it is at the time of writing, at the junction of Market and North Streets, with living accommodation upstairs. Lloyds Bank was operative in Market Street in the early 1920s and then after a break returned and was then situated in the former Durants' premises, until finally closing in the 1990s.

National Provincial Bank, 1920s. Left to right:
T.N. Saunders (Manager), V. Ellis, Mr Breeze.

Veterinary Surgeons

There was a vet here at least by 1828 when Edward Knapman, who was born in North Tawton in 1799, is recorded as such at the baptism of his son. By the 1851 census he was still in the town living next to the doctor in The Square, where about 15 years later Edward Leach lived, vet, druggist and wine merchant mentioned later in this chapter who disappeared from the records in the 1870s. It is certain that Edward Knapman was unqualified as the Royal College of Veterinary Surgeons was not formed until 1844 and it is unlikely that Edward Leach was a qualified vet either. Indeed it only became illegal to practise unless qualified in 1949 and many horse doctors and others plied their trade unqualified, passing on their knowledge from father to son. Of course farmers swopped 'cures' with one another, as in 1930 when a local farmer wrote out a 'splendid remedy for colic in a horse', consisting of various strange ingredients and with the instruction to give a second drench in one hour if not recovered, 'but it seldom fails', and another for a horse with 'staring coat and off his feet.' North Tawton seems to have been able to manage without a vet for close on 80 years before Major Fred Fry 'put up his plate' in 1948.

Before the Second World War most veterinary work was connected with horses and to a certain extent dogs, as many farmers were reluctant to call for assistance for other animals because their worth hardly covered the fees. However, by the time Major Fry came antibiotics and many new synthetic drugs had come on the market, together with vaccines and the development of artificial insemination. Major Fry worked hard and built up the practice from scratch, taking a partner, Alan Taylor, in 1955, and the business grew large enough to expand into Hatherleigh. In 1960 Major Fry moved to work for MAFF (Ministry of Agriculture, Fisheries and Food, now DEFRA) and Mr J.C. Hindson (Jim) joined Alan Taylor, the practice enlarging in 1963 by amalgamating with the Bow-based practice of Mike McHugh. New premises were now required, Ivydale, the previous former forge in Fore Street having been outgrown, so a site was acquired where Gregory's office building is now and a pre-fabricated building erected.

Further expansion of the practice took place and the vets moved to their present site below the White Hart. With larger and more up-to-date premises further changes occurred, including a name change to the North Park Veterinary Group in 1984.

North Park Veterinary Group, 2002.

The Cheese Factory

When it was built this factory was said to be one of the largest mechanised cheddar cheese plants in Europe. Built on the site of South Week Farm, it was opened in April 1974 at a cost of £4.5 million. At first it was owned by Express Foods and some years later by Grand Metropolitan. The company underwent rapid expansion and a management buy-out occurred in 1992 when the Cheese Company Ltd was formed. There was another change of ownership in 1995 when it was taken over by Waterford Foods plc, who, after a merger, became Avonmore Waterford Foods plc (of whom the majority shareholding is owned by a co-operative of Irish farmers). Branded

'Taw Valley', its products are supplied directly to a number of major retailers and food processors. The name Glanbia Foods was launched in 1999. At the time of writing over 30,000 tonnes of cheese is produced annually, together with whey powder, the best of the latter used in biscuit manufacture and the rest in animal feed. Over the years many prestigious awards have been won at all the main cheese shows. The company employed about 130 people at the time of writing.

Recently a retail outlet was opened on the premises, where cheese is sold to the general public, and a mobile van delivers to shops and hotels.

Glanbia Foods, 2002.

Vital Dog Supplies (Trading as 'Vital Dog')

This company is one of the three largest employers in North Tawton and has been situated at The Barton since the early 1990s. It began trading from part of Gregory's premises in 1980 and was started by Douglas Steuart, who sold pet food from the back of a Land Rover. The turnover in 2002 is expected to reach £64 million. Agricultural and independent retailers, plus breeders, kennels and catteries are supplied with pet food and associated products throughout the south of England from five depots.

From the North Tawton outlet alone 140 tonnes are moved daily. At the time of writing the North Tawton site employs about 120 people, many living locally. The site is open 24 hours per day and does most of its buying and selling on the Internet. The company was named 'Wholesaler of the Year' in the trade in 1999/2000 and again the following year.

Vital Dog, 2002, inside one of the warehouses.

Shopkeepers

Butchers

In the nineteenth century North Tawton was still very self-sufficient with its butchers who bought from local farmers, had their own slaughterhouses, sold the meat in their shops and also delivered goods by pony and trap. Even up to the Second World War this went on to a large extent, as in those days refrigerators were not in common use and housewives shopped almost daily.

The Madge family in High Street had a large business, moving there from the neighbouring village of Exbourne in the 1880s. Although long since gone they were followed in the shop by other butchers, notably Eric Rowland until the 1980s. Another butcher within living memory was S.J. Saunders (next door to Church Cottage and today a leather business), of whom a hair-raising story is told. A bullock being led up by a rope from Bale's yard to the slaughterhouse in Exeter Street took fright, turned around and bolted for home, dragging with it Mr Saunders, whose feet became entangled in the rope. On reaching The Square he realised he might well be seriously injured or even killed when the bullock turned the sharp corner into the yard in Fore Street, so took out his knife and cut the rope, thereby freeing himself, while the bullock raced home.

Other butchers whom many will remember were Charles Davey in The Square and Fred Hockey in Market Street, the latter succeeding a member of the Gibbings family who had transferred his business from North Street. The Hockeys lost their only child, Tom, an airman, in the Second World War. He had not followed his parents into the meat trade but had started a successful radio sales and repair shop. After several changes of ownership, at the time of writing the Market Street shop belongs to A.L. Martin & Sons and is managed by Roger Cudlip. It is now the only shop selling fresh meat in the town.

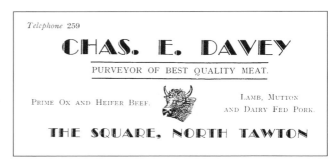

Chas E. Davey's billhead.

Roger Cudlip, one of the last ten contestants of the Daily Mail 'Shop Assistant of the Year' competition in 1988, with customers. Left to right: Roger Cudlip, Jane Field, Marion Pratt and Mandy Ruby.

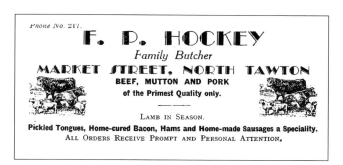

F.P. Hockey's billhead.

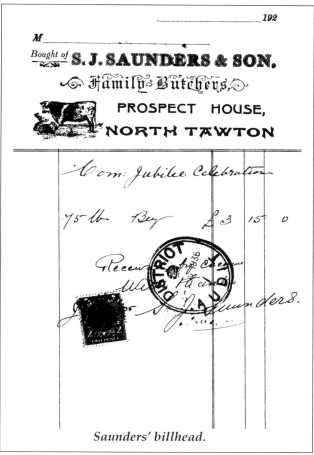

Saunders' billhead.

Fishmongers

In the 1930s Jim Holman and his wife, operating at first from a room at the back of the pannier market and later from a shop next to the butcher's in Market Street, sold wet fish and also fish and chips. There is still a fish and chip shop, run by the Grayling family in the High Street, once the site of Madge's butchery.

Grocers

During the twentieth century there were always a number of grocers. Mr Long, who survived the Boer War, set up a shop at the bottom of Fore Street, a few doors up from the White Hart. This was eventually taken over by his son-in-law, Herbert Parsons, who later moved to The Square.

All the grocers sold their produce loose from large bags or sacks and weighed out portions as required. Mrs Polly Taylor was one of these, in High Street, and her husband also kept cows and sold his milk in the shop and did a milk round. Her shop had previously been in the hands of the Heath family, who took over the Ring of Bells.

Moving up to the top of the town there was Mrs Florrie Day and her husband, Frank (he also had a taxi business), together with their daughter, Joy. She later married a serviceman, Ken Hands, who was stationed in North Tawton during the Second World War. They took over Mrs Taylor's shop post-war and renamed the premises Kayden House, which was an anagram of Ken and Day. They turned this into a small, thriving hotel and also did outside catering, plugging a gap in the market. This is still successfully run as a hotel and restaurant.

In Barton Street there was the Co-operative stores, which was run by a committee with Mr and Mrs Bennett in charge. Besides erratic opening hours, it could take nearly all morning to get served, as there was so much weighing up to do and only Mrs Bennett to do it. They also operated a country round. This building was converted for use as an Over 60s club in 1965 and is now private houses.

Perhaps the largest of the grocers was Skinners, which combined a grocery business with a pharmacy and was situated in The Square, where Cowley House Café is in 2002. William, a son of the original Frank Skinner who started up in the nineteenth century, having qualified as a pharmacist, was well known for his waxed moustache, as well as his habit of wiping his finger round the rim of the big medicine bottles in use and licking his finger.

Today there are only two grocers in the town; Spar in High Street, where Muller's bakery once stood, and the Stores in The Square, which has been a grocery shop since the last war. Many will remember Jim King, who ran the Stores for many years.

William Skinner was not the first pharmacist in town as, on the same site, there had previously been Mr J.M.H. Stanton, who was listed in the 1851 census. He was followed by Edward Leach, who combined being a veterinary surgeon, druggist and wine and spirit merchant, which must have kept him busy. When William Skinner retired, he was succeeded in different premises by Mrs Johns, trading as Annal & Johns, whose advice and potions were very highly rated, as were those of her successor, Claude Holcombe. He was then succeeded by Hugh Spence, a highly popular man. Today North Tawton still has a pharmacy, in the corner shop, which opens in the mornings only.

On the site once occupied by Hugh Spence is now a most successful shop selling almost everything except foodstuffs, namely Linfords. Shoppers come from far and wide and always seem to find a bargain.

Nearly all greengrocery was home grown or grown locally and Lee's shop in High Street catered

Heath's grocery, 3 High Street, 1890s.

Taylor's grocery, 3 High Street, 1930s.

Above: *Kayden House, 3 High Street, 1997.*

Above: *The Co-op, 1960s, Barton Street.*

Below: *Chemist's in The Square, 1960s.*

Muller's shop in High Street, 1950s.

Jim King in the Stores, 2 The Square, 1990s.

The Bakery, Fore Street, c.1939. Left to right:
Mrs Attwell with Jennifer, Winnie Johnson,
Les Finch and Redvers Ford.

for those without gardens, as well as selling seeds and flowers. Most farmers allowed their workmen to have a piece of ground to grow potatoes and many gave their employees milk and eggs and allowed them firewood. Of course many people kept a pig and a few hens in their backyard anyway. James Pillman tells in his diary that he:

... bought a pig of Mr Ware for £2.10s.0d., he gave me sixpence for luck. Commenced fatting the pig 9 October 1820 ... killed the pig I bought of Mr Ware the 20 December 1820, 14 score and 6 pound.

An entry dated 17 May 1823 tells how he also 'tilled 20 yards red potatoes in Mr Dunning's field.'

Bakers

The earliest baker for which we have evidence, from a billhead dated 1888, is Fildew and according to *Kelly's Directory* of 1893 he was by then also proprietor of a Temperance Hotel in the town. In 1939 there were three bakers, one of which was Muller's in High Street who sold groceries and was run by a Swiss family with eight children, some of whose descendants still live in the town. Mr Muller senr also doubled as a hairdresser, having his shop just above the corner shop near the Fountain Inn. The other bakers were Attwell's at the bottom of Fore Street and Fred Rounsley in The Square, who came from Coldridge daily with his bread.

Until the coming of the railway in 1865, coal was a rare commodity, so people very much relied on wood for cooking and heating. Even when gas was produced in North Tawton it was some time before gas stoves came on the market and the use of electricity for cooking took even longer to become popular. So the bakers helped out by cooking folks' Sunday dinners for them, a practice that went on well into the twentieth century. One man who imbibed a little too freely at the pub while waiting to collect his Christmas dinner of goose from Attwell's, dropped the whole dish outside Melhuishes in The Square on the way home. Charlie Attwell's daughter, Jennifer, thinks people took their dinners to the bakers because it was cheaper and better, and she describes a wonderful atmosphere at the bakery on Christmas Day, to say nothing of the aroma.

Before the Second World War people could take fat, sugar and dried fruit to the baker, who turned it into cakes, known as Cauly cakes in North Tawton. Everyone had their own individually made as some 'only put in enough fat to grease the tin', while others were 'full of goodness'.

Dairymen

There were a number of farmers-cum-dairymen, all on a small scale, and people took their own jugs to them to be filled with milk or bowls for cream. Although Pasteur had made his discovery in the mid-nineteenth century, none of the milk was pasteurised. One such dairyman was Walter Bale, whose home and shop were in Fore Street, with his cattle sheds opposite and his fields spread about, including some on part of the Ashridge estate, so before the war it was a common sight to meet his cows being driven through the streets at milking time. One of his daughters, Joan, recalls:

... the milk was brought indoors in large pails and poured through a wire mesh strainer lined with butter muslin, into enamel pans. Some milk was sold the same day but some was left to stand overnight to be scalded next day to make cream. This entailed it being lifted into another pan of cold water and slowly brought to near boiling point on the cooker. Then, after cooling overnight the cream was skimmed with an enamel skimmer. Cream was mostly sold at weekends, although there must have been some sale at other times as people bought skimmed milk because it was cheaper.

Cyril Down and David Knott delivering milk by tractor at Barton Hill, 1977.

Bale's Yard, Fore Street, c.1930s.
Left to right: *Samuel Bale, Rose Martin, Walter Bale and Gyp the dog.*

101

There were obviously no thoughts of dieting or cholesterol in those days.

Fanny Knott also had a dairy in Lakeway (North Street) and drove her cows through the streets to outlying fields, selling her milk direct from the farmyard. Others who sold milk included Andrew Ash at Slade and the Hobbs family at South Week, where the cheese factory now stands. Annie Vanstone had a dairy business in Fore Street and she made ice-cream with ice which came by train. Cornets could be purchased in cones for a halfpenny each in the 1930s.

Norman Watkins with his brother-in-law, Cyril Down, started a dairy in the 1950s, buying in their milk and delivering door to door, including to the neighbouring villages of Bow and Spreyton. When the country roads were almost impassable because of snow they put chains on their tyres, in order to negotiate the lanes. Snowploughs were in their infancy in those days.

Drapers

As well as dressmakers who worked from home, there were always several drapers, notably the Letheren family whose shop was on two floors at the corner of Exeter Street and The Square, with living accommodation next door on the Fountain Inn side. They sold all types of clothing, as well as groceries, and also did a country round, as the following extract from the *Exeter Flying Post,* dated 1 August 1883, shows:

An employee of Mr Letheren's, draper and grocer, absconded with £8.2s.6d. while delivering goods and collecting the money owed and was accused of embezzlement. He had been arrested at Liverpool on board a steamer about to sail for New York. His wages were said to be £15 p.a. plus expenses for refreshment. A lady from South Tawton gave evidence against him, and he was sentenced to 6 months hard labour.

As he had absconded on a Thursday and been apprehended on the Saturday, the police must have been extremely efficient. The Letherens ceased trading in the 1920s.

Meanwhile, the Martin family, whose shop and home was half way down Fore Street, had built on a derelict site where some cottages had burnt down. The building was constructed with concrete blocks made in the wool factory immediately after the First World War. Opened in 1923 by Bert Martin, who had trained as a tailor with Mr Phillips at the Devon Serge Warehouse in Essington, this shop was an Aladdin's Cave to many in North Tawton, with the latest fashions, material by the yard (metre), hats and haberdashery. They also employed a tailor, Harold Stoneman. Longer ago buying ready-made clothing was thought to be somewhat inferior and even those not particularly affluent preferred to have their clothes tailor-made.

Another tailor pre-war was Mr Alfred Davey in The Square and there were one or two others who, having trained with Mr Phillips, undertook tailoring from home. Home dressmakers too were always in demand not only for making new clothes, but also for repairs and alterations, clothes often being 'cut down' for younger or smaller members of the family.

Ironmongery

The Tamlins were ironmongers in The Square, at least since the 1870s and well into the twentieth century, while other members of this family were drapers and grocers.

Another ironmonger was Tom Manning, who came from Plymouth having been in the Navy and married a North Tawton girl. He first started his business where the Post Office is now and then only in half of it. As well as helping behind the counter, his wife baked pasties for the market traders and their customers who came to the market next door on Thursdays. The Mannings then moved to Broadhall Stores, almost next door to the Tamlins' ironmongery business. Tom was succeeded by his son Percy, who

Martin's draper's shop in Fore Street, 1930s.
Pictured are: Rose, Ronald and Bert Martin.

Manning's ironmonger's shop on the right,
early 1900s.

was a talented photographer in his spare time and also owner of one of the first motor cars seen in North Tawton, although it is said he always hated driving. His sister Ethel was very musical and had much success teaching the piano to her private pupils. Just before the war Percy Manning retired and his wife's sister and her husband, Mr and Mrs Herbert Sampson, took over the shop. They were followed by Gilbert Avery, who having started his business in Exeter Street, then moved to the Corner Shop, now occupied by the chemist, and then to Broadhall. Since then several businesses have occupied the premises, most recently a café and craft shop. At the time of writing this enterprise, run by Mike and Pam Jordan, has sadly proved unviable and ceased trading. In 2002 there is a builders' merchant, Mike Shipton, who occupies the site of the old market at the bottom of Fore Street and caters for many hardware and garden needs.

Shoemakers
There were always several shoemakers in the town, repairing as well as selling shoes. Samuel J. Taylor was one, as was his father before him. Samuel had been in the Royal Flying Corps and was also an accomplished photographer, and it is thanks to his hobby that we have many of our photographs.

Another shoemaker was Fred Harris, whose shop was on the corner of High Street and Barton Street, now named the Corner House. He continued to ply his trade until well into his eighties living to a very great age, which was all the more remarkable when one learns that he was kept in bed for about a year in his childhood due to tuberculosis, from which he was not expected to recover. Fred Harris was also an enthusiastic bee-keeper and a member of the bell-ringers. He had taken over the shop in the mid 1930s which was formerly run by John Lee, who as well as his trade as shoemaker was a popular entertainer with his concertina, also playing in the band.

Harold Cornelius, another shoemaker, whose wife was always in great demand as a pianist at concerts, had a shop in Fore Street, having learnt his trade with his maternal grandfather, Mr Knight of Sampford Courtenay, the adjoining village.

Stationers
The stationer opposite Mr Cornelius was Miss Squire, aided by her brother Harry, the latter also an insurance agent and a stalwart of the fire brigade. They had taken over the shop from their parents. This has continued as a stationers ever since and at the time of writing is owned and run by Alan and Pat Davies.

Saddlers
Next door, in what had once been a saddler's shop run first by the Tolley family and later the Attwell family, was Les Gale, who was a tobacconist and hairdresser and played in his father's dance band based in Okehampton. Opposite was Miss Banbery who kept a small confectioner's shop. Florence Heath followed her until 1974 when it became the shop of the Morris family who ran an electrician's business. It is now a private house.

The Post Office
It is not known exactly when North Tawton first had a postmaster, but by 1850 William Collihole, who was born in Winkleigh, is described as saddler and sub-postmaster. He was living in the town ten years before this, as in the 1841 census he is described as a shopkeeper and may well have been postmaster at that date as well. He lived in The Square, where the Stores are now. He continued as such at least until 1873, but by 1878 he had been succeeded by Frank Skinner, also described as grocer and chemist. The latter seems to have taken over Cowley House, the shop of the previous chemist Joseph Stanton.

Some time between 1902 and 1906 William H. Rattenbury became the postmaster and although the directories do not give his address an old North Tawtonian remembers going, as a child, to the Post Office at the bottom of Fore Street (probably the house named the Post House).

By 1919 Mr Francis had taken over as postmaster and the Post Office had moved back to The Square, where it is presently situated, this being the opposite side of The Square from its former site. Mr Francis was an excellent photographer and many picture postcards of the town bear his name.

The telephone reached North Tawton in 1912 and the Post Office had the distinction of a telephone number of one. This, of course, was a manual exchange then, operated by the postmaster. Only a few people had telephones before the wars, so telegrams were often used instead and were a very quick means of communication. In the 1930s Israel Lee and Ginger Woods sat on the seat in the clock tower outside the Post Office vying with each other to have the privilege of delivering a telegram, for which they received 6d. (2½p). Israel Lee in particular is a well remembered character who also officiated as the unofficial director of traffic. One wonders how he would get on today when the traffic in the vicinity of the clock tower resembles 'Spaghetti Junction'. Many postmasters have been and gone since then, all, like the present incumbents, Rosemary and Nigel Davies, also selling sweets, cards and fancy goods.

From the above it is apparent that North Tawton has kept up with the times and although many small-scale businesses have disappeared in the last 100 years, others, on a scale undreamed of then, have materialised. As well as those mentioned, there are of course still many other small businesses both providing employment and meeting most shopping needs in the town.

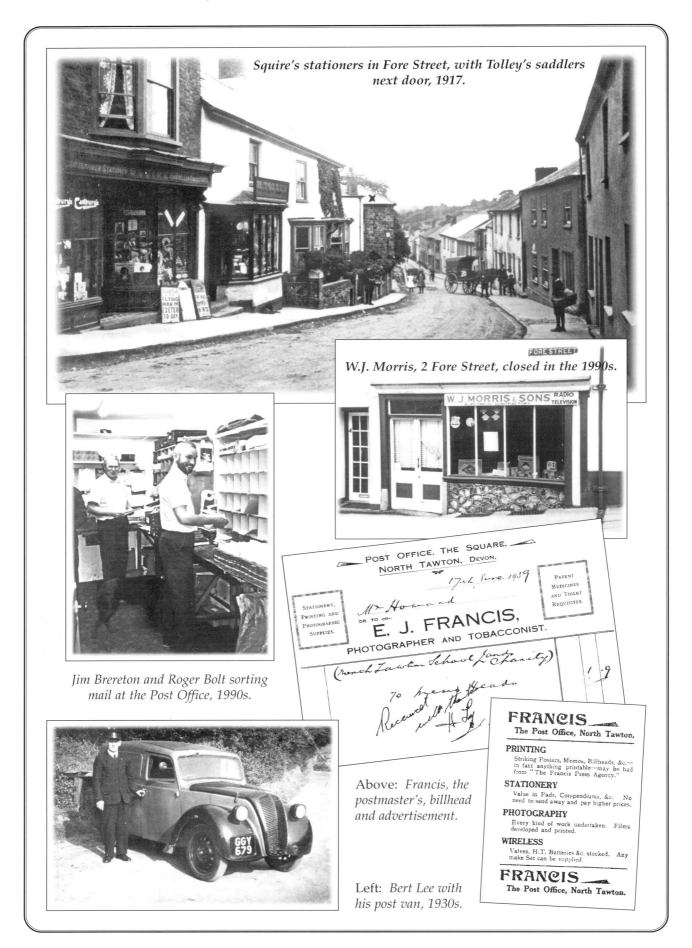

Squire's stationers in Fore Street, with Tolley's saddlers next door, 1917.

W.J. Morris, 2 Fore Street, closed in the 1990s.

Jim Brereton and Roger Bolt sorting mail at the Post Office, 1990s.

POST OFFICE, THE SQUARE, NORTH TAWTON, DEVON,

17th June 1939

STATIONERY, PRINTING AND PHOTOGRAPHIC SUPPLIES.

PATENT MEDICINES AND TOILET REQUISITES.

Mr Howard

DR. TO

E. J. FRANCIS,
PHOTOGRAPHER AND TOBACCONIST.

FRANCIS
The Post Office, North Tawton.

PRINTING
Striking Posters, Memos, Billheads, &c.— in fact anything printable—may be had from "The Francis Press Agency."

STATIONERY
Value in Pads, Compendiums, &c. No need to send away and pay higher prices.

PHOTOGRAPHY
Every kind of work undertaken. Films developed and printed.

WIRELESS
Valves, H.T. Batteries &c. stocked. Any make Set can be supplied.

FRANCIS
The Post Office, North Tawton.

Above: Francis, the postmaster's, billhead and advertisement.

Left: Bert Lee with his post van, 1930s.

Chapter 9

WARS

Early Wars & Skirmishes

As far as is known North Tawton has had very little direct involvement in wars, although the town has always played its part in various ways. In 1549 at the time of the Prayer Book Rebellion, magistrates from North Tawton, Alexander Atwood of Ashridge and Mark Slader of de Bathe (accompanied by Sir John Pollard of Kingsnympton, brother of our then rector), were three justices who went to Sampford Courtenay and attempted to quell the mob, to no effect, and were imprisoned in the church house for their pains. They were released unharmed and some ten weeks later there was a skirmish between the retreating rebels and the Government troops near North Tawton; a field named Blood Acre near Wardens Farm is thought to date from this time. In Tudor times when this country was under threat of invasion from Spain, beacons were set up which, when lit, would alert the populace. The nearest to North Tawton was just outside the parish boundary at Beacon Cross, Sampford Courtenay. In addition, part of the preparations required each parish to keep a list of those aged between 16 and 60 years who were ready to fight. This, known as the Muster Roll, survives for North Tawton for the year 1569, showing that there were 19 more affluent inhabitants who, in the event of war, would be required to provide horses,

Territorials outside the Gostwyck Arms, 1914. Left to right, back row: E. Long, J.S. Sandercock, T. Adams, W. Barrett, W. Long, (J. Ford in pony and trap); front row: W. Stoneman, G. Avery, W. Branch, W. Bolt, W. Fry.

armour and guns. Names included Wood of Ashridge, Cottle of The Barton, Slader of de Bathe and Bouchier.

There were 24 named archers, who were very skilled and would have trained at the Butts; 16 harquebusiers (who fired a kind of musket); 10 pikemen (the pike was similar to a long spear); and 10 billmen (a bill resembled a scythe), totalling 60 able-bodied men. Some of the names mentioned, such as Avery and Skinner, are still to be found in the town today (although of course not necessarily descendants of those listed).

During the Civil War, according to a diary kept by one of the Royalist officers writing in September 1644 when Charles I was in Devon, 'His Majestie lay this night at Okehampton ... the troope at North Tawton five myles further.' But so far no account of this event has been found in the North Tawton records.

In 1793 France declared war on England and this war continued, except for a brief interval at the Peace of Amiens in 1802/3, until England won the Battle of Waterloo in 1815. During these years England was under threat of invasion, particularly in 1804/5, and at home, along with every other parish, North Tawton was preparing to combat any such attack. There are some surviving documents to show how this was done. Arrangements were made to supply bread and flour to the Army and the 'nobility gentry and yeomanry' agreed to supply wheat, oats, straw, wagons, carts, horses and drivers. For instance, Francis Cole who rented Melhuishes, Holmes and West Down agreed to provide a wagon, four horses and one driver. On receiving instructions they were to proceed to Ashridge Moor, avoiding use of the public roads as these were to be left open for the use of the Army. They were also to send two days' provisions for horses and drivers plus a set of shoes and nails, together with pickaxes and other tools. In a Government directive dated 1798, all cattle were to be driven away to prevent them falling into enemy hands. There are inventories of live and dead stock, for example Thomas Seaward of de Bathe had six oxen, 50 sheep, six steers, seven cows and calves, four labour horses, one hackney, one cart and driver, 13 acres of wheat, ten of oats and 12 of barley, ten swine hogs and one acre of potatoes.

Although there was only a small army, men were drawn by lot to serve in the Local Militia (roughly equating to the Home Guard in the Second World War) for three years, as when William Hooper, serving in the North Devon Regiment, was on active service and the overseers of the poor were obliged to support his wife, Grace, and two children in consequence.

According to Fulford Williams in *Devon Notes and Queries* North Tawton celebrated the Peace of Amiens in 1802 with a huge banquet in The Square where:

1,000 of the inhabitants partook of 830lbs of beef and mutton, 700lbs of pudding, 2015lbs of bread and 4 hogsheads of cydar. Next day 2 Hogsheads of beer and the fragments were distributed to the sick.

(One hogshead equals 54 gallons.)

There were also the Volunteers, formed in North Tawton in 1799, which comprised 120 men by 1803 and was commanded by Mr Snell. These could be called on in case of invasion or rebellion. Although disbanded and reformed more than once, they were still in being in 1893 when a newspaper account reports the results of the annual prize shooting of the D Company of the Devon Rifle Volunteer Battalion (which included North Tawton) at the Yeo range (presumably Yeo Farm).

In 1809 North Tawton was a parole town for Napoleonic prisoners of war when around 100 French officers were billeted there and are said to have been accommodated in the upper part of High Street, consequently known as 'The Barracks'. These men were received in the town between September 1809 and March 1810 and were in the charge of an agent named Tozer. They had an allowance of 1s.0d. (5p) to 1s.6d. (7½p) daily according to rank and were allowed limited freedom within one mile of the town. They could also receive money from home. They somehow contrived a printing press and printed bogus identification papers, but were let down by the misspelling of prisoner, rendering it 'prisonnier'. Things came to a head when one, M. Montalant, was arrested in London with a false pass signed by Mr Tozer and a counterfeit passport, causing the Board to sack the agent and move all the PoWs to Moretonhampstead. No doubt this was a blow to the inhabitants of North Tawton from a business viewpoint. Perhaps it is because they were here for only six months that so little information about them has been handed down.

A few parishioners took part in the Boer War (1899–1902), one of whom, Samuel Long, died in South Africa and is remembered by a handsome brass memorial in the church. The fact that he died, rather than being killed in action, demonstrates the sad fate that befell so many of his comrades, when disease was a greater threat than the enemy. His brother also served and survived to return home and set up a provision shop in Fore Street. After the Boer War the Militia and Volunteers were combined to form the Territorials in 1907.

The First World War: 1914–18

There had been a premonition of war in the editorials of the church magazine for the two years previous to 1914. When war broke out there were soon lists of names of those 'who had answered the call' and recruitment meetings were held.

On the Home Front everyone kept busy. Two families of Belgian refugees were taken in by the town, housed at 13 Fore Street, and a committee formed to provide them with furniture and living expenses. The younger members worked in the wool factory and all returned home after the war. The house, however, remains known as Belgium House to many older inhabitants of the town.

Belgium House, where Belgian refugees were housed during the First World War.

A linen league was formed both to collect articles for the Red Cross, such as sheets and bandages, and to knit for the serving men. Sandbags were filled and money continually raised for the war effort. Mrs Matthews of Nichols Nymett was in charge of the Red Cross VAD unit, which had been formed in 1912. At least five of these ladies went on to work in various military hospitals during the war, including one, Annie Pillman, who reached the rank of Sister-in-Charge.

There was a homily in the church magazine in 1915 of those who had failed to join up and then, in November, an announcement of the compulsory conscription for the 15 to 40 year olds. In April 1915, 25 National Reserves were billeted in North Tawton, their main task to guard Newland (railway) Viaduct night and day. The Daws of Greenslade and Taveners of Newland Mills offered them hospitality and the Reading Room invited them to make use of their premises free of charge. They were also provided with weekly entertainment in the form of concerts. A notice dated 22 March 1916 reads:

In the event of a Raid by Enemy Air Craft the factory hooter will blow 5 times. Will the Public particularly note that immediately the Alarm is sounded, the Gas will be cut off at the Main.

Some memories of those days include the collection of horses, which were sent off to the Front from North Tawton Station, and on one occasion the parade through the town of a mounted Army unit, which had been housed overnight at the former barkyard.

As the war progressed, news became more gloomy and although a number of servicemen wrote home and the letters printed in the parish magazine, because of censorship they were not very informative. The tally of those killed and wounded continued to rise. Of 336 men who served, 52 never returned. A number were awarded decorations including three Military Crosses, two Distinguished Conduct Medals, four Military Medals, one Mentioned in Despatches, two Croixs de Guerre and two Legions d'Honneur. Several of these medal holders were treated to a public reception on their homecoming, as in 1917 when Sergt J. Bolt, DCM, Sergt Walter Martin DCM and Sergt Maj. S.H. Taylor MM 'were accorded very cordial receptions at a public meeting and received gifts and gave accounts of their experiences.'

The Red Cross VAD Detachment at the rectory during the First World War.

On Armistice Day news reached the Post Office at 10a.m. and was displayed in the window:

Soon the town was filled with masses of excited people all keen to read the good news for themselves. All the shops immediately closed down, and the bells of St Peter's pealed forth. The whole place was soon ablaze with flags. The schoolchildren marched through the streets headed by Mr Pierce and an improvised brass band. Thanksgiving services were held in church and chapel, and the ever to be remembered day wound up with a dance in the Town Hall at 9 o'clock.

One elderly resident remembers that 'there was a lot of drinking went on.'

In 1919 the late Frank Henson Gibbings, FRCVS, a native of North Tawton which he had left many years

Guarding the railway at the Viaduct, near Newland, June 1915.

Mounted soldiers in The Square, First World War.

Signaller Arthur William Bale, 3rd Hants, wounded twice in France.

Sergt Fred Chowings, RASC, who served in France.

2nd Air Mechanic, Samuel James Taylor, RFC.

before, bequeathed in his will a meadow of three acres in Barton Lane for a War Memorial Park and also £500, of which £300 was to be used for the memorial and the residue for laying out the grounds. A further £200 was to be invested and the interest used for maintenance. A row of cottages in Barton Street was purchased for £100 by the Parish Council to make an entrance and another row in High Street, already demolished, was to make a second entrance. Local builder Mr Samuel Sampson drew the plans for the memorial which was made of granite. Plans to make a lodge were abandoned due to a lack of money and the Park was officially opened in 1921 by Mr Arthur Gibbings, while the memorial was unveiled by George Lambert MP (later Lord Lambert). This monument was moved to the cemetery in 1948 and names of those who lost their lives in the 1939–45 war were added. Today the Park, which has an unrivalled view of Dartmoor, contains a children's playground and an open space for football. This is a charity of which the Town Council is sole trustee and at present the income from the investment realises 89p annually towards the cost of grass cutting!

The War Memorial at the Park, c.1925.

The Second World War: 1939–45

In the mid 1930s the Government had begun to take some steps towards preparing for war and in 1937 created an Air Raid Warning service. The first time this was sounded in North Tawton, David Bale remembers, he was playing in a tent in the garden and was chased indoors to sit on an old wooden bench in the coal hole.

Men joined the Territorial Army (TA), as did Ron Martin of Stockwell in Fore Street, who was called up at the time of the Munich crisis in October 1938. A month later a schedule of reserved occupations was issued (these exempted people in essential jobs from being called up) and by July 1939 conscription had been introduced. When war was declared on 3 September 1939 some of our men were already in the Services and others in the TA.

Reading the Parish Council minutes one would hardly guess there was a war on during 1939–45, so taken up were the members with parochial affairs. This was not the case for the parish magazines, which made constant references to the war and urged everyone to pray. As in the First World War, many men joined up, but happily a higher percentage returned. Four men from North Tawton were captured in July 1942, following the fall of Tobruk in North Africa. These were: Private James Piper of the Queen's Royal Regiment, who was reported missing but in fact had been taken prisoner; Cyril Down, a gunner; George Glover of the East Yorks Regiment and Lawrence Muller, a RASC (Royal Army Service Corps) driver. James Piper ended up as a PoW in Germany, Cyril Down was helped to escape into Switzerland and arrived home in October 1944, Lawrence Muller was a POW in Italy, while George Glover escaped and fought with the Italian Partisans, was wounded, developed tuberculosis and after some time in

hospital was eventually demobilised in 1949.

In all, 142 North Tawton men and women joined the Forces and 11 of these never returned. Their names are on the War Memorial and also on a plaque by the altar rails in St Peter's Church. Among those who served with distinction were Lieut Col Robert Arundell OBE, who was mentioned in Despatches, as was Tom Arscott, RN, in 1944, who served in HMS *Keppel* in Atlantic Convoys and then in the Far East. Bill Wright, a regular soldier pre-war who served in India and throughout Europe reaching the rank of Company Quartermaster Sergeant, received the Commander in Chief's Certificate for Gallantry in 1945. He was sent to North Tawton in 1940 to train North Tawton's Home Guard, was billeted with Mr and Mrs Samuel Taylor and married their daughter, Enid, in 1942.

The 'welcome home' gift to the men and women who served in the war was distributed by messengers to their homes on Victory Day. An envelope with a card thanking them for their services to the country and wishing them all the best in the future contained £3.15s.0d. (£3.75).

On the Home Front, meanwhile, an Invasion Committee was formed and there were 20 fire-fighters, seven ARP (Air Raid Precautions) Wardens, 15 First Aiders and 13 WVS (Women's Voluntary Service) personnel, plus many more with designated tasks.

After the retreat from Dunkirk in June 1940, when our troops returned to England, a unit of the RAOC (Royal Army Ordnance Corps) set up a camp in fields between de Bathe Cross and North Tawton Station, putting up a Nissen hut and also a number of tents. This was a depot for stores to replenish the Army, which had lost almost everything in the retreat. Their stores were guarded by a unit of the Manchester

Sergt R.W. Moore (Bob) joined the Devonshire Regt in 1938, serving in Burma where he was severely wounded.

Pte Royce Stoneman, 6th Battalion, Devonshire Regt.

Alfred Jones, Les Finch, Charlie Bolt and Clifford Westlake, all from different regiments, met up at Deolali, India, in 1945.

The Martin brothers. Left to right: W.O. Alan (RAF), Capt Ronald (Indian Army), Co Sergt Major Ronald Martin (Paratrooper).

Driver Gilbert Avery with his Army lorry.

Ivy G. Chowings, WAAF.

Lieut (later Capt.) Herbert Sampson, RE, c.1942.

Cpl (later Sergt) Albert Vanstone, RM, 1941.

Owen Bolt served as a fitter in the RAF.

LAC Harold Hancock, RAF 1940–5, on left, saw service in India.

Tom Arscott RN, mentioned in Despatches.

Reg Fry, Catering Corps, at Rawal Pindi, India 1942–5.

Wartime wedding of Enid Taylor and Sergt Bill Wright, 1942.

Harry Bloor, RAOC, 1941.

Men of 48 Division RAOC, who were stationed at North Tawton, 1940. Several of them married local girls.

Regiment. After about six months the field became waterlogged and they moved into the Town Hall, later to be dispersed throughout the town. Others were stationed at Week Farm. Some of the soldiers married local girls, among whom were Harry Bloor who married Mabel Bolt, Ken Hands who married Joy Day, and Jock Murray, a driver attached to the RAOC, who married Cicely Stoneman.

Writing many years later, following a reunion in 1985, more than one said that their time here was the best time they had in the Forces and, in particular, George Critchell, who was billeted with Mr and Mrs Davey in The Square, and Charles Lock and Horace Shalless, who were placed with Dr and Mrs Isard, said they were treated as sons by their hosts.

The WVS set up canteens, one in Exeter Street in Prospect House, now Tony Piper's leather shop, and another at the railway station, in a spare shed.

When the Americans arrived some were billeted at Burton Hall and others at the Ring of Bells. They took over the old open market, now the site of the Town Hall, and fixed up showers employing an old man named 'Ginger' Woods to tend the water heater. They also took over Gregory's Yard (which in those days was situated where the Vet's Surgery is now) as a depot for Army vehicles. The officers of this unit lived at 36 Fore Street and their food was prepared at Number 34.

There was an anti-aircraft searchlight detachment along the Wildridge/Ashridge Road which was manned by the Royal Artillery and housed in three Nissen huts. Part of their establishment later became Norman Watkins' yard.

As well as soldiers there were a number of Land Army Girls who went out daily in 'gangs' to farms, replacing men who had joined the Services. Some of the girls lived in lodgings in the town, while others lived on the farms where they worked. At a reunion in North Tawton in 1994 one former Land Girl, Marge Dean (née Simpson), came over from Australia and has written a book about her wartime experiences. Some of our local girls joined the Land Army too and others, such as Violet Adams, served in the NAAFI (Navy, Army and Air Force Institution).

German prisoners of war worked on local farms too. They came daily from a camp at Whiddon Down. At least one of these men still corresponded regularly with two families in North Tawton until his death in 1998 and he had also returned for a visit. He had a spell on the Russian Front and could never get over his great good luck in having been drafted to the Western Front and taken prisoner by the British, and was thus eternally grateful to this country.

The Home Guard started as the Local Defence Volunteers in May 1940, when local policeman Sergt Mallet enrolled members on 27 May in an empty room at Blackmore's Stores, where the chemist is located at the time of writing. Captain L.A. Shuter of Nichols Nymett was in command and was autho-rised to find a list from Police and British Legion sources to select a Platoon Commander and enrol suitable candidates between the ages of 17 and 65 years. The LDV was renamed the Home Guard in August 1940 and the North Tawton Battalion became the 3rd Devon HG, then in January 1941 became the 6th Battalion. Unbelievably, at first Devon was to have only 250 rifles and ten rounds of ammunition per rifle, with 12 men sharing one rifle. There were no officers or NCOs (non-commissioned officers) at this time. Two sections were formed, one under Mr J.O. Heard, the headmaster of the senior school, and the other under Mr Bill Heath of the Ring of Bells, a First World War veteran. A duty roster was drawn up and arrangements made for manning a post at a site near Wildridge on Bouchiers Hill. There was no shelter for those on duty so a fowl house was bor-rowed from Mr Sampson. It was manned all night which was very boring and cold work. Road blocks were prepared in readiness, sandbags filled and barbed wire rolled up. Gradually the men were equipped with uniforms and weapons and eventual-ly North Tawton became No. 1 Platoon in January 1941. Shortly afterwards ranks were introduced into the Home Guard which was, by that time, its title. As all the men had uniforms, regular parades were held. Their task was to defend the town, or at least delay an enemy invasion, and for this contingency plans were drawn up. By that time the Royal Observer Corps was formed and some of the Home Guard transferred to that unit, which took over the outpost near Wildridge. This is still in existence although much enlarged and now a cattle shed.

According to Captain Heard's diary:

... needless to say the shelters were seldom used as the men were too eager not to miss anything, and usually all six were on guard duty together and the yarns were spun. It was no place for those with sensitive feelings. The long night watches provided the old sweats with an opportunity to outdo each other with tales of the last war, and putting the wind up those with no previous experience ... age began to tell, and some of the older men found they could not stick the cold nights. We fear poor Henry Woolacott's death was hastened by his strict attention to duty.

It was decided that they needed a better lookout position and chose Hayne Hill, where a hut originally used for housing dogs was erected.

By May 1941 the platoon strength was 72. Various courses were held in map reading, first aid, arms drill, shooting, gas mask drill, etc. and exercises took place. Guard duties were discontinued from October 1942, presumably when the immediate threat of invasion was over, but parades, practices and mock exercises continued. They practised shooting in the entrance drive at Devonshire House, resulting in an unfortunate incident when Private E.R. Sampson (of

Left: *The Land Girls during the Second World War, at potato harvest. Pictured are Edith Knott (far left), Hilda Sanders (3rd from left), Eileen Anstey (4th from left).*

Below: *NAAFI girls. Violet Adams (Marsh) is pictured on the left.*

Below: *Some members of the North Tawton Home Guard outside the Secondary Modern School, 1943/4. Left to right, back row: Bill Jewell, ?, W. Mortimer, C. Arscott (Bow); front row: ?, J.O. Heard, W. Blight, H. Chapman, ?.*

Below: *Bill Stoneman, Royal Observer Corps, 1943.*

Reg Stoneman, Royal Observer Corps, at the Observer Post at Ashridge during the Second World War.

Waterloo Cottage) was injured. A .22 rifle bullet ricocheted off a tree and struck him in the face during practice there. He was blinded in one eye as a result and had poor vision in the other.

At the beginning of the war they stuck rigidly to their rules and the late Mrs Marjorie Lee, who had recently moved to Wylands, recalled going with her husband and children, the smallest of whom was in a pushchair, to collect the milk from Mr Mondon on Hayne Hill when they ran into the Home Guard post by Ashridge Lodge. In response to 'Halt! Who goes there?' they explained their mission, were asked for their identity cards, which they had not brought with them, and after a lot of argument Mr Lee and the smallest child were allowed through while the rest of them had to return home.

In the 1943 Honours List Major Blight of Spreyton, a schoolmaster in North Tawton, was awarded the MBE for his services to the Home Guard and Sergt Walter Mortimer was awarded a Certificate for Good Service.

In 1944, someone writing in the parish magazine strikes rather a sad note:

... we really hoped there would now be a job of work for us, something to make worthwhile all the hours of slogging we had put into our training. Instead began the decline and we are gradually being relegated to the scrap-heap.

On 2 November that year a standing-down parade of the Home Guard was held at Chulmleigh.

The Royal Observer Corps, located on a hilltop ridge east of Wildridge near the searchlight battery, was responsible for detecting and identifying all aircraft and reporting the height and course to Fighter Command. This operated from July 1940 until nearly the end of the war. Most members were former 1914–18 servicemen. The post was well organised with a hut in which to rest and eat and the watch platform was raised and partly sheltered. The shifts were arranged around the men's working life, e.g. Walter Bale sometimes did the 4a.m. to 8a.m. shift then brought the cows home from a nearby field for milking.

Young Clive Ridyard won a competition for making a model aeroplane and the prize was a visit to the Observer Post, after which he was a regular visitor. There were also the Special Constables who undertook guard duty and helped the regular police. At one time when fears of invasion were at their height, the 'specials' manned the 'Iron' bridge near Greenslade, sitting all night in a car, which must have been very cold as there were no car heaters then.

Farmers, too, played their part and much pasture was turned into arable land on the instructions of the War Agricultural Committee, whose local representative was Arthur Knapman of the Barton. Every village had a quota of crops and he had the task of seeing that it was fulfilled. Mechanisation increased and tractors replaced horses and towards the end of the war Mr Knapman's son, Harry, introduced the first combine harvester in the district, people coming from far and wide to see it. Unfortunately, it was later parked too near the railway line and a spark from a passing train set light to the surrounding straw, destroying the combine as well.

Of course there have been other wars since, indeed we never seem to be without a war. One combatant, Sergt Nigel Stapleton, won the BEM (British Empire Medal) in 1991 for services rendered in the Gulf War. At the time of writing we are engaged in a war against terrorism and who knows what lies in store.

Members of North Tawton Home Guard outside the Secondary School, 1943/4.

The Royal British Legion

It was reported in the parish magazine on 19 March 1920 that, following a meeting called on the initiative of Mr Charles Baker (who had served with the RASC and been wounded in France and was now a railway signalman), a branch of the 'Comrades of the Great War' had been founded. Capt. Shaw, owner of the wool mill, was Commandant; the Secretary was Walter Gardner, then licensee of the White Hart who had been in the Royal Marines for over 20 years; and the treasurer was E. Weekes. The committee comprised Messrs W.J. Heath, E.J. Carnell, A. Martin, W. Lee and W. Edworthy. It was reported that the Memorial Book (already mentioned in Chapter 2) was completed. This association was the forerunner of the British Legion (later the Royal British Legion), the North Tawton branch of which was formed in February 1922. Over the ensuing years many fund-raising activities were held in the form of whist drives, dances, sports and 'smokers' (smoking concerts). One of the latter took place at the Ring of Bells in 1924 when songs and recitations were given by W. Branch, W.J. Bale, P. Day, R. Armstrong, R. Arscott senr, Reg Lias, R. Arscott, Reg Letheren and T. Arscott. Mr J.C. Pierce presided, Mr Saunders was treasurer and Mr Coveton was secretary. Annual armistice parades were held, when the members marched to the church, then to the War Memorial when the Last Post was sounded, as in 1926 when the trumpeters were H. Lee and James Stoneman. This tradition continues today.

Struggling on through the Second World War, the branch was moribund at the end of the war and for some years afterwards and it was largely due to the efforts of the late Clifford Westlake and Reg Farley that it was resurrected. At the time of writing it meets monthly at the Kayden House Hotel and has about 45 active members.

As the number of war veterans declines and post-war National Servicemen are getting older, the branch increasingly depends on Associate members who have not served in the Armed Forces. Despite this, the number of collectors for the annual Poppy Appeal has never faltered and neither has the generosity of the general public.

The Royal British Legion, marching to church on the fiftieth anniversary of VE day in 1995. Left to right: Alan Martin, Clifford Westlake, Colin Payne, Alf Bolt, Reg Fry, Bernard Bale.

Alf Bolt, former Royal Marine, on the fiftieth anniversary of VE Day 1995, at the Park gates.

Royal British Legion Flower Show, August 1971. Left to right: Monica Simons with Jane and Ian, Mary Lee, Audrey Ruby, Mary Fry, Pat Slater, Annette Ruby, Joan Lee, Reg Fry, Aubrey Ruby, Bill Stentiford, rest unknown.

The Royal British Legion (Women's Section)

This group was formed in 1925 and meetings were held in the upper room of the Ring of Bells. The Misses Heath, whose brothers had served in the Forces and two of whom were currently the landlords, were faithful members. Over the years the meetings have been held at various venues and at the time of writing are held in the Mortimer Room at St Peter's Church. These meetings are held on the second Monday of the month, usually with a speaker, followed by tea and biscuits. Outings and walks are also arranged.

The men and women's sections have always worked well together, the women often doing the catering for flower shows, sports and other events organised by the men. They also participate in collections for the Poppy Appeal and a number of members have been awarded a certificate and special brooch denoting 25 or 50 years' service. They participate in church services on Remembrance Sunday, with their standard bearer in 2002 being Mrs Enid Westlake.

In 1951, following the re-siting of the War Memorial in the cemetery, the chains and granite posts surrounding it were given by the women's section.

Parties are held for the children and grandchildren of members and the ladies take it in turns to visit the sick. In recent years, darts, skittles and quiz evenings have been held with other branches.

In over 75 years, many are those who have held office, but deserving of special mention is Mrs Elsie Avery, the widow of Gilbert Avery who, as Driver with the 4th City of London Yeomanry, saw service in North Africa, Italy, France and Holland between 1942–6. She was president in the 75th anniversary year, at the age of 94 years.

Royal British Legion (women's section) at the 75th anniversary, June 2000. Left to right, back row: Elsie Avery (president), Mrs Stevens (county chairman), Enid Westlake (chairman), Joan Scott, Mrs Bowden (county treasurer), Greta Stoneman, Mabel Bloor, Winnie Hancock, Mary Fry, Joyce Vallance, Helen Balsdon, Margaret King; front row: Shirley Turner, Mrs Jones, Olive Delve, Grace Lawrence, Gladys Pyke, Kathy Tonkins.

Evacuees and Other Visitors

A number of strangers came to the town because of the war, including the evacuees from London and other places who stayed with local families. Everyone had to report how many empty bedrooms they had in their house to the WVS billeting officer, Mrs Daisy Tucker, who lived at Crooke. Evacuees, soldiers or Land Army girls were then allocated to fill them. Those who remember her will know that excuses never sufficed.

Some who came have told about their impressions of North Tawton. Clive Ridyard, who had known the town pre-war while on holiday, was brought with his brother Peter to stay with their great-aunt, Polly Taylor, at her grocery shop in High Street, and they later lived with Mr and Mrs Reg Lias.

Settling-in memories are somewhat vague; apart from the lighting of the living room kerosene lamp, the candles at bed time, and the weekly bath in the scullery supervised by Kate Ford and the ever piercing eyes of Winnie Luscombe, made worse by her thick lenses.

His days were filled with school, Cubs, joining the church choir with Mr Newcombe, pumping the

Evacuees billeted with Mrs Bolt at 13 Barton Hill 1941/2. Left to right: Leslie Wills, George and Frank Mintrum, Audrey Minell.

organ, watching the bell-ringers under the charge of Jim Bennett and trying to understand and interpret the 'changes'. On Saturdays he helped in the shop, spooning out the mice droppings from the large cardboard boxes filled with rice (the shop was next door to Durant's, seed growers and a happy hunting ground for rodents) and setting aside the mouldy bits of cheese, long past their sell-by date, for Tom Long. Clive enjoyed:

... riding on Farmer Ash's milk float with the eventual thrill of being allowed the reins and I recall his two lovely daughters, Rosemary and Pamela. I visited Farmer Sanders and his wife in Exeter Street, drove their cows to pasture, learning milking, suckling calves with my fingers and even slitting chickens' throats – ugh! Learning to avoid cockerels and geese and then ferreting for rabbits. Great fun! I remember the thrill of 'cutting out' time in the cornfields and chasing rabbits, as the corn was cut, then the ride back with a handlebar of rabbits to sell at sixpence each; blackberrying at Ashridge Moor, mole trapping, sledging on the slopes behind the Drakes' farm, following the Devon Hunts on bicycle and on foot – and still coping with school homework.

He also remembers going to the station and seeing the exhausted troops coming home from Dunkirk, leaning out of the windows during brief stops when they were plied with food and drink. The stationmaster, Mr Cornall, watched proceedings, immaculate in his uniform.

Schoolchildren, 1940s. Left to right, back row: *Margaret and June Mallett, Rosemary Knott;* front row: *Joy Bird, with evacuees Clare and Lesley Stillman in North Street.*

After winning a place at Okehampton Grammar School he and his fellow pupils cycled to the station, where sometimes they 'squashed' half-pennies on the line, in the hope of transforming them into pennies. Others have mentioned this pastime. Then he made friends with Dr Isard's family, which opened up a whole new world where he learnt to swim in their pool, became familiar with the rudiments of gardening from the resident gardener, Fred Skinner, rode horses, enjoyed picnics, and accompanied Dr Isard on his rounds, opening gates for him when he visited remote farmhouses.

Clive helped Reg Lias, his great friend and the caretaker at the Town Hall, to clean the snooker room and iron the table at the billiards club there. He also made up a regular foursome with local members, the Revd Siviter, Mr Tavener and Harry Bradley. All so different from life at home in Southampton whence he returned at the end of the war.

Another unofficial evacuee, Sheila Leech, came with her parents to Devonshire House where her father's firm of stockbrokers had moved at the onset of war. Whilst at Devonshire House she enjoyed many new pastimes and much time was spent in the vicinity of the river, where she learned to swim. She also played on Neptune, the town's original fire engine, outside Essington Park Farm where it had been placed in a strategic position to repel enemy forces. She remembers that:

We used to stand each side on the pump bars and ride up and down rather like a see saw. The Home Guard were important; all ablebodied men left behind were involved. Devonshire House had a long wide drive leading up to the front door, and it was at the widest part that the Home Guard had its rifle practice. I can remember being told by my mother to always pass behind the guns, not in front! Imagine that happening today.

This was wise advice, bearing in mind the fate of Private Sampson, mentioned above in the section on the Home Guard.

When the troops arrived in the town in 1940, a group of the Devonshire House ladies took over the old chapel off Fore Street and turned it into a canteen/nightclub, which was extremely popular. Food was served in spite of the premises having no running water or toilet. Dances were held there and many people remember 'The Pantry', as it was known, with nostalgia.

Richenda Lee, not an evacuee but a member of the family who in 1940 moved to Wylands, an isolated smallholding, now living in the USA, recalls her indignation, when five years old, at being referred to as 'the little maid', a term of endearment in Devon. She particularly remembers when American soldiers camped for a few days in the field next to their house and offered them chewing gum, which they had never previously encountered, and after they had gone digging up all sorts of buried 'treasures', mostly food in tins and packets. She too remembers all the country delights; the flowers, the birds and the walks by the river, and her brother Graham, now living in Australia, comments 'what a quiet happy place North Tawton was with a lot of lovely people.'

Barbara Westlake came with her mother to live with relatives, Miss Smerdon and Mrs Western, at 'Yorklea' (now York House) in High Street, where it seems that:

... there was no electricity, only gas light in the two downstairs rooms, no bathroom, an outside loo decorated with icicles in winter and big spiders in summer, a big copper boiler in the kitchen, and a coal hole to the left of the back door which was home to even bigger spiders ... all North Tawton knew when we had a bathroom fitted ... we were so excited. Baths were a bit thin on the ground, so Uncle Bill and Aunt Audrey Martin and Miss Beavis used to come on Saturday nights to play cards with the whole family, then slip away, one at a time to have a bath. The bathroom was nice but not as nice as the tin bath in front of the range.

After comments on her school-days Barbara continues:

One year my birthday coincided with Good Friday. I went down to the baker's shop and there in the window was a pink and white iced cake, with 'Happy Birthday Barbara' on it. I was ecstatic! Then Uncle Bill and Aunt Audrey and all our family took the cake on a picnic, to where wild daffodils grew in profusion by the river which tumbled through boulders. We picked the daffodils for decorating the church the next day, hundreds of them, for jam jars all the way up the main aisle, and ate the cake. Heaven has got to be pretty fantastic to better that afternoon.

Like the other newcomers Barbara has very vivid memories of North Tawton which all seem very positive, but the ones quoted were living with families or friends already known to them. It must have been different for others who were living with hosts who were less welcoming.

Mrs Bolt of Barton Hill, who had a knack with homesick children, had a number of evacuees, some of whom have kept in touch ever since. Her daughter remembers that some of the children who came to North Tawton had little or no parental support and all had very few clothes. They were only allowed to bring the bare necessities and indeed would have been unable to carry much anyway, so knitting parties were organised to provide for them.

Betty Oldrieve came to North Tawton in 1943 when her family's farm at East Allington was taken over with others in South Devon for D-Day training. In total, eight villages with their farms were evacuated. In October 1942 they were given just six weeks' notice to pack up and take everything, including their livestock, fodder and root crops in the ground, but were helped to move by soldiers from the British Army. After a short spell at another farm, her father bought a butchery business in The Square, later resuming farming at Broadpark, North Tawton. They never returned to East Allington; Betty married locally and still lives here.

Cup for the best-kept allotment, c.1950. Left to right, back row: Jack Arscott, Will Stevens, Fred Sanders, Walter Gerry, ? Bailey, Cyril Knott, Fred Pope, Leon Squires, Archie Kendal, Will Bolt; front row: Will Day, Sergt Squires, George Venton, J.O. Heard, Bill Stoneman, Winifred Davies.

North Tawton AFC at Battishall's Plain, 1921. Left to right, back row: Will Lee, Reg Lias, Cuddy Knott, Bert Woods, Harold Stoneman, Ern Arscott, Revd Wallace, Len Lias, Hector Whittet, Jack Merchant, ?, Jim Shopland, Tom Day, Reg Lee; front row: Percy Mondon, George Arscott, Ern Ford, Wilf Stoneman, Charlie Stapleton.

North Tawton AFC, spring 1998. Left to right, back row: Pat Ward, Paul King, Colin Cornwall, Keith Steward, Mike Brock, Colin Bissett and baby, Renia, Paul Burrows, Steven Paddon, Mark Seton, Dean Garrett; front row, kneeling: Adrian Rice, Darren Nicholls, Jamie Prouse, Steven Ward, Chris Field, Martin Quick, James Gosney, Stuart Cann.

Chapter 10

LEISURE

Clubs and Societies

Like most communities there has always been a large number of clubs and societies in the town, especially during the last 100 years. Fortunately newspaper cuttings and photographs have been saved and put in scrapbooks and albums to give a good idea of how folk spent their leisure time, and of course still do.

Allotment Association
This club flourished before the Second World War and until the 1950s. Many people spent much of their spare time cultivating vegetables, especially during the war when food was scarce. Competitions were held and cups given to the holder of the 'best kept allotment'.

Association Football
The club was founded in 1910, playing in green and white in a field at the top of Bouchiers Hill. A flashback to those times is the report that they were all ready for action on the field one Saturday in October when they received a telegram from South Tawton to say they could not raise a team. However, South Tawton came a few weeks later and the home side had the satisfaction of winning by four goals to one. Later the club's ground was at Battishill's Plain.

At some point the club ceased to exist but was reformed in 1966, playing at South Week and later at de Bathe Cross until 1982, when they moved to a field at Wardens where a clubhouse was erected. They fielded one or two teams and at one time had a boys' team who played on Sundays and a ladies' team. Their colours are now tangerine and white and they enjoy some success.

Badminton
A badminton club was formed in the 1980s and subsequently located at the Manor House Hotel in Okehampton. It then closed but a new club was started in 2000, playing weekly in the Town Hall, with about 15 members.

Billiards
This club had its origins in the Reading Room, which was established in Fore Street in the early 1880s by Dr Deans who was the first president. In 1908 the building burnt down and the club moved into The Square, where the dentist now has his surgery. By 1914 it also had a billiards table and had moved to the Town Hall, where the room was located in what is now the kitchen. Darts were also played there. This club was for men only but there was a well stocked library and lady members could borrow books for a nominal sum. Surviving primarily as a billiards club, it continued for many years until the mid 1960s when it ceased through lack of support.

Brass Band
The first mention of a band in North Tawton was in 1803, when members played at the street party celebrating the Peace of Amiens, but we do not know what sort of band this was.

In 1877 a band marched from the town to the races (see section headed Horse Racing, below) and there are frequent references to it in newspaper reports and the parish magazine after that date. It seems to have kept going throughout the First World War and a lady born in about 1900 remembered the band playing in The Square in the 1920s on Saturday nights and everyone dancing.

Throughout the band's history the Lee family have been prominent members. The band is thought to have been started by a shoemaker, Mr James Lee, who was followed by his son John, then John's son Esau. When Esau moved and took over the Buckfastleigh band, he was followed in North Tawton as bandmaster by his brother Herbert, who was a fine cornet player and had played in the Services Band at Cranwell while in the RAF during the First World War. The Stoneman family, also very musical, provided many players, as the photograph *(see p.122)* shows. One of this family, James, died aged 46 in March 1932 due to wounds received at the battle of Loos in the First World War. The cortège was followed by the bandsmen in uniform and members of the Royal British Legion also attended.

Left: *The Billiards Club with their shield, having won at Beaford in 1936. Left to right, standing: Reg Lias, R. Stoneman, J. Steer; seated: Gilbert Avery, Will Long, Mr Nicholls (vice president), Reg (Dickie) Lee.*

Right: *The Brass Band, outside Town Hall, before 1939. Left to right, back row: Jim Stoneman, Walter Stoneman, Bert Lee (bandmaster), Gordon Vallance, Harry Densham; middle row: Harold Stoneman, Bill Stoneman, Roy Lee, Philip Stoneman, Horace Pope, Ron Stoneman; seated: ?, Percy Day, Jack Taylor, Bert Fewings, Sid Coombes.*

Left: *North Tawton v. Devon at the bowling green, 1995.*

Right: *Ladies Bowling Club, 1980s. Left to right, standing: Sue Squires, Donna Vallance, Joyce Vallance, Margaret Arscott, Elizabeth King; seated: Frances Brookes, Joan Lee, Bill Stoneman, Monica Simons, Jane Simons.*

The band was discontinued at the outbreak of the Second World War and was not restarted, following the death of Herbert's son, Roy, who was also an accomplished cornet player, in an air crash during the Second World War.

However, in 1954 a Silver Band was formed and this continued for some years until dwindling numbers caused it to cease in the late 1970s.

A popular dance band was Gale's, started in Okehampton by Jimmy Gale, whose daughter Betty was a saxophonist and son Les was a trumpet player. These two had a hairdressing shop in Fore Street where the ladies' salon was in the front of the premises and the men's section at the rear.

Bowling Club

This club owes its foundation to the late Mr Walter Martin, who was secretary for 25 years. In 1952 the club started to play in the Old Rectory garden where they had one rink, nearer to Market Street than their present green, which is on the site of the Old Rectory tennis court, purchased by them from the Church Commissioners for £125. At that time the annual subscription was 10s.0d. (50p) and there were four rinks. They were soon playing matches and holding fund-raising events.

In 1972 the club entered its first county competitions and in 1978 a ladies' club was formed, followed some years later by an Over 60s section. A new pavilion was opened in 1983 and in 1993, due to a generous benefactor, an extension to the green provided six rinks. At that time the club had 48 male and 23 female members and by 1999 the subscription had risen to £40 annually, an 80-fold increase in less than 50 years. In the winter months some members play short mat indoor bowling at various venues.

This is a thriving club which has received generous support and hard work from its members throughout its history.

Brownies and Guides

The Brownies pack of North Tawton, which was started in 1927 by Brown Owl Miss Bertha May, was discontinued in around 1939/40, but was revived with the Guides in 1952.

Although the organisation was founded in 1910 by Agnes Baden Powell as the Girl Scouts, the North Tawton Guides was not started until the 1920s. Miss Olive Gibbings was Captain and the Lieutenants were Bertha May and Ruth Blair. Not much is known of these early Guides, but there is a reference to their visit to a pantomime, *Jack and the Beanstalk* in Exeter in 1926, followed by tea in the magical Deller's café, which was destroyed during a bombing raid in 1942. Mr E. May financed the outing and presented prizes to Evelyn Baskerville and Nancy Edworthy for the best accounts of the day.

Lapsing during the war, the Guides was restarted in 1952 by Scoutmaster Mr de Leysin, helped by Mrs Avery and Mrs B. Hart, while Mrs Wilson of Bouchiers Hill was appointed Captain. In subsequent years they have held sports in the Butts, and have organised jumble sales, coffee mornings and other fund-raising activities. They have provided much entertainment, one example being in 1978 when they entertained the Over 60s Club with a programme of games and songs. They go camping every year and have been as far afield as St Lucia in the West Indies. They also participate in parades and district events. There have been many changes of leadership and at the time of writing Miss Jane Simons is in charge, helped by Mrs Lorraine Dunn, and there are currently 28 Guides.

The Bale family, c.1938. Bernard (Cub), Joan (Brownie), Hazel (Guide), David (Scout).

The Brownies on Revel Day, 1977.

Cottage, Horticultural and Poultry Association

The only reference to this club that has been found was in a scrapbook and reports of the fourteenth annual flower show, which was held on 24 July 1891 in a field lent by Mr W.S. Bickham. The weather was favourable and a new feature was a lawn tennis tournament.

Cricket

Cricket has been played in North Tawton since at least 1862, as a newspaper of that date gives an account of a match between North Tawton and Okehampton, when the scores were very low, no doubt due to the poor pitch (this was before the lawnmower had been invented). The club was formed in 1886 playing at the Hams, South Week, in the early days, near to where the pitch is at the time of writing. Between the wars they played at The Barton in various fields and at that time North Tawton had a team that could provide a contest with any in the area.

Preparing the ground was a case of all hands on deck and the bucket and spade gang were very important in clearing all evidence of animals. Those who did not do their share might not find a place in the team come Saturday. Travel to away matches was by an ancient bus known as 'Noah's Ark' which had to stop from time to time to cool off.

Among the players of the 1920s and '30s were Revd Bevan, Drs Bastard (of Bow) and Isard (of North Tawton), Messrs M. Densham, H. and R. Fry, F. Gill, L. Horn, H. Knapman, ? Matthews, F. Pope, J. Reddaway, A. Lugg, F. Skinner, H. Stoneman and John Tucker, to name but a few.

During the Second World War the club was suspended, but it reopened at the Barton, playing near the lido at first, but as with many rural pitches it had to move due to crop rotation, so that the wicket was at various sites over the ensuing years. Other venues have included a field at de Bathe Cross, the Butts, the school playing-field and where Gregory's buildings are now situated, though not necessarily in that order.

In 1977 the club opened their new ground, complete with pavilion, changing rooms and flush toilets, but before any cricket could be played, Dr Webb, Master of the Molehounds, was invited to hold his Opening Meet there and the ground became known as Mole Park. In 1980 the clubhouse was damaged by flooding and money was raised for its repair. Over the years many fund-raising events have been held, including a whist drive in the 1950s when the first prize was a live pig! How times have changed.

Many are the legends connected with the club, as when Reg Fry took 6 for 37 in 1934 at Dolton; Reg Farley hitting a four off the last ball of a limited overs match to win by one run; and the farmer who dashed in to bat in wellington boots, only to dash off again to finish the milking.

By 1986 the club had a ladies' and a youth team. Of recent years the club has not found life easy, with difficulty in finding sufficient players, owing to competing demands on people's time. In the summer of 2001 they were unable to play at all due to the restrictions imposed by the foot and mouth disease outbreak which affected Devon so badly. In 2002 the club has ceased, hopefully only temporarily, due to lack of support – potentially a sad end to over 100 years of cricket in North Tawton.

During the 1980s and '90s, and possibly earlier, there was a ladies' cricket team who, in 1994, notched up their first official win in ten seasons, but this did not in the least detract from their enjoyment.

North Tawton Cricket XI at The Barton, early 1950s.
Left to right, standing: *Bill Wright, Maurice Orchard, Derek Clifton, Frank Berwick, Wally Bines, Bill Long;* front: *Bill Pyke, Dennis Fewings, Reg Fry, Leonard Lee, Jack Gregory.*

North Tawton Ladies Cricket XI at Hatherleigh, c.1980.
Left to right, standing: *Marion Pratt, Mary Tucker, Corinne King, Mary White, Jane Field, Celia Boughton;* kneeling: *Jane Simons, Carol Dennis, Frances Brookes, Bridget Dennis, Angela Botham, Janice Thwaites.*

Fountain Inn Darts 'A' Team League Winners at Duke of York, Iddesleigh, 1965/66. In doorway (left to right): Gordon Paddon, Leonard Lee; back row: Arthur Brookes, Maurice Horn, Patrick Burns, Clifford Bolt; front row: Eric Rowland, Reg Fry, George Potter, Harold Bradley.

The Fountain Ladies Darts Team, 1980/81, 'Wooden spoon' winners. Left to right, back row: *Hilary Knott, Carol Cudlip, Jane Lake, Muriel Leach, Elizabeth King, Ethel Paddon;* front row: *Bessie Stoneman, Greta Stoneman.*

The chorus in ANTS production of Snow White, 2000. Left to right, back row: *Doreen Hiscock, June Maybury, Jane Simons, Keith Badman, Sue Weedon, William Speak, Irene Ward, Paul Hannaford, Gill Hoggins;* middle row: *Emma and Sam Scrace, Alice Willatt, Megan Warre;* front row: *Hannah Ward, Donna Hicks, Zoe Phillips.*

YANTS production of Bugsy Malone, 1999. Left to right: *Janet Lanchberry, Adam Smith, Tim Warre, Adam Courtier, Tamsin Woodland.*

The North Tawton Specimen Angling Club Dinner at the Pretoria Vaults, Okehampton, in 1980. **Left to right:** *Peter Ruby, Pat Ward, Mandy Ruby, Pete Heal, Ted Tuckerman, Albert Farley, John Avery, Annette Andrews, Norman Ruby, Paul Whiteley, Anthony Heal, David Hoare, Michael Edwards.*

Right: *Frank Skinner at the rear of Cowley House, c.1930.*

Below: *Ann and Daniel Hoare at Spires Lake, 1994.*

Laying out the golf course in 1913. Left to right: Sam Hoyle, ?, Mrs Mary Gibbings, W.D. Gibbings, W. Edworthy, Sammy Skinner.

Darts

As already mentioned above, darts was originally played in the Reading Room in the Town Hall. At one time or another every pub in the town had at least one darts team, most playing in the Lane League. The season ran from September to March, with games played weekly on different nights for the ladies' and men's teams. Every team in the League played twice, home and away, and refreshments were liberally supplied by the host pub. In the beginning the finals were held at the Duke of York, Iddesleigh, but later on moved around the different pubs or halls in the area, with a dance often finishing off the evening when held in halls. Darts matches were always very sociable and well-supported events. Unfortunately there is no coverage of this game in the extant parish magazines, so when it started in North Tawton is not known.

Drama

Drama has always been a popular pursuit in North Tawton and the parish magazines bear eloquent witness to the many events held in the Town Hall over the years. The earliest written record is from 1909, when a performance of two plays, *Box & Cox* and *The Coming Woman*, was advertised to take place in the Town Hall. In that year tickets were priced at 1s.6d. (7½p), 1s.0d. (5p) and 6d. (2½p).

In December 1931 *Daddy Long Legs,* the Amateur Dramatic Society's sixth production, was held, produced by Miss Pratt of Dawlish. The cast included Mr Mortimer, Miss M. Bragg, Miss O.P. Gibbings, Misses E. and R. McCombe, Miss B. May, Mr R.G. Saunders, Miss D. Sampson, Miss O. Priest, Miss Ford, Messrs H. Lee, Way, Delve and Master B. Bale. In a scrapbook there is an undated reference to the 'newly formed dramatic club', but in 1983 the drama group ceased to function after 11 years and:

... a nostalgic members evening was held at Letherens by kind permission of Mrs G. Gregory. All materials and props were dealt with and Mrs Peggy O'Loughlin is compiling a records pamphlet on the various entertainments. It was arranged for the cast to have a farewell dinner and social.

However, in November 1985 a newly formed ANTS (Actors of North Tawton Society) arranged a fundraising coffee morning and this group has been very active ever since, regularly putting on plays and pantomimes to packed houses. Their producer is Twiggy Lake. They have an offshoot called Young ANTS which is equally successful.

Fishing

The Angling Club was formed in 1975 and originally had 12 members, growing to 45, but has now contracted again. Its first meeting was held in the Congregational Hall, after which it moved to the Fountain Inn. Competitions are held fortnightly for game (trout and salmon), coarse fish and beach fish. There is a presentation for the biggest specimen. An annual dinner is held, at which some 60 cups are presented.

Others have fished quietly on their own in the Taw, catching both trout and salmon. From an 1866 directory, we learn that the:

River Taw furnishes excellent fishing, for which permission may be had by ticket, on application to the host of the Gostwyck Arms.

In more recent times, fishing can be had from artificial lakes such as Spires Lake.

Girls' Guildry

Mrs Northam, who also ran a small school, started the Guildry in the 1920s. It was a Scottish version of the Girls' Life Brigade, with similar aims and activities as the Guides. They wore navy skirts with red bow ties and sashes. This organisation gave scope for her talent for drama and she put on many entertainments. Remembered performers include Margaret Shaw, Olive Knapton, Hilda Page, Lily Evans and Muriel and Phyllis Down, among others.

Golf

In 1912 a meeting was held regarding the formation of a nine-hole Golf Club at de Bathe Moor. A committee was formed, Mr W.D. Gibbings was appointed secretary and 20 people put down their names to join. By November arrangements had been made with the occupier, Mr Gatley James, an expert was engaged to lay out the course and the Earl of Portsmouth had agreed to be patron. The subscription was one guinea (£1.05) for men and half that amount for ladies and juniors. The course was opened in April 1913, when a large crowd gathered, and afterwards there was a luncheon in the club room at the Railway Hotel.

The first home match was a friendly against Bude, who beat North Tawton soundly, but by August they were able to win against Stafford Moor, Dolton. Things went well for a time, but by 1916, in the darkest days of the First World War and with a change of tenant who was not so sympathetic to the idea of moving his sheep and cattle off the 40 acres covered by the links as his predecessor had been, the club disbanded. However, in 1927 Mr and Mrs Bragg opened a nine-hole golf course at the Burton Hall Hotel and for a subscription of one guinea members could still engage in this ancient game, which was certainly being played long before Mary Queen of Scots indulged in it, though probably not in North Tawton.

Above: *Boy handbell-ringers.*
Left to right: *Brian Balsdon,
Chris Delve, Geraint Vanstone,
Albert Vanstone.*

Above: *The Tennis Party, probably behind Crispins, c.1895.* Left to
right, back row: *C. Letheren, F. Goss, A. Goss, A. Letheren, Mary
Skinner, S. Hellier, John Gibbings, E. Carpenter;*
third row: *Ernest May, A. Clare, ? Worth,
F. Tavener, J. Tavener, Mrs Durant, ? Burridge;*
second row: *L. Goss, Mrs Letheren, A. Clare,
E.P. Skinner, ? Barrett, May Tavener, L. Gibbings,
Mrs Davies, Mrs May;* front row: *Charlie Letheren,
Frank Skinner, F. Tucker, R. Carpenter.*

Above: *Girl handbell-ringers.*
Left to right: *Linda Chapple,
Sue Armstrong, Paula Crawford,
Elizabeth Fry.*

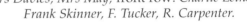

Above: *Tennis Court at 'Clarks', 1930s.*
Left to right: *?, Thelma Hill, ?, Greta Perkins,
Cliff Martin, ?.*

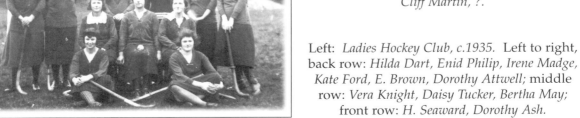

Left: *Ladies Hockey Club, c.1935.* Left to right,
back row: *Hilda Dart, Enid Philip, Irene Madge,
Kate Ford, E. Brown, Dorothy Attwell;* middle
row: *Vera Knight, Daisy Tucker, Bertha May;*
front row: *H. Seaward, Dorothy Ash.*

Handbell-ringers

This club was formed in 1948 by Mr and Mrs Albert Vanstone who bought the bells for £1 each. It started with the Scouts, of which Mr Vanstone was Scoutmaster at the time, then girls became involved. Over the years they have raised a lot of money for charity and have played in concert halls, at weddings, carnivals and in hospitals in Exeter, Plymouth and Okehampton. They have been on radio, TV (including 'Opportunity Knocks') and have won many prizes and certificates, including the South West of England Cup. On one occasion they rang for 14 hours non-stop in relays to raise money for their trip to Blangy, our twin town in Normandy.

Sadly, in 2000 Mr and Mrs Vanstone, then aged 84 and 82 years respectively, had to 'call it a day' and the group was disbanded.

Ladies' Hockey

In the 1920s and '30s a ladies' hockey club started up in North Tawton. At first games were played in a field near the station, they then transferred to The Barton and finally to a field at de Bathe Cross. Many matches were played and those against Okehampton Columbines were always needle matches when both teams had to watch their ankles!

Fund-raising dances were held in the Town Hall and on at least one occasion they had a dinner-dance in the Sunday-school rooms, with the food served upstairs and dancing on the ground floor, together with a men's ankle competition judged by Miss Lizzie Skinner. Herbert Sampson was the winner. This was a very successful club, but like many other organisations, it ceased because of the war and never restarted.

The Over 60s' Club, in the upper room of the Town Hall, 1969.
Left to right, back row: *Mr Durston, Miss Pillman, Amy Fewings, Mrs Wood, Susan Adams, Mrs Fry, Mrs Young, Mrs Bird, Win Stoneman, Mrs Densham, Archie Gregory, Miss Brealey, Mrs Rowland, Mr and Mrs Arthur Friend, Miss Adams, Mrs Pike, Sid Yeo, Annie Way;* front row: *Miss Nellie Sampson, Mrs Windrum, Mrs Bale, Mrs Bailey, Mrs Mallet, Mrs Winifred Davies.*

Lawn Tennis

Tennis has been played in North Tawton since at least 1890 and there were over a dozen privately-owned grass courts and a club which played at 'Clarks', adjacent to Gregory Distribution. Tennis parties were a regular feature in those days, at any rate for the more leisured classes, and North Tawton had two noted players in Mrs Arundell, who won Devon county championships, and her son Robert Duncan (later Sir Robert), who won the singles lawn championship in Tanganyika in 1934.

The other courts were situated at the Rectory, Court Green, the Holmes, Melhuishes, Stoats (on the site of the present fire station), Crispins, Bouchiers Hill, Burton Hall, Week Farm, Crooke Burnell, Nichols Nymett, de Bathe, and Newland. The National Provincial (now NatWest) Bank had a court opposite Crispins. All but one of these has now disappeared, although additional courts have been built at the school and at Wildridge.

After the Second World War the club was revived, playing at the old rectory (now Essington House). The court was rented by the Town Council in 1950, but the lease was not renewed by the rector, Revd Searle Barnes, after 1951. Subsequently the North Devon Water Board leased the court and the club was restarted with Mrs Young as secretary. Unfortunately for the tennis players, the newly formed bowling club bought the site. The tennis club, unable to find anywhere else to play, was reluctantly disbanded amid controversy.

In 1985 a new club was formed which played on the school court, but this did not have many members and folded after a few years because of the lack of support. Some years later, yet another attempt was made to start again, but with the same result.

Over 60s' Club

Founded by Nurse Winifred Davies in 1965 on behalf of the Women's Voluntary Service (WVS later WRVS), meetings took place in the upstairs room of the Town Hall, where members played whist and bingo, sometimes had a speaker and enjoyed a chat over a cup of tea. A draw was held with tickets costing one penny each. There was an annual coach outing, a Christmas party and an annual birthday party, when Win Hancock always made the birthday cake. By 1968 the club had outgrown the premises, so a move was made to the old Co-operative grocery shop in Barton Street. The WVS kindly bought the property for £450, gave £100 for conversion and lent another £500. This entailed

Left: *RFC at the Butts, 1912. Left to right, back row: ?, Harry Bradley, Jim Browning, Will Attwell, Harry Squires, Walter Bennett, Charlie Setter, Harry Long, Ralph Bennett, Bill Lee, Frank Attwell, ?, Ern Mann, Henry Day (Secretary); middle row: Sam Ash, Edwin Long, Will Skinner; front row: Fred Delve, Sid Ash, Fred Moore (Capt.), Walter Stoneman, Sam Skinner, Jack Skinner, Frank Heath.*

Above: *North Tawton Rugby Club, winners of the Junior Cup, 1947/8. Left to right, back row: E. Arscott, D.C. Philip (President), G. Avery, R. Workman, W. Heath, S. Palmer, J. Skinner, E. Ford, L. Squires, J. Piper, A. Bolt, N. Bolt, P. West, J. Bennett, C. Evans; middle row: S. Arscott, W. Bolt, G. Stevens, D. Tucker, C. Heyward, R. Arscott, P. Reddaway, A. Hoare, F. Muller, W. Axworthy; front row: L. Scorer, L. Skinner, R. Fry, J. Tucker (Capt.), C. Bolt, L. Lee, L. Gardner, R. Lias and R. Lee (joint hon. secs).*

Right: *Last game played at the Butts v. Ilfracombe, 1997.*

much fund-raising and a lot of hard work by very many willing volunteers. Capt Pat Slater, RN, retired, was in charge of the conversion and Revd Lane, the rector, was very handy with pick and shovel, among many other men who gave freely of their time and expertise, right down to the piano tuner, while various organisations such as the handbell-ringers gave concerts in aid of funds. All went well for about 20 years and then in 1988 it emerged that £3,500 was needed to bring the building up to the standards required by law. This was a blow to the club who could not raise that much and although the Parish Council intervened on their behalf, the WRVS sold the property in 1989, giving £5,000 to the club to be invested so that they could use the interest for the rent of an alternative venue. At first they moved to the United Reformed Church (URC) schoolroom and then back to their original meeting-place, upstairs in the Town Hall, where they still meet at the time of writing, having about 15 members, who at last can reach the meeting-room due to the introduction of a stair lift.

Pig Club

Perhaps this club started in the Second World War, when meat was rationed. It certainly continued into the 1950s and '60s and outings were held (presumably the pigs being left at home).

Rugby Football Club

The club is thought to have been founded in 1885/6 by Mr Lucas, a schoolmaster and organist at St Peter's Church, together with Mr Frank Attwell, a local baker, although rugby has been played here since at least 1876. A photograph which was unfortunately destroyed by fire, showed the team with a matchball of this date.

As a working town with a farming community there was always a supply of fit young men on hand to fill the various positions. There is a reference to the club in the parish magazine of 1910 and another to the quaintly named 'Annual Dinner and Smoking Concert', held at the Gostwyck Arms in June 1912, when between 40 and 50 people sat down to the meal. There were no less than 11 toasts and speeches, yet they still had time for a concert to which a number contributed, including the president, Dr Deprez.

In the early days the club played at de Bathe Farm, then Drake's Field, eventually settling at the sloping field at the Butts by permission of the Tucker family, themselves no mean rugby players. David Tucker was selected for a Devon trial in 1946. A grandstand was erected and opened in 1930.

The club won the Devon Junior Cup on several occasions, including 1914, 1931/2, 1947/8, 1948/9 and 1950/1, and were runners-up in 1989. There was a time in the early 1960s when the club disbanded through lack of players, but it reformed in 1967 and also boasted a supporters' club for a few years.

At one time the HQ was at the Ring of Bells, as the photograph *(see p.130)* shows, and at another time it was at the Fountain, where the bath was in the cellars. Then the old club 'hut' in the field next to the Butts was used as the changing room. This was followed by a nomadic existence when they changed at the back of Eric Rowland the butcher's premises and drank in any pub that would have them.

At that time the 'committee', which consisted of everybody, decided to have a clubhouse and one of Laings' redundant motorway buildings was purchased for £2,000, funded by selling hot-dogs and hamburgers every Friday and Saturday on the old A30 bypass for three long summers. This clubhouse was formally opened in September 1980 by Mrs Joan Tucker and many good times were had in that old wooden building.

In July 1991 the Devon Rugby Football Union made history by electing their first woman committee member, Mrs Gill Hoggins of North Tawton RFC.

Rugby Supporters Club, 1949. Left to right, back row: *W. Phillips, S. Arscott, F. Hart, W. Wright, H. Manuel, R. Fry;* seated: *W. Hancock, E. Merchant, H. Stoneman, O. Vicary.*

Tag Rugby team, 1999. Left to right, standing: *Jack Preston, Lucy Wilson, Kylie Matravers, Fred Bolt, Robert Crisp, Luke Honeychurch, Richard Bolt;* kneeling: *Melissa Poynton, Austin Healey (England player), Vicky Skinner.*

Since 1979 the club has run two senior sides and a mini rugby team.

At last the club achieved the long-awaited purchase of its own ground in 1994, when, with the kind co-operation of the Webber family, Richard Ash bought the site on its behalf. With the help of a grant a large new clubhouse was erected with all mod cons, including separate accommodation for the referee, a ladies' changing room and a large function room with bar. The new ground, named Taw Meadow, was officially opened on 3 May 1998 and it is hoped the club will continue to go from strength to strength.

Opening of the new Rugby Ground, 3 May 1998. Left to right: Gill Hoggins, Richard Jackson, Reg Fry, David Knott.

Scouts, Cubs and Beavers

The Scouts movement was started by Baden Powell on Empire Day in 1909 and there was certainly a pack in North Tawton by January 1913, when a note in the parish magazine stated that the Scouts' 'entertainment is postponed because of an outbreak of scarlatina in the town.' By the 1920s and '30s those in charge were Walter Martin, Walter Mortimer and Mr Heath. They met in the old Sunday-school building and camped most summer weekends in a field belonging to the Drakes in Essington.

In 1932 there is an account of a party they held:

... which went on till midnight, when the Guides, Rangers and friends were the guests. The Rangers gave a return party four days later when dancing, games and supper made a very entertaining evening.

They held rallies, as in 1939 when one took place in a field between the town and de Bathe Cross, probably in Northam's Field.

Disbanded during the Second World War, the Scouts (with Scoutmasters Messrs de Leysin, Mortimer and Vanstone), and the Cubs, Guides and Brownies, were reformed in 1952, still meeting in the Sunday school. They then took over two cottages in Essington (later becoming the site of Dr Webb's surgery) for storage. Among other fund-raising activities they collected waste paper and sold it.

North Tawton Scouts and Cubs on the steps of the Town Hall, 1952, with Scout and Cub Masters Albert Vanstone, Walter Mortimer and Mr de Leysin.

Again the Scouts were disbanded in 1982, but five years later were reformed and continue to date, with an average attendance of about 15, meeting in the Town Hall with their Scoutmaster, Brian Crisp.

It is not known when the Cubs were formed, but it was probably around the same time as the Scouts. Reformed in 1952, they met in the cottages belonging to the Scouts as above. In 2002 Colin Sharp was their Cubmaster and, like the Scouts, they meet in the Town Hall. There is also a Beavers group whose leader is Jackie Phillips.

Beavers building a suspension bridge with help from Professor Harvey, 2000. Left to right: ?, Kayleigh Stuart, Peter Folland, Gary Down, Cyran Guy, Joshua Speak, Ben Tabiner, Stuart Badman, Paul Sercombe, Joshua Cassells, Alex Norman, James Speak, Jack Edwards, Martin Hann, with leader Sue Molyneux in the background.

Table Tennis

In the 1950s there was a thriving table tennis club in North Tawton, which played in the old Sunday school in New Road, when Reg Farley was noted for being the most accomplished player. Among others who played were Derek Clifton, Brian Long, Richard Lee, Lawrence Finch and Lew Lacey. After some years this club folded up and a few of the players transferred to the Okehampton club.

Women's Institute

The aim of the WI (founded in Canada in 1915) is to improve the conditions of rural life for women and to enable them to play an effective part in local and national life. In pursuance of these aims the North Tawton branch was formed in 1929. Two founder members, Mrs Phyl Lewis (née Bragg) and Mrs Hilda Powlesland (née Dart), have told how the meetings were first held in a room known as the Market Room at the Railway Hotel. They subsequently moved to the kitchen of de Bathe Farm, where the ladies sat on forms around a large scrubbed wooden table and after business was concluded heard a speaker and enjoyed a social 'cuppa', a format still followed.

At the time of writing the meetings are held in the Town Hall, although the Sunday-school rooms were also the venue at one time. In those early days the hostess was Mrs Lily May, who was very keen on drama, and much time was spent learning lines and practising for concerts, even on a train journey to Exeter for a competition, when the time was well spent rehearsing.

On Mrs May's death in 1939 her daughter, Mrs Daisy Tucker, took over as president, becoming County Chairman in 1947, thus keeping the North Tawton branch in the forefront of county and national events. Many members still recall the annual garden party at Crooke Burnell, where her daughter-in-law Mrs Betty Tucker helped to prepare a delicious home-made feast and the weather was always fine!

Minutes from meetings held in the 1940s show that the WI lived up to its reputation, having a canning plant for fruit and jam making in the corner shop in Exeter Street, making clothes for the Devonshire Regiment and later for European children who had been liberated.

Members have always been involved in local issues and represented on the Town Council; indeed Mrs Tucker was the first lady vice chairman of the Parish Council. Throughout its history there has been a strong drama group and many and varied classes in upholstery, Devon architecture and computers, to name but a few. Latterly due to an outstandingly talented craft teacher, Gisela Banbury, many have learnt new skills and taken part in local and national competitions. In 2000, to celebrate the Queen Mother's 100th birthday, Gisela made a quilt containing a piece of one of the Queen Mother's dresses, which was raffled at a coffee morning and won by the daughter of long-time member Mrs Maureen Drake.

Christmas Crackers, 1980, by the Afternoon WI. Left to right, back row: Marjorie Cornelius, Mary Harris, Jean Lawrence, Winifred Sanders, Enid Westlake, Ivy Lambert, Grace Hayman, Mrs Rozee, Gladys Gregory, Lol Lias; front row: Biddy Watson, Joyce Milton, Ray Lawrence, June Phillips, Florence Heath.

Heritage walks have been held, followed by cream teas when over 100 have participated and, under the presidency of Mrs Dorothy Stoneman, there was a Second World War exhibition and another entitled 'Within Living Memory'. North Tawton had 14 entries in the WI book of that name, gleaned from members' recollections of days gone by.

A high point was when North Tawton boasted two Institutes with over 100 members, the newer Evening WI opening on 9 Jan. 1979 in the URC room. At the first meeting Monica Simons was elected as President. This eventually closed in 1999 due to lack of support, many of the members transferring to the Afternoon WI, which is currently as strong as ever.

Young Farmers Club
An account of this club can be found in Chapter 3.

Youth Club
There have been various youth clubs in the town, but none seems to have lasted very long. In July 1994 a notice in the parish magazine stated that, 'the resurrected Youth Club now has 54 members and meet at the Barn in the White Hart.' In July 1996, with the aid of a £180,000 lottery grant, they were able to purchase the former Methodist chapel in Barton Street, which, as well as having a coffee bar, is equipped with computers. One of the rooms is used by the pre-school group.

Evening WI's fourth birthday party, 1983.
Among those pictured: *Noreen Crocker, Hazel Quick, Margaret King, Barbara Watts, Pam Evison, Chris Watts, Marilyn Rowland, Gill Hoggins, Margaret Partridge, Mary Fry, Jo Fear, Shirley Armstrong, Teresa Rugman, Mary White, Valerie Whiteley.*

The Youth Club, 2001.
Left to right: *Melissa Poynton, ? Mookes, Robert Crisp, Simon Weekes, Tom Davis, Cassie Smith, Adam Davis, Verity Heffer, James Sullivan.*

High Days and Holidays

Carnivals
A carnival was first held in 1913, when the idea originated with Dr Deprez, who was President, and Mr W. Durant Gibbings, who was the honorary secretary of the carnival committee. In those days the proceeds were always given to the Royal Devon and Exeter Hospital, which at the time was maintained by voluntary contributions. It started with an evening procession led by the band from Taw Bridge at 7.30p.m. and the many tableaux were illuminated by 150 torches. All the tableaux were horse-powered in those days.

The festivities were held in abeyance during the First World War and were later restarted, but again lapsed for six years until a revival in the 1930s. Then the Carnival Queen was Emmie Underhill, attended by Ruth Lias and Win Fry. It was in aid of the District Nursing Association and a tableau devised by Nurse Biggs, 'The Future Generation', attracted considerable interest. Discontinued again during the Second

World War, it restarted in 1946 when there were 11 consecutive carnivals, all in aid of the refurbishment of the Town Hall.

From a newspaper report dated 24 August 1946 we learn that the carnival which coincided with VJ Day (when victory over Japan was celebrated) was opened in brilliant weather by Mr T. Lawley of Ashridge Court. Miss Rosemary Ash was crowned Carnival Queen by Mrs Sedgewick Rough, with Miss Phyllis Dart and Miss Joyce Horrell as her attendants. The carnival was in aid of the Town Hall (which for a short time was renamed the Victory Hall, but subsequently reverted to its former name) and they hoped to raise £400 through the event.

The following year the Town Hall committee still needed a further £2,000 to £3,000 to provide a club room, dance hall and cinema to seat 400 people. Again a carnival was held to help raise this large sum. On this occasion the King and Queen were William Goodman of Fore Street and Miss Myra

Above: *The Carnival Queen and attendants, 1947.*
Left to right: *Betty Breadmore, Kathleen Stevens, Edith Cole, Joan Bolt, Mary Long.*

Above: *Walter Martin (Scoutmaster) with a cow at the carnival, 1930s.*

Below: *'The Firefighters' in the 1956 carnival. Left to right: Arthur Arscott, Roger Bailey, Anthony Burns, David Lee, Graham Vanstone.*

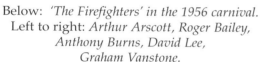

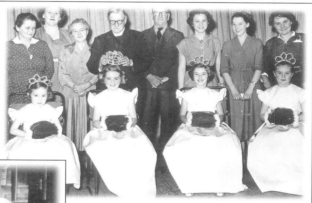

Above: *Crowning the princess, 1955. Left to right: Mrs Goodman, Edith Cole, Mrs Bale, Revd Searle Barnes, A.J. Gregory, Lily Jones, Monica Avery, Julie Phillips; seated: Janice Farley, Rita Lovering, Pam Day, Judy Phare.*

Right: *Carnival, 1945. Pictured are Rosemary Ash (Queen) Phyllis Dart and Joyce Horrell (attendants); standing on the left is Frank Skinner, Special Constable.*

Carnival, 1948. Uncle Tom Cobley. Left to right: *Jimmy Stentiford, Raymond Arscott, Maurice Bailey, Allan Bolt, Peter Fewings, Ern Arscott, Will Bolt.*

Edwards, domestic-science teacher at the school. Having been chosen by popular vote, they were crowned by Mrs T.H. Lawley. The princesses were Estelle Coles, Iris Sandercock, Ivy Yeo, Sheila Westlake and Elizabeth Slater.

The annual carnival was a really momentous event in which nearly everyone took part and there are more carnival photographs than any other category. After the carnival some of the tableaux would have been taken to other venues and so much fun was had by the participants that perhaps it is time for a revival.

Christmas in the 1890s

Miss Kate Pillman, true to the family tradition of diary keeping, wrote many years later about Christmas in the 1890s. She recorded that the celebrations:

... started on the first Tuesday in December with the Annual Fatstock show. The valuable silver cups and salvers offered as prizes were on show in Mr Skinner's window for a week before the show. The show was followed by a luncheon at the Gostwyck at the then large price of 3s.6d. (18p) and was attended by some of the nobility such as the MP and Lord Portsmouth.

After the cattle were gone and the cleaning up was finished, sweet stalls were erected around the clock, with overhead awnings. Miss Pillman recalled:

How we used to enjoy those sticks of home-made rock, only a penny, the gingerbread and strips of liquorice we pulled and stretched to make last longer. Then there was a cheapjack stall selling all kinds of things like halters, horse brasses and some sort of embrocation which he said was useful for animals or humans. These stalls were lit by kind of hanging lanterns, which got blown about and looked really dangerous, but nothing ever happened. There were several charities distributed about this time ... and a blanket club run by Mrs Hole. People paid 4d. per week all the year and got a blanket made at our factory at Christmas. Coal was given away too, it was 1s.0d. a cwt then. In Sunday School we paid one penny a week and if we made full attendance it was made up to 6s.8d. to be spent on boots or clothing. But I think the most outstanding thing of all was the Soup Kitchen. This was cooked in a big copper boiler in the wash house at The Nook, whole shins of beef and knuckles and plenty of good vegetables. People had to fetch it and were given a quantity according to their needs, also a loaf of bread.

Christmas morning as now, the band played in The Square, then church, which was decorated with garlands of holly and ivy. We thought it was wonderful in those days. The afternoon we usually spent comparing our presents with our friends, and after tea we had the burning of the ashen faggot, seeing who could stay by the fire the longest was great fun, and the sticks burning used to make it so hot. After a few more fireside games we went to bed perhaps not until 10 o'clock, tired but happy.

On Boxing Day the band used to play in all the streets, the postman used to come to every door collecting his 'Christmas box' and in the Public Houses free meat sandwiches were given to all the customers, and the day always finished with a dance for the band. The price was 1s.0d. each and the music was supplied by Mr Lee playing his concertina.

Circuses and Menageries

There is mention in the Pillman diaries that menageries came to North Tawton in pre-Victorian times, as this extract dated 14 May 1818 shows 'the wild beests here'.

On one occasion within living memory there was a circus in The Square, with caged animals including an elephant. Subsequently circuses were held behind George Madge's butcher's shop, where there are houses now in Butts Way, and later a move was made to the Butts Field.

The late Walter Martin, born in 1890 at Roseberry in Fore Street, spoke of German bands, an organ grinder with a monkey and a dancing bear. He also described an Italian woman with a barrel organ and 'coloured birds picking out your fortune from cards on a tray, we'd call them budgies today.'

Country Fair

For a few years in the 1990s a country fair was held at de Bathe Farm. Originally organised to raise funds to refurbish the Town Hall, it was then continued by the four main sports clubs as an annual fund-raising event. There were horse and dog shows, ferret racing, archery, clay pigeon shooting and children's races, craft tents, etc., and there was also a major attraction each year, such as a hot air balloon or parachute display.

There was a Flower Show and Fête in 1914, with sports and a two-mile cycle championship for Devon and Cornwall, which took place on the North Tawton track, although where this was situated is unknown. Steam roundabouts, swings and shooting galleries were hired for the occasion.

There was always a church fête in the rectory garden, a custom which is still maintained. Other organisations had similar events from time to time, usually held at the Butts.

The Country Fair at de Bathe Farm, 1990s.

Friendly Societies' Annual Festivities

These mutual benefit societies were in being long before the Welfare State, so that those who were old, ill or unemployed were able to claim relief and thus avoid destitution or the poorhouse. These were of particular prominence in the eighteenth and nineteenth centuries and there were several in North Tawton, including the Oddfellows' and the Tradesmen's Societies.

There is a reference in the parish documents showing that William Day was admitted to the Tradesmen's Society on 24 February 1800, around the time that it is thought the society was formed in North Tawton, and in 1808 there was a balance of £16 with 30 members paying 7s.7d. (38p) each and younger members in proportion.

The Exeter Lodge of the Oddfellows was formed in 1845, but there are no records of when the North Tawton branch started. However, it is known that their meeting-place was the Gostwyck Arms and as the reference to horse racing below shows, they had an annual day of festivities. This club still exists in North Tawton, on a much reduced scale.

There was also a 'tent' of Rechabites in the town as the photograph below shows. This was started on the Isle of Man in 1835 and was a teetotal Friendly Society, formed because most societies met in public houses and it was thought members were tempted to spend their money on alcohol. It flourished in North Tawton at the turn of the nineteenth century, meeting at Court Green.

Independent Order of Rechabites at Court Green, c.1892–5.

Horse Racing

This was a popular sport in times gone by and was held at various venues. The earliest recorded event is in a diary of the Pillman family dated 1818. The event took place on Broadnymett Moor when:

... some thousands of spectators attended and several large booths were erected. A band of 13 musicians played and were paid the illiberal subscription of fifteen shillings a dam poor job.

THE NORTH TAWTON
RACES
AND
Steeple Chase,

WILL TAKE PLACE AT THE BARTON, NORTH TAWTON,

On TUESDAY, the 17th. of SEPTEMBER, 1861.

THE NORTH TAWTON SWEEPSTAKES,

1 Sovereign each, with 15 added,

For Horses *bona fide* the property of Gentlemen, Farmers, or Tradesmen, residing within a radius of 15 miles from North Tawton, such Horses having been in their possession 6 months previous to the day of Racing.

Three Years old to carry 8st. 7lbs.; Four, 9st.; Five, 9st. 9lbs.; Six and Aged, 10st. 5lbs.; Thorough-bred Horses, 14lbs. extra.   One-mile-and-a-half.

THE BARTON STAKES,

(Hurdle Race,) 1 Sovereign each, with 10 added,

For Horses bred within a radius of 15 miles from North Tawton, and *bona fide* the property of Farmers, or Tradesmen in that District.

Three years old to carry 8st. 7lbs.; Four, 9st.; Five, 9st. 9lbs; Six and Aged, 10st. 5lbs.; the Winner of any Public Race to carry 7lbs. extra, and of Two Races, 14lbs. extra ; Thorough-bred Horses, 14lbs. extra.   One-mile-and-a-half over Five flights of Hurdles.

THE OPEN RACE,

2 Sovereigns each, with 20 added,

Three years old to carry 8st.; Four, 9st. 5lbs.; Five, 10st.; Six and Aged, 10st. 7lbs.; the Winner of any Race above £30 in value to carry 7lbs. extra · £100, 14lbs extra.   All Horses bred within 15 miles of North Tawton to be allowed 7lbs.   Heats.   About One-mile-and-a-half.

THE STEEPLE CHASE,

2 Sovereigns each, with 20 added, the Second Horse to save his Stake,

For Horses that have been regularly Hunted with LORD PORTSMOUTH, or the HON. MARK ROLLE, during the Season of 1860, 1861, and that have during that time been in the possession of Persons residing within the respective Hunting Districts, or within 15 miles of North Tawton.

Four years old to carry 10st. 7lbs.; Five, 11st.; Six and Aged, 11st. 7lbs.   Over about 3 Miles of fair Hunting Country.

THE GALLOWAY RACE,

1 Sovereign each, with 10 added,

For Horses *bona fide* in the ownership of Gentlemen, Farmers, or Tradesmen for 6 months prior to the day of Racing, or bred within 15 miles of North Tawton.—14 and half hands.

Three years old to carry 7st. 7lbs.; Four, 8st. 12lbs.; Five, 9st. 7lbs.; Six and Aged, 10st.; Winners of any Public Race to carry 7lbs. extra ; and of Two Races, 14lbs. extra ; Thorough-bred Horses, 7lbs. extra.   Heats.   About One-mile-and-a-half.

THE PONY RACE,

10s. each, with £10 added,

For Ponies belonging to Gentlemen, Farmers, or Tradesmen, residing within 15 miles of North Tawton.   13 hands.   Catch Weights.   Heats.   About 1 mile.

RULES AND REGULATIONS.

The Horses to start for the first race at 12 o'clock precisely, and all Horses not ready to start when the second bell rings, to be excluded from all right to run in the race.

No Entrance Money to be returned, and no person will be allowed to ride without Colours.

Professionals to carry 7lbs. extra.

Three Horses to start in every Race, or no Race.

All disputes to be settled by the Committee, or whom they may appoint, whose decision shall be final.

All Horses to be entered and named before 9 o'clock p. m. on *Saturday, the 14th of September*, at the "GOSTWYCK ARMS," NORTH TAWTON, where the Clerk of the Course will be in attendance.   The Entrance Money to be paid at the time of Entering, and Colours named.

AN ORDINARY will be provided at the TOWN HALL, NORTH TAWTON, after the Races, when and where the Prizes will be awarded.

MR. W. SALTER,   MR. C. TAVERNER,   } COMMITTEE
— W. DENSHAM,   — H. C. BOLT,   } OF MANAGEMENT.
— RD. HOLE

G. LUXTON, Esq., (Winkleigh,) Judge.   J. CHAPPLE. Esq., Treasurer.

Dated, July 20th. 1861.

Thomas Simmons, Printer, Okehampton.

Poster advertising races in 1861.

In 1861 races were advertised at The Barton and in February 1862 an account in the *Exeter Flying Post* tells of the aftermath, when the landlord of the White Hart at Bow, 'wishing to cut a dash' at the forthcoming races in North Tawton, after some discussion with a few of his customers hired a band carriage and band leader from Exeter and four musicians from Okehampton. On the morning of the races 'having drunk some vinegar to sober himself' he drove off in splendid style causing a sensation on his arrival. He subsequently entertained the musicians and band leader overnight and then sued his cronies for their contribution to his costs. The judge, however, found in favour of the defendants, who with three witnesses were allowed 5s.0d. (25p) costs each.

Another account in July 1877 shows the races to have been held at de Bathe after a lapse of five years, when the day, being that of the Annual Revel and the fêtes of the Tradesmen's and Oddfellows' Societies, was a general holiday:

When first mooted nearly 300 persons signified their approbation by sending in subscriptions and a licence was applied for to sell liquor in the Race Field. This was refused by the Justices, and a second application also, but most people took their own.

The Oddfellows had their lunch in the Market Hall, served by Mr German of the Gostwyck, and the Tradesmen held theirs at the Ring of Bells. Then they marched with the Band from the town to the Race Field.

Some inconvenience was occasioned by there being no race cards printed. Length of the course was ¾ mile and most races went twice round. There were 4 races all well contested but the many petty disputes and delays somewhat detracted from the enjoyment of the day. Booths were pitched in the centre of the field and in the evening a dance was held.

Again in August 1919, after a lapse of nearly 40 years, races were held at de Bathe with Mr Ernest May as President. A card of half a dozen events attracted a field of 60 and some keen racing was witnessed. Music was provided by the Town Band under Mr J. Lee and a dance was held in the evening in the Town Hall. Subsequently the races returned to the Barton, near the river, and hurdles were erected, with Mr Frank Coles of Skinnersland, Bondleigh, a farmer and butcher, in charge of events.

Hunting

North Tawton is situated in the Eggesford Hunt country and the pack of foxhounds so named seems to have been started in about 1798 by the Honourable Newton Fellowes, later to become Lord Portsmouth, North Tawton's lord of the manor. Originally it included some 300 square miles and hounds were housed, as they are at the time of writing, at kennels in Wembworthy, near Eggesford House. It seems that in the early days, even though various masters were appointed, the hunt was supported or at least

The Eggesford Foxhounds in The Square, before 1917.

Dartmoor Otterhounds at Newland Mills, 1959.

A street market in The Square at Midsummer Madness, 1996.

Midsummer Madness, 1997. Pictured are Mrs Ann Brereton, Chair of the Town Council with Robert Brett turned Town Crier.

Schoolchildren enjoying a ride on the miniature railway, c.1960.

Maurice and Gwyneth Densham at Melhuishes.

140

guaranteed by members of the Portsmouth family.

A reference to a meet at North Tawton Station in 1910 lists the names of 27 riders and 13 of the more prominent foot followers, the latter, without motor transport, must have been left miles behind as the pack ran to Kennerleigh Woods, a distance of some ten miles as the crow flies. Also in 1910 hunt concerts were held in the Town Hall, organised by Mrs Matthews of Nichols Nymett. In later years hunt balls were regularly held, first at the senior school – one can imagine the outcry if this were mooted today – and after the Second World War in the Town Hall. Huge annual jumble sales also took place in North Tawton, all of which helped to aid funds.

The opening meet in November has been held at North Tawton for very many years, when there is always a large following. The foot and mouth outbreak stopped hunting in 2001 and at the time of writing this ancient pursuit is held in the balance, due to impending governmental legislation.

Otter hunting was popular too, when visiting packs hunted along the banks of the River Taw, accompanied by foot followers.

Midsummer Madness

Commencing in 1987, when it was first organised by the Town Council to celebrate the centenary of the clock tower, this has become an annual event. There is a Midsummer Queen, a street market, treasure hunt, street party and other events on the Saturday, followed by an open-air service in The Square for the combined churches on the Sunday, accompanied by the Hatherleigh Silver Band.

Miniature Railway

The establishment of this railway was entirely due to Mr Maurice Densham (1909–98) who had a lifelong interest in trains. Moving from Broadnymett to Melhuishes in The Square in 1948, he constructed a 10-inch-gauge line in his garden with redundant track from the clayworks at Peters Marland. He also built a viaduct and a station and was much helped in these endeavours by Eric Stoneman, Bill Nicholls, Cyril Matthews, Charlie Stapleton and Jack Stoneman, the latter building the station.

Many alterations and additions to rolling-stock, including the introduction of steam, took place over the next 25 years and at its peak it could carry 50 adults at a maximum speed of 10mph for over 1,100 yards. Before every trip the engine had to be cleaned and it then took at least an hour to get up steam, for which a hundredweight of coal was required, and the boiler had to be filled with over 30 gallons of water.

There was only one accident causing injury and this was to an exuberant boy who leant out of the carriage and hit his head on the station building, there being very little clearance. After a couple of stitches in his head the young man in question was soon back on the train! There was also one derailment when some mischievous passengers leaned out and changed the points.

An exceedingly generous couple, the Denshams, held open days to raise money for various local and national causes and many people recall their train rides with nostalgia. In 1977 the railway had to be dismantled and sold, much of it to St Austell railway, although some of the sleepers stayed in the parish, going to Nichols Nymett for use as fencing.

Nanny Knight's Revel

This was an important annual event, which was said:

... to have been celebrated since time immemorial but revived in 1910, and is derived from a story that an old woman called Nanny was lost, her relatives and friends after an extensive search finding her asleep in a cornfield. So overjoyed were they, that when they got back to the town they held great rejoicing and it eventually became a revel and for the last 20 years the event has been held in aid of the Hospital Fund.

This was written in 1934 in the parish magazine, although there are other versions of the story. It is probable that this revel became amalgamated with the Feast of St Peter, which had previously been celebrated every June. It started with races in the street from the Globe (Copper Key), up Fore Street around the clock tower and back again, later moving to two fields near the Barkyard in Fore Street for a variety of competitions.

Mr Attwell, the owner of one of the fields, organised races and handicapped the children according to size and age. He also prepared a bran tub containing coins and similarly a tub of water, in which some of the children nearly drowned in the frenzy to win the coins. There was skittling for a pig, which apparently a well-known Sampford Courtenay resident, Leonard Horn, always won. There was also a fair, and the day culminated in the 'best dance of the year', a sixpenny hop in the Town Hall (in an upstairs room over the present Town Hall, reached by a stone staircase just inside the main doors on the right).

Shows

There were many concerts held in the Town Hall over the years. Magic lantern shows, and later films were screened too.

Twinning

The year 2001 marked the 25th anniversary of the twinning of North Tawton with Blangy-le-Chateau in Normandy, which came about on the initiative of Clifford Westlake, supported by Roger and Monica Simons, closely followed by Rose Dadds, Brenda Gerry and, of course, Enid Westlake. Clifford was chairman for 20 years and is much missed. He and M. Gaston Leon signed the Twinning Charter on 2 May 1976.

Bon Appetit! Blangy-le-Chateau, 1996. Left to right: *Jane Lake, Marion Pratt, Monica Simons, Christine King, Bill Robertson, Roger Simons, Mike Thwaites.*

Rabbiting in the 1940s. Left to right: *Will Bolt, Clifford Bolt, Allan Bolt, Leonard (Dipper) Lee.*

Out for a walk, 1917-style. Left to right, standing: *Ned Woolacott, Jack Merchant, Harold Stoneman, Roland Moore;* seated: *Reg Lias, Bill Martin, Jack Stoneman.*

Handbell-ringers and friends, off to Blangy-le-Chateau on a twinning trip, 1970s.

Many trips have taken place and the hospitality received is second to none. Other organisations in the town have become involved and our soccer team have played Blangy both at home and away, with honours about even. The firemen and the handbell-ringers have also taken part in exchange visits.

One of the most successful outcomes has been the involvement of our primary school, thanks to Neil Hallam the headmaster and Christine King (current Twinning chairman). The first visit took place when pupils from Blangy came to North Tawton in June 1982 with their then headteacher Mme Bernadette Piaczinski, followed by a return trip a year later. These exchanges, which still continue, have proved a rewarding experience for the children and have helped to foster the *entente cordiale*.

Wrestling

Wrestling took place on Court Green Meadow, on the east side of the churchyard. The churchyard was enlarged and consecrated for burials in 1871, the present wall was built and a footpath leading from Court Green into the churchyard was closed.

The following extract from the *Exeter Flying Post*, dated 5 August 1824, is quite illuminating, but it seems strange that people could spare two days from work at what must have been a busy time on farms. However, the prize-money would have been well worth having:

A grand match for 10 sovereigns took place at North Tawton on Thursday and Friday last. So strongly was it contested and the balance of power so equal at 4 o'clock on the last day, when no less than 16 laid claim to a share in the prize, and the skill and science displayed on both sides so equal that it was left in doubt who should wear the laurel. After hard struggles till midnight, 1st prize was awarded to James Stone, 2nd to Robert Jackman, both of Colebrooke, and 3rd to William Smale of Monkokehampton. The play throughout was good and the enlivening band made the scene truly delightful. The good order and harmony throughout the whole arrangement reflects great credit on the managers, who have resolved to renew this Grand National Exercise in the following year.

The Pillman diaries refer to the same match which took place on 28 and 29 July 1824. According to Walter Mortimer's book the beribboned hats for the winners were hung in the church porch, but when wrestling contests ceased is not known.

Country Pastimes

As elsewhere longer ago, children and adults amused themselves in many simple ways. Les Skinner, for example, tells how he spent many happy hours:

... messing around by the river, [seeing] birds nesting in the spring, and swimming in the summer at the lido

on the Taw in The Barton fields. We lashed bits of wood together to make craft that were carried all the way to Bondleigh Bridge.

He went on to say he found that:

Ferreting for rabbits was good fun too, there was an abundance of rabbits before Myxomatosis came, and most farmers were agreeable to us ferreting and if they weren't we did it just the same. Then at corn harvest in the days of binders, we could go to the fields being harvested and as the area of corn in the middle got smaller and smaller the rabbits congregated in the centre and got easier and easier to catch. Most farmers would let you have a couple each and any way you probably had one or two hidden under a machine or in the hedge, then we used to sell them.

They helped with the harvest too, stacking the sheaves in 'stitches'. For adults, shooting rabbits was a popular sport, with a dog and maybe a ferret. Alan Martin remembers mole-trapping as a boy and sending the skins away for sixpence each for the best ones, less for others. Skins of larger animals too were saleable, but he once got in quite severe trouble for cutting the horse's tail and selling the horsehair!

At the lido on the River Taw in 1938. Left to right: Les Skinner, Dennis Cornall, Ron Martin.

Some boys, according to the late Sanders brothers (born in about 1900), could make some pocket money helping to drive cattle to the station on market days or holding a horse's head while its owner went into a shop. One lady horse-rider told a story of inadvertently giving such a lad a gold sovereign instead of a lesser coin, but not realising it until she got home.

Many people, just as today, enjoyed walking. The girls went walking and picked primroses, violets and daffodils in season and made daisy chains. In the summer they picked blackberries and in autumn mushrooms. One old lady said, 'you never came home empty handed, even if it was winter you could pick up a few sticks for the fire as you walked.' Win Hancock remembers playing in the streets with hoops, skipping-ropes and tops. Traffic was not much of a problem before the war. They also played 'weddings' in the churchyard and sometimes a gang of older girls would walk to Sampford Courtenay Station and return by train. The boys sometimes dressed in their best and went walking too, although probably not to pick flowers.

Outings
As well as outings by train, sometimes Archie Gregory would clean out a lorry and put some temporary seats in place, taking people out for the day. Newland Mills did the same with a Foden's steam wagon. They generally went to the seaside or to Belstone on Dartmoor.

Celebrating National Events
The earliest record we have of a street party is 1803, as mentioned in the previous chapter, when the Peace of Amiens was celebrated. There is reason to believe that Queen Victoria's Golden and Diamond Jubilees were celebrated in similar fashion. We have a full account of the celebrations at the time of the coronation of King George V on 22 June 1911.

At 5.30a.m. an impromptu Feu-de-joie was fired in The Square, at 6a.m. the bells were rung, then at 8a.m. the Band gave a selection of patriotic music in The Square. At 10 the children massed in the school playground and sang patriotic songs. A procession, led by Sam Skinner, followed by the band, Boy Scouts, schoolchildren, Church Wardens, District and Parish Councillors, Friendly Societies and Fire Brigade with decorated Fire Engine processed to Church which was packed for a Service. 400 mugs were distributed to the schoolchildren by the Tavener family. Then 370 males over 15 years sat down to a meal of beef, ham salad, beer and cider.

In the afternoon, sports were held followed by tea in the Town Hall for 300 children and then the women and girls. More sports took place in the evening and at 10p.m. huge crowds assembled in a field next to Staddon Moor where:

... by kind permission of Mr Wallace Cheriton we were able to take part in the bonfire celebration conducted throughout the land. The Devon Gas Co. gave 80 gallons of tar, while Mr J. Ford did the haulage free of charge.

Special prizes were awarded for best decorated house.

Meanwhile, it was reported that Miss May Tavener:

... has consented to collect for the 'Queen Mary Coronation Gift.' All those named Mary, Maria, Marian, Marion or May will be able to contribute towards the gift.

There is no record of how much was collected.

The coronation of George VI is not as well documented, but similar celebrations took place, although on a lesser scale. At the coronation of Queen Elizabeth II in 1953, as well as the usual festivities, a television set was hired for the general public and placed in the Town Hall, which was the first time many people had ever seen one.

Millennium Celebrations
Always ready to enter into the spirit of the occasion, North Tawton laid on a full programme for this once-in-a-lifetime event. A committee comprising Gill Hoggins, John Kinsey, Lin Ford, Irene Ward, Nicola Compton and Rose Dadds was formed, to oversee fund-raising and make the arrangements.

The festivities began with a family disco including a magician and other events for the children in the Town Hall, culminating in the crowning of the queen, Kimberly Lenthall, the prince, Rory Honeychurch, and princess, Holly Buckley. This was followed by an adult dance both in the hall and under awnings draped between the hall and the Jubilee Clock. Of course it rained and the water collected on the awning and had to be released at regular intervals because of the weight, invariably cascading down on Roger Cudlip's barbeque! About 750 people enjoyed the evening and took part in the countdown to the new year.

Other events followed during 2001, including a millennium service when the churches combined for a special service led by Revd Michael Winter, St Peter's Church being interregnum (the interval between the appointment of ministers) at the time, and Revd Andrew Sowden. There was a tea party for the children and an Over 60s' supper and entertainment on the occasion of the Queen Mother's 100th birthday.

A successful local history exhibition was held and a revival of beating the bounds was carried out. This was an ancient custom when the parish officers and others, accompanied by the children, checked the boundary stones were in position and that no encroachments of parish territory had occurred in the preceding year. It traditionally took place at Rogationtide (the three days before Ascension Day) and is said to have ceased in North Tawton in 1870. On this occasion the group managed to do it in two days when Paul Baker, John Bennett, Graham King and John Wright led over 50 people around all 20 miles of the parish boundary during a hot August weekend.

Left: *Coronation day, 1911, in Exeter Street.*

Right: *The coronation of King George VI and Queen Elizabeth, 12 May 1937. The South Week milk float in the charge of Tom Arscott and his father Tommy.*

Left: *Millennium tea party in The Square, August 2000.*

Right: *Beating the bounds (southern section) for the millennium. John Shields (in foreground) steps out at Spires Lake.*

Samuel Budd, 1772–1841.

William Budd, MD, FRS, 1811–80.

Richard Budd, MD Edin, 1809–96.

Chapter 11
PEOPLE & PLACES

North Tawton has been the home of some notable people over the centuries, as well as ordinary folk. This chapter gives a brief history of some of them together with an account of some of the more interesting buildings to be found in the town.

North Tawton Families

The Budd Family

The first of that name to come here was Samuel, born in 1772 in Cornwall where he attended Truro Grammar School. He was apprenticed to a Mr Haywood, surgeon of Bideford, and then studied in London. He entered the Royal Navy and served on HMS *Victorious* and HMS *Venerable* in 1794. At some time between then and 1796 he settled in North Tawton, marrying Catherine Wreford, a farmer's daughter from Bow in 1801. They had ten children, nine of whom were boys and six of these entered the medical profession.

John, George and Christian went to Cambridge, Christian also studying in Paris, while Samuel, Richard and William went to Edinburgh, the last two also studying in Paris and London. All were distinguished both in looks and learning, attaining higher degrees and winning numerous prizes. Both George and William were Fellows of the Royal Society (FRS). Of the rest, Octavius was a Fellow of Pembroke College, Cambridge, like his medical brother John, and became a wine merchant; while Nonus, a Fellow of Caius College, Cambridge, was a barrister and JP. Septimus, although going to university does not appear to have obtained a degree and went to seek his fortune abroad, dying young in Toronto. Their only sister, Catherine, married and settled in Suffolk.

William Budd, the sixth child, born in 1811, had a spell studying in Paris after qualifying, where he became ill with a fever, possibly typhoid. He returned home to convalesce and subsequently helped his father in the practice. While thus occupied he was able to chart an outbreak of typhoid fever in the district and came to realise that typhoid was a contagious waterborne disease, spread by drinking-water contaminated by infected sewage. He then moved to Bristol where he became well known, becoming Physician at St Peter's Hospital and then the Infirmary. Here, seeing typhoid and typhus side by side, he was one of the first to recognise the difference between them. He did much work on tuberculosis, cholera, anthrax and various animal diseases. During the cholera epidemics in Bristol he managed to reduce the mortality considerably by various public health measures, such as the disinfection of the clothes and bedding of patients, and drains and sewers, together with speedy disposal of infected corpses. He tried hard to persuade the War Office to adopt such measures in the Crimean War, but to no avail. Ironically in view of recent events during the foot and mouth epidemic, his recipe for animals infected by rinderpest was 'a pole axe and a pit of quick lime.'

He took an active part in the formation of the Bristol Waterworks Company in 1844 in an effort to improve the water supply. He married in 1847 and had nine children, his second son Arthur also became a doctor and excelled in Rugby Football, becoming President of the RFU (Rugby Football Union) in 1888/9.

The other member of this remarkable family who concerns North Tawton is Christian (1813–91), who joined his father in practice and took over on the latter's death in 1841, continuing to live in the family home at Melhuishes. Surprisingly little is known about him, except that he never married and had a glass eye, which he sustained in an accident. Nonus came to live in the house on his brother's death and remained there until he died in 1899.

The remaining doctor brothers were all eminent in their profession: John Wreford Budd practised in Plymouth; Samuel was Physician to the Devon and Exeter Hospital for 40 years; George was a Professor of Medicine in London; and Richard was a highly respected doctor in Barnstaple. In the next generation, Samuel's son W.A. Budd, also became a surgeon at the Devon and Exeter Hospital (which incidentally was granted the prefix 'Royal' in 1899), while the latter's daughter, Katherine Rose Budd, was the first woman driver to be granted a driving licence in Exeter on 25 February 1904.

The Gostwyck Family

Originating in Bedfordshire where they attained high office in the time of Henry VIII, one of the descendants of this family was appointed as the rector of Sampford Courtenay in the early-seventeenth century. His son settled in North Tawton and five generations lived here, until the name became extinct in North Tawton when the last, Edward Gostwyck, died in 1793, young and unmarried.

His five sisters were his co-heiresses who, unsurprisingly, quickly found husbands so the family's influence continued for some years, until in 1827 the following advertisement appeared in the newspaper:

For Sale Lot 1. All that large and extensive dwelling house, malthouse, courtilages and garden, containing nearly one acre of land and situate in the centre of North Tawton, late residence of the Gostwyck family in which a very considerable business has been carried on in drapery, grocery and malting and is in a most desirable situation for a person carrying on those trades or for a person to build upon, fronting the south and commanding a principal part of the town. The premises are so spacious as to provide sufficient room for three or four good dwelling houses each having a very good backlet (sic).

From the above it would appear that this south-facing house was where the Cowley House Café and the adjoining properties, including the old Ring of Bells, are now. The old eighteenth-century map (3) of North Tawton also confirms this. As the Ring of Bells was built in the 1830s and the chapel at the rear in 1833, this explanation fits the known facts.

This family is said to have had their own tokens. These were issued in times of money shortage and used locally in exchange for goods in the seventeenth, eighteenth and early-nineteenth centuries. Their name lives on in Gostwyck Close, which was part of the garden of the Gostwyck Arms.

The Hole Family

As detailed in Chapter 1, the advowson of North Tawton was purchased by the Holes from the Cottles in 1716 and for the next 200 years they appointed a member of their own family as the rector. The Holes were a large Devonshire family, many of whom were parsons and considerable landowners. Not all those appointed as rector lived here, as several employed a curate. In general the Hole family were benefactors of the town. For instance, Revd Richard Hole endowed the Charity School in 1746, while his descendant Revd George not only built a new rectory, but also enlarged the church by building the present chancel at his own expense.

The last of this family to serve the parish was Revd Robert Hole, who was born in 1824 at Chulmleigh in Devon. He attended Eton and to get there boarded a

The Hole family in the rectory grounds on the occasion of Revd and Mrs Hole's golden wedding anniversary, and Revd Robert Hole's diamond jubilee as the rector of the parish, 1910.

coach at Exeter at 5p.m. arriving at Eton at 10a.m. the next morning. As an undergraduate at Oxford by his own account he was keen on shooting, hunting and racing and got into various scrapes, which is hard to reconcile with his exemplary behaviour while in North Tawton.

Ordained as a priest in 1847 he was appointed three years later to the living at North Tawton and ten years later he married Kate Fulford, granddaughter of the woollen manufacturer who started the North Tawton factory. They had eight surviving children.

Robert had inherited from his father estates said to be worth £40,000, but in the agricultural depression lost money and by the time of his death had sold a lot of his property. He took an active part in the life of the parish being a JP and chairman or trustee of many organisations. Every year he gave a dinner to all those aged 65 years and over and presided over it until the year of his death.

He was somewhat autocratic, as indeed were most men in his position at that time, but was well respected locally and he and his wife were considered to be good employers. One of the most prized possessions of the late Mrs Ethel Merchant, a one-time employee at the rectory, was a painting given to her by Mrs Hole, who was a gifted amateur painter. Ethel Merchant was a descendant of the Pike family

– see picture below.

Revd Hole numbered the Portsmouth family among his many friends and he and the then Lord Portsmouth were said to be keen on wagers. A story, probably apocryphal, is told that on one occasion after a dinner party at the rectory, when the ladies had retired, clean plates were called for, together with spiders contained in matchboxes. A spider was given to each diner to place on his plate and bets were laid as to whose spider would scramble off the plate first. After several rounds of this game it was apparent that Revd Hole's spider always won. Afterwards it was revealed by one of the maids that all the plates were cold except his!

In 1910 Robert and Kate Hole celebrated 50 years of marriage and his 60 years in North Tawton. It was said he had only been absent for three Sundays in all that time, a truly remarkable achievement. They were presented with a 'handsome silver salver' and an illuminated album with the names of over 400 subscribers. The latter still exists and the names in it make interesting reading.

Robert Hole died in 1916 and has been regarded as the last of the Devonshire 'squarsons' (squire parsons) and is said to have been the oldest incumbent, magistrate and Etonian in England. His death certainly marked the end of an era in North Tawton.

The Pike family at 21 Park Terrace, Essington, on the occasion of Mr and Mrs John Pike's ruby wedding, married 31 December 1869. Left to right, standing: *James, Sidney, Jane, William, Mary, John;* seated: *Emma, Mary, Mr and Mrs John Pike, Eva (school teacher), Louise.*

Above: *Double wedding, 29 June 1923, when two sisters married two brothers. Thomas Edwin Day married Edith Martin, Frank Day married Florence Martin.*

Above: *Wartime wedding, 1941, when station-master's daughter Marjorie Cornall, married draper's son Pte (later Co Sergt Major) Clifford Martin.*

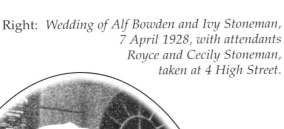

Right: *Wedding of Alf Bowden and Ivy Stoneman, 7 April 1928, with attendants Royce and Cecily Stoneman, taken at 4 High Street.*

Above: *Bob Gerry with his daughter Judith outside the United Reformed Church on 16 September 1972, before her marriage to Brian Weeks.*

Above: *The wedding of Carron Burns and Richard Collyer at the United Reformed Church, 6 July 1996, attended by handbell-ringers. Left to right: Emma Iles, Hayley Ruby, Lindsay Skinner, Emma Jelley, Claire Quick, Lucy Cudlip.*

Ted Hughes, OM, OBE

Edward James Hughes was born in Mytholmroyd, near Halifax in Yorkshire on 17 August 1930 and died on 28 October 1998. After attending Mexborough Grammar School he won an Open Exhibition to Pembroke College, Cambridge, where he graduated in Archaeology and Anthropology in 1954. Having previously done his National Service in the RAF, in 1961 he moved to North Tawton.

He was awarded the Queen's Gold Medal for Poetry in 1974 and the OBE (Officer of the Order of the British Empire) in 1977. In December 1984 he was appointed Poet Laureate to Her Majesty Queen Elizabeth II. In August 1998 he was awarded the Order of Merit and received the Insignia two weeks before his death.

His first book, *The Hawk in the Rain*, published in 1957, was widely acclaimed and followed by many others. *Tales from Ovid* won the Whitbread Book of the Year award in 1997 and also the WH Smith award. *Birthday Letters* won the 1998 Forward Prize, TS Eliot Award and the South Bank Award. In the same year he again won the Whitbread Book of the Year prize. He also wrote books for children, of which *The Iron Man* is best known and has sold over one million copies.

He was a noted fisherman and a founder trustee of the Westcountry Rivers Trust. He was also a great lover of the countryside and its wildlife, having farmed at the neighbouring village of Winkleigh for a time.

He injected new life into English poetry and will be remembered as one of the greatest poets of the twentieth century and a great countryman of whom North Tawton is justly proud.

The Sampson family of Wildridge with their Sampson cousins, c.1910. Left to right, back row: *Harold, ?, Nancy, Marjorie;* front row: *Mr Samuel Sampson, Tim, Dolly, Aubrey, Norman, Herbert.*

Ted Hughes.

Presentation of a cheque to the RNIB from various clubs in the town, 1981 at the Fountain Inn. Left to right, standing: *Twiggy Lake, John Avery, Greta, Alistair and Tony Stoneman, Reg Fry, John Leach, ?, Steven Stoneman, Mike Thwaites, Jane Lake, Gill Hoggins;* seated: *Bessie Stoneman, Muriel Leach.*

Sylvia Plath

This American-born poet, Ted Hughes' first wife, lived in North Tawton in 1961/2. She wrote numerous poems, short stories and books of which perhaps the best known is *The Bell Jar*.

Burton Hall before the Second World War.

Broadhall in The Square, early-twentieth century.

Left: *Presentation of a TV set to Sam Howard, Parish Clerk (left) by D.C. Philip, JP, chairman of the Parish Council, with A.J. Gregory (centre).*

The Town Hall Committee, 1951. Left to right, back row: *Frank Day, John Collins, Clifford Westlake, Bill Martin;* middle row: *Bill Nicholls, Charlie Stapleton, Tom Roberts, Fred Underhill, Archie Gregory, Revd Searle Barnes, Bill Stoneman, Ken and Joy Hands, Sam Howard;* front row: *Kathleen Ford, Dorothy Isard, Edith Coles, Honor Muller, Gladys Gregory, Sybil Hamilton, Mrs Dawe, Enid Westlake, Nellie Sampson.*

North Tawton Buildings

Broadhall

Very little is known about this prominent house in The Square, but it must be one of the oldest and most interesting in the town. The date 1689 on the front is misleading as this was reputedly found in the garden by a former owner. In fact the house is thought to date from the fifteenth century. Perhaps it belonged to the lord of the manor or his steward. Dean Milles, writing in about 1755, says 'The only other public work of which mention may be made is a house standing in the town where the lords held their Courts, and bringed criminals.' Broadhall could well have been this house, so too could the seat of the Valletorts in Essington. Local legend has it that there is an underground passage leading from Broadhall to the church, but it is hard to see what purpose this would have had.

It is shown on the eighteenth-century map (*Map 3*), which seems to indicate that it projected further into the street, but it is quite possible that the houses beside it which were once part of it, were in fact further back from the road than we see today. It had a second arched doorway within living memory which was removed to enlarge the shop window. The gabled end fronting the street has a bay window of eight lights, which has had some of its mullions replaced, but the rest are finely carved with perpendicular foliage, indicating a grandeur not found elsewhere in North Tawton. Being so close to the road it has suffered the inevitable effects of pollution. The house is much altered inside and the roof has been renewed, but there remains a brick chimney-stack, possibly dating from the sixteenth century, and a massive granite fireplace very close to the bay window, so close in fact that one wonders if it was moved there from elsewhere.

In the eighteenth century, Broadhall was owned by many people. One owner was a butcher named Robert Medland who lived there and this family seem to have occupied it for many years. Later, one of the residents was William Densham, a surgeon who died in 1839, who was followed by another surgeon, John Birom. It was put up for sale in 1856 in three lots, one of which had 'a stable, coach house, garden and premises' and also 'three houses recently and substantially erected and in an excellent state of repair.' From the deeds and the wording of this sale notice, it would seem that Broadhall included all the premises down to the Gostwyck Arms. There is evidence of yet another house in the garden at Broadhall. One of the later occupants was another doctor, named John Deans, who was still in residence in the 1881 census. The later history of the occupants is covered in Chapter 8.

Burton Hall

This unique house, which stands on Bouchiers Hill overlooking the town, was built of wood in Norway for Mr Fulford Vicary, owner of the wool factory, in 1872. It was then dismantled into sections and brought to this country by ship, which sailed up the Exeter canal. It continued its journey by train and wagon and was then re-erected. Fulford Vicary had rented salmon fishing in Norway for several years previously and much admired their style of building. His new house cost under £2,000 and it was said a similar house in stone would have cost £4,000. After several changes of ownership it became a hotel run by the Bragg family and during the Second World War was occupied by American troops. Run as a hotel again post-war under various owners, it has now reverted to use as a private house.

The Bragg family came to Burton Hall in 1923 from Chulmleigh in Devon. At that time the charge for residents was £5.5s.0d. (£5.25) per week with full board. The hotel could seat 50, but could not sleep as many so guests were 'boarded out' in the big houses on Bouchiers Hill nearby. Mr Bragg, who owned a large stretch of the River Taw, took the residents fishing, shooting and hunting. There were bowling and putting greens, a tennis court and a nine-hole golf course. All the Bragg children had to help in the hotel, so it was 'family run' in a very real sense. After the Second World War it reverted to a hotel and among other owners was Ed Murray, who had been Winston Churchill's bodyguard. It is now once again a private house.

The Market House (Town Hall)

This building was erected in 1849 by John Parish of Bow on a site previously occupied by cottages which were demolished to make room for it. It was paid for by £5 shares and its purpose was to revive the market in North Tawton, 'wherein meat, corn, butter and poultry markets will be held.' This pannier market with cobblestone floor survived until 1939 in a much reduced form. The building was mostly uncovered, although there was an upstairs meeting-room reached by a stone staircase to the right of the main entrance.

A contemporary newspaper account reveals that on 28 October 1849:

... the day the market was opened the bells rang merrily all day, the weather was fine and it was estimated that 2,000 persons were present. 300 sat down in the upstairs room for dinner at 3 o'clock, provided by Mr Bickham of the Gostwyck Arms ... and many excellent speeches were made.

Tolls were fixed as follows:

Every butcher occupying a stall 1s.0d.
Bagmaker, confectioner, shoemaker, jeweller,
* cheesemonger, fruiterer, and others 6d.*
Each basket 1d.
Pigs by carcass 1d., for weighing 1d.
For each bag of wheat 1d., barley and oats ½d.
For each living pig 1d., sheep and bullock ½d.

The building was fully roofed after the Second World War, major improvements were completed in 1951 and have been carried out since, but it lacks off-street car parking, and requires expensive maintenance. Added to which it now has competition from the Rugby Club as a venue for dances and other functions, but it has served the town well for over 150 years.

The Jubilee Clock Tower

This red-brick clock tower with freestone dressings was erected by public subscription in 1887 to commemorate Queen Victoria's Golden Jubilee. It was made to designs by Robert Medley Fulford, an Exeter architect who had North Tawton connections, and was built by Mr Samuel Ellis, a local builder, for £71. It occupied the site of the old town post, then in use as a lamp post, which was relocated in the churchyard. The clock itself cost £80 and there were a few other bills outstanding, which were met by the generosity of Mr Snell of Broadnymett.

Described in a newspaper as a Gala Day, there were great celebrations in June 1887 when the foundation stone was laid. The houses and streets were decorated, the band played and a special service was held in the church, followed by a procession. At 1p.m. 450 men sat down to dinner, followed by 450 children, and then 520 women were given tea. In the evening all the houses had lighted candles in their windows and a bonfire was lit, together with a fireworks display.

Under the foundations, 'in a glass' various items were placed, such as newspapers, coins and autographs of the committee and builder. Only three months later the clock tower was dedicated and opened by Mr Snell's ten-year-old daughter, Maude.

One hundred years later it was decided to celebrate the centenary with 'Midsummer Madness', which has since become an annual event (see Chapter 10).

Under the Jubilee Clock at midnight, 31 December 1999.
Left to right: Les Skinner, Bill Dadds, Percy Hunt,
Allan Bolt.

BIBLIOGRAPHY & SOURCES

Books and Articles

Adams, Ann 'Devon Buildings Group', *Newsletter No. 17*, Broadhall, 1999.

Billings', Kelly's & White's Directories.

Bovett, Robert 'Historical Notes on Devon Schools', 1989.

Budd, William *Typhoid Fever*, 1873.

Carbonell, Barbara 'Notes on the History of the Parishes of Bow and Broadnymet', *Transactions of the Devonshire Association* (*TDA Vol. 60*, 1928).

Cherry and Pevsner *The Buildings of England, Devon*, 1989.

Cresswell, Beatrix 'Notes on Devon Churches', 1921.

The Devon & Cornwall Record Society, New Series, Vol. 23 1978 *The Devon Cloth Industry in the 18th Century, Sun Fire Office Inventories, 1726–1779*, edited by Stanley Chapman.

Domesday Book, Devon, published by Phillimore, 1985.

Fulford Williams, Revd Henry 'Memories of a Devon Childhood', *TDA Vol. 92*, 1960.

Fulford Williams, Revd Henry 'North Tawton. A Devon Market Town', *TDA Vol. 86*, 1954.

Fulford Williams, Revd Henry 'Devon & Cornwall Notes and Queries', *Vol. 28*, 1961.

Gentry, F.D. *Take Care of your Fire and Candle*, 1985.

Griffith, F.M. 'Devon Archaeological Proceedings', *No. 42*, 1984.

Horn, Keith 'Monograph on Miniature Railway at North Tawton'.

Hoskins, W.G. *Devon*, 1954.

Jope, E.M. and Threlfall R.I. 'Excavation of a Medieval Settlement at Beere, North Tawton'.

Lysons D. *Magna Britannica, Vol. VI*, 1822.

Mortimer, Walter *The History of North Tawton*, 1978.

Nicholas John and George Reeve *The Okehampton Line*, 2001.

Oswald, Neville C. 'The Budds of North Tawton', *TDA Vol. 117*, 1985.

Risdon, T. *Survey of the County of Devon*, 1620.

Russell, P.M.G. *A History of the Exeter Hospitals, 1170–1948*, 1976.

Sellman, R.R. *Devon Village Schools in the 19th Century*, 1967.

Sellman, R.R. *Some Aspects of Devon's History*, 1962.

Tate, W.E. *The Parish Chest*, 1946.

Vancouver, Charles *General View of the Agriculture of the County of Devon*, 1808.

Wesley, Revd John *The Journal of Revd John Wesley, Vol. 5*, edited by Nehemiah Curnock, 1938.

Worth, *History of Devonshire*, 1886.

Establishments

Devon Record Office.
North Tawton Town Council Archives.
Okehampton Library.
Okehampton Museum of Dartmoor Life.
The Public Record Office, ADM 98 (re Napoleonic PoWs).
Westcountry Studies Library.

Photographs

Admart Ltd, The *Crediton Country Courier*, The *Express & Echo*, The *Okehampton Times*,
The *Western Morning News.*
Bertram Authers, High St. Studios, Crediton.
Chris Beglin, Polytask, North Tawton.
Barrie Hall, Braetor Studio, Okehampton.
Cinnebar, The Arcade, Okehampton.
Gowan, North Tawton.
Percy Manning, North Tawton.
R. Pengelly, Market St., Hatherleigh.
C. Ridge, Castle Hill Studio, Torrington.
Ian Snell, Okehampton.

LIST OF SUBSCRIBERS

Ann Adams, Zeal Monachorum, Devon
Patricia M. Adams (née Hollands), Great Torrington, Devon
Roy S. Allison
Annette Andrews, North Tawton, Devon
Arthur and Helen Arscott, Crediton, Devon
Rene L. Arscott, North Tawton, Devon
Hilda D. Arscott, North Tawton, Devon
Robert and Margaret Arscott, North Tawton, Devon
John R.H. Arundell, Perth, Western Australia
Keith and Irene Badman, North Tawton, Devon
Mrs Joyce Baker, Culmstock, Devon
Colin R. Baker, North Tawton, Devon
David Bale, Fore Street
Bernard Bale, Swindon
Mrs Rose Ball (née Swain), Welling, Kent/Women's Land Army North Tawton
Mr and Mrs J.B. Banbury, Bondleigh, Devon
Michael Edward Bath, Charlesbourg, Quebec, Canada
Mr D.J. Beeby, North Tawton, Devon
John Bennett, Exeter, Devon
Mary Bennett, Great Haywood, Staffordshire
Georgina Bentley, Bishops Tawton, Devon
Mrs Hilary and Samantha Biggs, Callington, Cornwall
Mr and Mrs R. Blaber, former landlord of Ring of Bells, North Tawton
Steve Blood and Chris Selman Blood, North Street, North Tawton, Devon
Sarah J. Board, North Tawton, Devon
Roger Bolt, North Tawton, Devon
Rita Bolt
Mrs Betty Jean Bolt, North Tawton, Devon
Fred and Veronica Bolt, North Tawton, Devon
Victoria A. Bond, North Tawton, Devon
Alexander D. Boughton, Cheltenham, Gloucestershire
Celia F. Boughton, North Tawton, Devon
Ivy M. Bowden, North Tawton, Devon
Alan A. Bowden, Crediton, Devon
Mrs C. Bowden, Butts Way, North Tawton, Devon
Norman C. Bragg, North Tawton, Devon
Frances and Arthur Brookes, North Tawton, Devon
Nicki Budd, North Tawton, Devon
Patrick A. Burns, North Tawton, Devon

K.J. Burrow, Bucks Cross, Devon
Mark Butchers and Hilary Burr, Oxford
Frank and Brenda Bye, North Tawton, Devon
Lorna Campbell (née Pike), Pinhoe, Exeter, Devon
Ann Cann, Crediton, Devon
Robert Carr, Tavistock, Devon
Edna Carr, Tavistock, Devon
Georgina F. Cheffings, North Tawton, Devon
Dorothea Clark, Tiverton, Devon
Lawrence Clark, Bickleigh, Devon
Mrs Margaret Clifton, North Tawton, Devon
Stephen W. Cockerham
Christine Cockwill (née Hollands), Devon
Bill Coles, Barton Street
R. and J.B. Collett, North Tawton, Devon
The Compton family, North Tawton, Devon
Terence B. Cook, Down St Mary, Devon
Annie Coram, North Tawton, Devon
Denis J. Corney, Totton, Hampshire/North Tawton 1934–38
George Critchell RAOC (TA), 48 Division, Reading, Berkshire
Mary E. Cross, North Tawton, Devon
Mr and Mrs R. Cudlip
George Cutland, Mary Tavy, Devon
Mr Bill and Mrs Rosemary Dadds and Carole, North Tawton, Devon
June and Bryn Dando, North Tawton, Devon
D. Davis, North Tawton, Devon
Madeleine Davis (née Pyke), Talaton, Devon
Mrs Marjorie M. Dean (née Simpson), Perth, Australia/Women's Land Army
Christopher J. Delve, Exeter, Devon
Mr and Mrs P. L. Delve
Steve and Karen Dennis, Billericay, Essex
Peter and Beryl Dennis, Argyll and Bute, Scotland
Neil and Carol Dennis, North Tawton, Devon
Derek and Diane, Nicholas Nymet, North Tawton, Devon
Jill Dilley, North Tawton, Devon
Andy Down and Debbie Whittle, North Tawton, Devon
Brian and Maureen Drake, North Tawton, Devon
Teresa J. Dunster (née Bolt), North Tawton, Devon
John Durant, Adelaide, South Australia
Mr Alan Eames, North Tawton, Devon

Ray Edworthy, Shaldon, Devon
Christopher and Joanna Fear, North Tawton, Devon
Simon and Peter Fear, North Tawton, Devon
Paul (Joe) Fewings
Malcolm D. Fewings, North Tawton, Devon
Derrick Field
Amma and Chris Field, Crediton, Devon
Doreen M. Field (née Day), Hill View Park, Eastleigh, Hampshire
Valerie Ford (née Stoneman), Hawkhurst, Kent
Barbara W. Fordyce (née Westlake), Chorleywood, Hertfordshire
May Madge Durant Forsyth (née Gibbings)
M.M.D. ('Trixie') Forsythe (née Gibbings), Holt, Norfolk
Mrs Margaret Fosket, Feniton
Reg and Mary Fry, North Tawton, Devon
Mr J. Gardner, Bell Hill, Petersfield, Hampshire
Mr P. Gerry, Chawleigh, Nr Chumleigh, Devon
Brenda Gerry
The Rev Anthony Gibson, former Rector 1988/93
Mrs Vivienne Glanfield (née Heard), Exeter, Devon
Mrs R. Gooding, Ipplepen, Devon
Brian D. Gorman, Bishop's Stortford, Hertfordshire
Simon and Linda Grainge, North Tawton, Devon
Casper and Ruben Gray, North Tawton, Devon
Graylings Fish and Chips, High Street, North Tawton, Devon
Allan and Margaret Grice, Milford Haven, Pembrokeshire
Jill D. Hall (née Smallbone), Senderhills, North Tawton 1949–55
Neil Hallam, North Tawton, Devon
Mrs W. Hancock, North Tawton, Devon
Jeremy S. Hannaford, Totnes, Devon
Eileen Harrison (née Day), North Tawton, Devon
Jo, Tom and Ian Hart
Keith and Val Hart, Bondleigh, Devon
Grace Hayman, North Tawton, Devon
Preb. F. Vere Hodge, for Richard and Richoard Hodge, North Tawton, Devon
Kevin and Sonia Hodge, Ian, Laura and Paige, North Tawton, Devon
Peter and Gillian Hoggins, North

NORTH TAWTON, *Nov 23 188*
AND AT
JACOBSTOWE & EXBOURNE.

Mr J D Gibuy

Bot of P. Madge & Sons.
WHOLESALE, RETAIL
AND
Family Butchers.
PRIME PICKLED TONGUES. HOME CURED HAMS & BACON.
Licensed Dealers in Game.

ESTABLISHED 1843.

					£	s	d
	Bal.	Cash			13	0	0
Sep. 23.		Buy	11	6		5	6
oct. 3º.		Beer qr.	5	5½		3	9
1888					4	4	4½
Jany 1.		Cash			13	0	0
Mar. 2.			6		16	9	0
	19º.				1	13	6
Credit					44	19	10½
		Creditors a/c.			41	6	1
					3	13	9½

Settled
Mr. C Madge

Tawton, Devon
Robin Holcombe, Appleford, Oxfordshire
Sally and George Holden, North Tawton, Devon
Nigel Hollands, Devon
Sandra Ann Hopkins (née Holland), Germans Week, Devon
Christine and Richard Humphrey, Nichols Nymet
Michael Hunt, North Tawton, Devon
Cdr David C.V. Isard RN (ret'd), Iwerne Minster, Dorset
Mrs Sue Jackson, Exeter, Devon
Rosalind A. James, Westhampton, NY, USA
Tony and Christine Jelley, North Tawton, Devon
Clifford H. Jones, North Tawton, Devon
Gary B. Kent, Canberra, Australia
Liz Keys, Chiswick, London
Graham and Christine King, North Street, North Tawton, Devon
Margaret J. King, North Tawton, Devon
James W. and Margaret J. King, North Tawton, Devon
Richard and Sheryl Kingsley, Brisbane, Australia
Richard and Carolyn Knapman, Sampford Courtenay, Devon
Mr and Mrs R. Knapman, Coryton House, Coryton, Devon
Jacqueline and Des Knight, Exeter, Devon
D.C. Knott, Newton Abbot, Devon
Richard J. Knott, North Tawton, Devon
The Knott family, Newbridge, South Wales
Mr and Mrs A. Lanchbery and family, North Tawton, Devon
Richard A. J. Lee, North Tawton, Devon
Doreen L. Leonard, North Tawton, Devon
Betty Letchford, Okehampton, Devon
Christopher Lewis, Bow, Devon
Mr B.J. and Mrs L.P. Lias, Crediton, Devon
Mrs Irene Lockyer, Exmouth, Devon
Thornton W.E. Madge, Barking, Essex
Paul R.P. Madge (Madge Family Historian), South Petherton, Somerset
William G. Mallett, North Tawton, Devon
Gloria M.C. Marley, Dawlish, Devon
Violet M. Marsh, North Tawton, Devon
Clifford W. Martin, Upminster, Essex
Mr and Mrs P. Martin, Paignton, Devon
Irene and Alan Martin, The Stables, North Tawton, Devon
Ron Mayo (Willcocks), Forster, New South Wales, Australia
Nancy Mead, Cornwall, New York
Nina J. Mills, North Tawton, Devon
I. Montgomery, Bath
Barry and Davina Moore, Haverfordwest, Pembrokeshire
Nick and Janet Morgan, Exeter Street, North Tawton, Devon
Claire E. Mortimer (née Bennett), Par, Cornwall
Mr and Mrs R. Nicholls, North Tawton, Devon
North Tawton Development Trust

North Tawton Pre School, Playgroup
North Tawton Twinning Association, twinned with Blangy-le Chateau, Calvados, France
Mr and Mrs Martin Orbell, North Tawton, Devon
Margaret E.H. Partridge, Bondleigh, North Tawton, Devon
Susan and Steven Paul, Egloskerry, Launceston, Cornwall
Christine A. Pavely, Okehampton, Devon
Kenneth H. Penny, North Tawton, Devon
Janice Phillips, Sampford Courtenay, Devon
Linda M. Pike, Coldridge, Crediton, Devon
Alan Pike, North Tawton, Devon
Norman J. Piper, USA
Mrs Stephanie Pouya, Honeychurch, Devon
Don Pridham
Elizabeth Pumford, Tavistock, Devon
Michael and Helen Purser, Killiney, Co. Dublin
Mr and Mrs D.W. Puttick, Eastbourne, East Sussex
Gladys Pyke, North Tawton, Devon
Stella Pyke, Strasbourg, France
Jane Pyle, Lower Nichols Nymet, North Tawton, Devon
Hazel and Michael Quick
Bill and Marian Quick, Loosebeare Manor, Zeal Monachorum, Devon
Patricia Randall, Barnehurst, Kent
Peter and Jeanette Raymont, Queensland, Australia
A.M. Reddaway
Stewart and Jose Reddaway, Honeychurch, North Tawton, Devon
Edith C. Rice (née Knott), Newton Abbot, Devon
Clive Ridyard, Skipton, North Yorkshire
R.W.A. Rivett
Deirdre N. Robbins (née Smallbone), formerly of Senderhills, North Taw
Jane Roberts, North Tawton, Devon
Jenny Rosser MBE, Twickenham, Middlesex
Mrs Audrey Ruby, North Tawton, Devon
W. Ryan, Coventry
Dr Andrew, Mrs Victoria and Jack Ryan
Barbara and Michael Sampson, Sticklepath, Devon
Julie Scoines, Bovey Tracey, Devon
Mary Sexton (née Hollands), Essex
S. Seymour and Z. Knight, Essington, North Tawton, Devon
John R. Shields, North Tawton, Devon
Mr M. A. Simmons, Devonshire House, North Tawton, Devon
Roger, Monica, Jane and Ian Simons, North Tawton, Devon
Mrs K. Smith, Broadwoodkelly
Catherine Smith, Kingsteignton, Devon
Ralph and Margaret Smith, Sampford Courtenay, Devon
Rose P. Smith (née Madge), Salisbury
Jill Snell, Chulmleigh, Devon
Betty Southcott (née Merchant) and Steven Southcott
William R. Speak, North Tawton, Devon
W.P. Speak

Andrea Squire (née Dinner)
Derrick and Sue Squires, North Tawton, Devon
Trevor and June Squires, North Tawton, Devon
Robin Squires, North Tawton, Devon
Elizabeth J. Stacey, Sampford Courtenay, Devon
Mr W. Stevens, London
Margaret Stevens (née Elworthy), Ashridge N.T.
Peter L. Stokes
Andrew M. Stokes, Bondleigh, Devon
Alastair M. Stoneman
Harold Mervyn Stoneman
Alison Stoneman, Crediton, Devon
Greta Stoneman, North Tawton, Devon
Terry and Jenny Stoneman, Feniton
David and Julie Stoneman, Exmouth, Devon
Lieutenant Colonel James Tarvit, North Tawton, Devon
David St John Thomas
Maureen Thomson, Westacott Barton, North Tawton, Devon
Mike and Ben Thwaites, North Tawton, Devon
Amy Thwaites, London
Gil Tregunna, The Pottery, North Tawton, Devon
Dorothy Tynan, Newton Poppleford, Devon
Joyce and Des Vallance, North Tawton, Devon
Doris and Albert Vanstone, North Tawton, Devon
Geraint Vanstone, Winkleigh, Devon
Dorothy R. Vanstone
Clive Vanstone, Eastbourne, East Sussex
Graham L. Vanstone, Devizes, Wiltshire
Joan and John Vaughan
Brenda and David Vaughan, North Tawton, Devon
Mr W.G. and Mrs J.M. Voaden, Exeter, Devon
John F.W. Walling, Newton Abbot, Devon
Jean Walls, North Tawton, Devon
Julia Walters, Salisbury
The Ward family
Ann and Barry Ware, North Tawton, Devon
Mrs Nicola Way, North Tawton, Devon
Dr and Mrs Hugh Webb, Mistlemead, North Tawton, Devon
Arthur G. Webber, North Tawton, Devon
Jeff and Sue Weedon
Mrs J. Weeks, Bow, Nr Crediton, Devon
Colin P. Westlake, North Tawton, Devon
Darren and Lorraine Westlake, North Tawton, Devon
Enid Westlake, North Tawton, Devon
Stephen Whiteley, North Tawton, Devon
Alan and Carol Woodrow, Broadhall Cottage, North Tawton, Devon
Hilary and Mike Wreford, Okehampton, Devon
John W. Wright, North Tawton, Devon
Roger and Jacqueline Yeates, South Tawton, Devon
A.J. Yeo (Sam), Albany, Lake Lane, Dousland, Devon

Titles from the Series

Forthcoming

For details of any of the above titles or if you are
interested in writing your own history, please contact:
Commissioning Editor Community Histories, Halsgrove
House, Lower Moor Way, Tiverton Business Park,
Tiverton, Devon EX16 6SS, England;
email: naomic@halsgrove.com

In order to include as many historic photographs as
possible in this volume, a printed index is not included.
However, the Community History Series is indexed by
Genuki. For further information and indexes to
volumes in the series, please visit:
http://www.cs.ncl.uk/genuki/DEV/indexingproject.html